£39-50

KV-559-712

BISHOP BURTON LRC
WITHDRAWN

THE LIBRARY
BISHOP BURTON COLLEGE
BEVERLEY HU17 8QG
TEL: 0964 550481 Ex: 227
T009981

Accession No. 15,857 ©

Class Number 307·12 Ref

Progress in Rural Policy and Planning

Volume One
1991

Progress in Rural Policy and Planning
General Editor: ANDREW W. GILG

Regional Editors:

Owen Furuseth (USA) Department of Geography, University of North Carolina, Charlotte 282233, North Carolina, USA

Andrew W. Gilg (UK) Department of Geography, University of Exeter, Exeter, EX4 4RJ, United Kingdom

David Briggs (Europe) Department of Life Sciences, Huddersfield Polytechnic, Huddersfield, HD1 3DH, United Kingdom

Robert Dilley (Canada) Department of Geography, Lakehead University, Thunder Bay, P7B 5E1, Ontario, Canada

Geoff McDonald (Australasia) Division of Australian Environmental Studies, Griffith University, Nathan, Brisbane, 4111, Australia

Progress in Rural Policy and Planning

Volume One
1991

Edited by
Andrew W. Gilg
and
David Briggs
Robert Dilley
Owen Furuseth
Geoff McDonald

Belhaven Press
London and New York

THE LIBRARY
BISHOP BURTON COLLEGE
BEVERLEY HU17 8QG
TEL: 0964 550481 Ex: 227

© The editor and contributors 1991

First published in Great Britain in 1991 by
Belhaven Press (a division of Pinter Publishers),
25 Floral Street, London WC2E 9DS

All rights reserved. No part of this publication may be
reproduced, stored in a retrieval system, or transmitted by any
other means without the prior permission of the copyright holder.
Please direct all enquiries to the publishers.

British Library Cataloguing in Publication Data

A CIP catalogue record for this book is available from the
British Library

ISBN 1 85293 106 X
ISSN 0956-4187

Library of Congress Cataloging in Publication Data

A CIP catalog record for this book is available

Typeset by Mayhew Typesetting, Bristol, England
Printed and bound in Great Britain by Biddles Ltd.

Contents

List of figures   vii
List of tables   viii
List of contributors   ix
List of abbreviations and acronyms   xi
Preface   xiii

Section I: United States of America
Introduction *Owen Furuseth*   3
1   Problems of resource dependency in US rural communities   5
    Richard S. Krannich and A.E. Luloff
2   On the threshold of the 90s: issues in US rural planning and
    development   19
    Mark B. Lapping and Irene Szedlmayer
3   *Dealing with change in the Connecticut River Valley: a design
    manual for conservation and development* by Yaro, Arendt,
    Dobson and Brabee, reviewed by *Owen Furuseth*   36
4   *Saving America's Countryside: a guide to conservation* by Stokes,
    Watson, Keller and Keller, reviewed by *Frederick Steiner*   38

Section II: United Kingdom
Introduction *Andrew W. Gilg*   43
5   Rural planning policies in the 1980s: an *aide-mémoire*   45
    Andrew W. Gilg
6   'Annual Review' of rural planning in the United Kingdom,
    1987–89   59
    Andrew W. Gilg
7   The social and economic restructuring of rural Britain   106
    Richard Munton
8   Countryside change: some Newcastle research programme
    findings at Year One   109
    Ken Willis
9   Splitting nature   112
    Ian Brotherton

Section III: Europe
Introduction *David J. Briggs*   119
10 Land consolidation and agrarian policy in the Friuli-Venezia
    Guilia region, Italy   120
    Franca Battigelli
11 Problems of Polish agriculture   131
    K.R. Mazurski
12 Conflicts caused by imbalances in forest policy and practice in
    the Basque Country   140
    Helen Groome
13 EC legislation on the environment and rural areas, March
    1989–September 1990   152
    David J. Briggs
14 Towards a European Environment Agency   157
    David J. Briggs

Section IV: Canada
Introduction *Robert S. Dilley*   175
15 Canadian agriculture and the Canada-US Free Trade
    Agreement: a critical appraisal   176
    Michael Troughton
16 Canada: the rural scene   197
    Robert S. Dilley
17 Promoting community development: Atlantic Canada group
    focuses on rural areas and small towns   206
    Floyd Dykeman
18 Alberta's Vision 2020: communities choosing futures today   211
    Tom Hong

Section V: Australasia
Introduction   215
19 The Murray-Darling Basin: a case study in cooperative policy
    development   216
    Neil S. McDonald
20 Recent developments in rural planning in Australia   228
    G.T. McDonald
21 Review of recent developments in rural planning in New
    Zealand   242
    Richard Willis

List of figures

 2.1 US drought severity, August 1988   25
10.1 The traditional pattern of fragmented and scattered holdings
      in the Commune of Pradamano, Udine, before consolidation   123
10.2 The rationalised pattern of holdings resulting from a
      second-generation consolidation scheme in Pradamano,
      Udine   126
11.1 Ecologically threatened areas in Poland   133
11.2 Health conditions of Polish forests   135
11.3 Extent of soil erosion in Poland   136
12.1 a. Forest policy model promoting maximum profitability   142
      b. Forest policy model promoting maximum welfare
         benefits   142
      c. Vertically and horizontally integrated woodland
         management options   143
12.2 Location of the southern Basque Country   144
12.3 Species composition of woodland areas, by province   146
14.1 Proposed structure of the European Environment Agency   163
14.2 Steps in the integration of multi-source data sets   168
15.1 Canadian agricultural trade, 1986   180
15.2 Projected shifts in production of intensive agriculture from
      Canada to the USA based on combinations of physical base,
      scale economies and surplus capacity in the USA   184
15.3 Newspaper advertisements for and against the Canada-US
      Free Trade Agreement   190

List of tables

1.1	Average unemployment rates in counties specializing in agriculture and natural resources, 1976–85	7
2.1	State programs for farmland preservation	22
2.2	State rural development programs	32
5.1	Expenditure on agricultural grants in the UK, 1979–90	49
5.2	Forestry Grant Scheme	51
5.3	Central government spending on countryside planning: actual and planned, 1984–93	58
6.1	Set-Aside Scheme	65
6.2	Farm Woodland Scheme	65
6.3	Expenditure plans for rural planning	72
6.4	Woodland Grant Scheme	80
6.5	List of new protected areas and designations	86
11.1	Health conditions of Poland's forests according to damaged zones between 1967 and 1986	134
15.1	Provisions of the Canada-US Free Trade Agreement with respect to trade in agricultural commodities	178
15.2	Some gross dimensions of the Canadian and United States agricultural systems (1986)	181
20.1	Contemporary policy documents in Victoria	233
21.1	Contemporary rural policy and planning issues in New Zealand	243

List of contributors

Owen Furuseth, Department of Geography, University of North Carolina, Charlotte 282233, North Carolina, USA.

Richard S. Krannich, Departments of Sociology and Forestry, Utah State University, Utah, USA.

A.E. Luloff, Department of Agricultural Economics and Rural Sociology, Pennsylvania State University, PA, USA.

Mark B. Lapping, Faculty of Planning and Associate Director, New Jersey Agricultural Experiment Station, Rutgers University, NJ, USA.

Irene B. Szedlmayer, Faculty of Planning, Rutgers University, NJ, USA.

Andrew W. Gilg, Department of Geography, University of Exeter, UK.

Richard Munton, Rural Studies Research Centre, University College, London, UK.

Ken Willis, Department of Town and Country Planning, University of Newcastle, Newcastle upon Tyne, UK.

David J. Briggs, Department of Life Sciences, Huddersfield Polytechnic, Huddersfield, UK.

Franca Battigelli, Istituto di Geografia, Universita' degli Studi di Udine, Italy.

K.R. Mazurski, Wrocław, Poland.

Helen Groome, Farmers' Union of Vizcaya, Euskadi Colon de Larreategui, Bibao, Spain.

Robert S. Dilley, Department of Geography, Lakehead University, Thunder Bay, Ontario, Canada.

Michael Troughton, University of Western Ontario, London, Canada.

Floyd W. Dykeman, Department of Geography, Mount Allison University, Sackville, New Brunswick, EOA 3CO, Canada.

Geoff McDonald, Division of Australian Environmental Studies, Griffith University, Nathan, Brisbane, Australia.

Neil S. McDonald, Water Branch, Department of Primary Industries and Energy, Australia.

Richard Willis, Department of Geography, Victoria University, Wellington, New Zealand.

Abbreviations and acronyms

ADAS	Agricultural Development and Advisory Services
AONB	Areas of Outstanding Natural Beauty
CAC	Community Advisory Committee
CAP	Common Agricultural Policy
CEPA	Canadian Environmental Protection Act
COSIRA	Council for Small Industries in Rural Areas
CSIRO	Commonwealth Scientific Industrial Research Organisation
CV	contingent valuation
CWB	Canadian Wheat Board
DOE	Department of Environment
EA	Environmental Assessment
EC	European Community
EPA	Environmental Protection Agency
ESA	Environmentally Sensitive Areas
FTA	Free Trade Agreements
FWS	Farm Woodland Scheme
GATT	General Agreement on Tariffs and Trade
GDO	General Development Order
GIS	Geographic Information Systems
GST	Goods and Services Tax
HC	House of Commons
HL	House of Lords
ITCM	Individual travel cost model
ITE	Institute of Terrestrial Ecology
IYRP	International Yearbook of Rural Planning
JNCC	Joint Nature Conservation Committee
LDP	Land development process
LEP	Local environmental plan
LESA	Land evaluation and site assessment
LFA	Less Favoured Area
MAFF	Ministry of Agriculture, Fish and Food
MUP	Minimum plot size
NCC	Nature Conservancy Council
NEPA	National Environment Protection Agency
NFU	National Farmers' Union

THE LIBRARY
BISHOP BURTON COLLEGE
BEVERLEY HU17 8QG
TEL: 0964 550481 Ex: 227

NNR	National Nature Reserve
NPA	National Park Authority
NRA	National Rivers Authority
NSCP	Natural Soil Conservation Program
PIRPAP	Progress in Rural Policy and Planning
RAC	Resources Assessment Commission
RDC	Rural District Council
REA	Rural Electrification Administration
REP	Regional Environmental Plan
RMC	River Murray Commission
RSPB	Royal Society for the Protection of Birds
RSTRSP	Rural and Small Towns Research and Studies Programme
SEPPs	State Environmental Planning Policies
SI	Statutory Instruments
SPA	Special Protection Area
SSSIs	Sites of special scientific interest
TCM	Total catchment management
TDR	Transfer development rights
UNEP	United Nations Environment Programme
USDA	US Department of Agriculture
WGS	Woodland Grant Scheme
ZTCM	Zonal travel cost method

Preface

Progress in Rural Policy and Planning is a new journal which will be published on an annual basis in 1991, 1992 and 1993 in the first instance. After 1993 it may move to a quarterly interval if there is enough interest from both contributors and subscribers. Although PIRPAP, as it is known to its editors, is a new venture, rural planning afficianados will recognise that three of the editors worked on the former *International Yearbook of Rural Planning*, and one of the other two editors was a contributor. Going further back, Andrew W. Gilg, the general editor of PIRPAP, was of course the editor of the *Countryside Planning Yearbook* between 1980 and 1986, when it expanded from its UK base into the *International Yearbook*.

There is therefore some continuity between PIRPAP and its predecessors, notably in the UK section. This partly reflects the nature of the UK with its national legislature, which allows an attempt to be made to produce a comprehensive review. In the other sections, however, we are dealing either with federal systems as in Australia, Canada and the USA or with over 20 countries as in the case of Europe. The editors in these countries have therefore come up with a more flexible structure for their sections than the UK, which follows a slimmed down yearbook format.

The aims for PIRPAP are to provide a regular review of both the progress of rural policy development, and the implementation of these policies on the ground. These reviews can take three broad forms in either case: first, considered reviews of developments over a fairly long time-span, normally about 10 years; second, reviews of events over a much shorter time-span, normally two years or less, in order to provide a framework of information for those people working in one branch of rural planning who need access to information in other areas but do not have the time to research new ideas for themselves; and third, short topical articles or reviews of books which can either contribute to an ongoing debate or report on current research. PIRPAP is not meant to be a primary research journal, but rather an intermediate stage between such a journal and an abstract or yearbook type of publication.

The contents of the Journal will be confined to the broad area of rural policy and planning. Rural policy is defined as legislation, government advice, government or judicial decisions involving case law or ministerial precedent, statements of policy by government organisations and the argument of rural policy pressure groups. Rural planning is defined as the implementation of these policies on the ground via plans, land-use designations, controls, quotas, grant aid, loans, incentive schemes, capital provision and programmes of various kinds. Clearly both these activities overlap and the definitions are provided only as a guide and not as a complete or rigid list.

In a similar vein, the coverage of issues and topics is loosely defined to cover the planning of extensive land uses and social and economic provision in rural (low population density) areas on the following topics: agriculture; forestry; conservation; recreation; extractive industries; employment; transport; general land-use planning; and social issues. The areal coverage is confined to five regions of the world purely because they have a common rural structure and a set of rural planning systems which are broadly the same, thus allowing comparative work to be assessed and a broad sense of unity for papers from otherwise quite spatially far apart parts of the world. If in 1994 the Journal expands to a quarterly format, then other parts of the world may then be brought in with the extra space allowed.

In the mean time, in a reversal of normal alphabetical order, material from the five regions of the world so far included is presented in reverse order, namely: the USA; UK; Europe; Canada; and Australia. The material is presented by region since it has been edited this way, rather than thematically. Comments and offers of papers can therefore be most effectively sent to the regional editors, rather than to me as general editor. In this role it remains only for me to thank all those who encouraged me to develop the *Yearbooks*, those who commented on draft proposals for PIRPAP and all those people who have worked so hard to bring this first issue to fruition. It is now up to you, the reader, to tell us how we can improve PIRPAP and hopefully contribute to its development through the 1990s.

Andrew W. Gilg
Exeter
29 November 1990

Section I:
United States of America

edited by
Owen Furuseth

Introduction

Owen J. Furuseth

The recent history of rural America has witnessed a 'roller coaster' pattern of socio-economic fortunes. During the 1960s, rural areas suffered economic stagnation and decline, and outmigration was widespread. The 1970s brought a dramatic reversal of conditions. The 'rural renaissance', an economic and demographic renewal, created optimism about the future of many rural communities. The industrialization of non-metropolitan areas was seen as a harbinger of long-term economic growth, and the emergence of strong, seemingly sustained, reversal in rural immigration.

The heady times, however, quickly ended at the beginning of the 1980s. The population and economic growth of the preceding decade turned out to be ephemeral. Despite the glowing reports of national prosperity eminating from Washington, economic decline and depopulation re-emerged as primary concerns of rural America. The events of the past several decades are symptomatic of the particular challenges facing rural America. In this inaugural issue of *Progress in Rural Policy and Planning*, the substantive article and legislative review in this section are focused on the legacy of rural economic and social change in the 1980s.

For resource-dependent rural areas community development opportunities, even in the best of economic times, are limited. The challenges facing local leaders and planners in these communities are the theme of Richard Krannich and Al Luloff's article. This provocative article analyzes the impacts that resource dependency have on the social and economic fabric of rural communities, and raises issues about how to provide for long-term improvement in rural well-being.

A political and policy-oriented complement to Krannich and Luloff is Mark Lapping and Suzanne Szedlmayer's legislative review. The two Rutgers' planners have synthesized a wide ranging set of Federal, State and Local legislative acts, judicial actions and policy guides into a finely tuned legislative and policy review for rural specialists.

Finally, the two book reviews in this section reflect the renewed interest in environmental issues in the USA. Perhaps one of the most exciting facets of the new environmentalism is the broadening interest in environmental issues related to rural issues. The intersection of rural planning and environmentalism is best evident in the two books, *Saving America's Countryside* and *Dealing With Change* which are reviewed here. This new genre of research bodes well for the future.

In our next issue of *Progress in Rural Policy and Planning*, the theme of

THE LIBRARY
BISHOP BURTON COLLEGE
BEVERLEY HU17 8QG
TEL: 0964 550481 Ex: 227

this section will shift to a discussion of new technologies and rural policy and planning initiatives. The impact of GIS and decision support systems on rural planners and elected officials is likely to be profound. What lessons can be learned from early adopters; what opportunities or pitfalls should be noted? These are topics for our next issue.

Because we are a new serial, we are especially open to involving a wider group of contributors. Please contact me with your ideas and comments. Contributions of articles and review materials are encouraged.

1 Problems of resource dependency in US rural communities*

Richard S. Krannich and A.E. Luloff

Introduction

A central issue addressed by social scientists and planners concerned with rural well-being involves the responses of rural communities to changes associated with growth or decline. The past three decades have witnessed major shifts in the way that the rural social science and planning literatures have addressed the prognosis for attaining well-being in rural community settings. This fluctuation in focus and interpretation is linked to corresponding shifts in the patterns of change affecting rural America.

During the 1960s, much of the work undertaken by rural social scientists and planners reflected concerns about the fates of communities left behind by the forces of urbanization, modernization and industrialization (Whiting, 1974). Rural outmigration was widespread, reflecting both the pull of employment opportunities in urban areas and the push of limited life chances throughout rural America. Rural communities were viewed as places which would, inevitably, experience a 'self-perpetuating downward spiral of economic stagnation and population decline' (Lovejoy and Krannich, 1982, p. 475; also Brinkman, 1974). As a result, much attention was focused on the problems of adaptation in what were often viewed as dying rural communities (Gallaher and Padfield, 1980).

However, the 1970s brought a fairly dramatic shift of emphasis, as attention was focused on an unanticipated renewal of growth in many rural areas. The industrial invasion of non-metropolitan areas of the USA created new optimism about the economic future of many rural communities (Summers et al., 1976). In addition, a great deal of attention was directed to the emergence of a strong and seemingly sustained turnaround of long-standing patterns of net outmigration from non-metropolitan areas (Beale, 1975; Zuiches and Brown, 1978). Suddenly, attention was shifted from the problems of decline to the changes associated with this unexpected rural renaissance (Morrison and Wheeler, 1976). Although

* An earlier version of this paper was presented at the annual meetings of the Rural Sociological Society, Seattle, Washington, August 1989. This research was supported in part by the Utah and New Hampshire Agricultural Experiment Stations.

researchers also identified a variety of problems associated with unexpected and, in some cases, undesirable growth (Price and Clay, 1980;
Weber and Howell, 1982), in general the dual themes of rural decline and
the death of rural communities gave way to more optimistic perceptions
of the potential for revitalizing rural America.

With the arrival of the 1980s the focus of rural social scientists and planners shifted once again toward concerns about the problems of economic
decline and depopulation. The population turnaround of the 1970s turned
out to be somewhat ephemeral, with the emergence of slowed growth in
some rural areas and substantial decline in others (Beale and Fuguitt,
1986; Luloff, 1990a). Many rural sociologists turned their attention to the
implications of the 'farm crisis' for rural communities and families
(Heffernan and Heffernan, 1986). Others noted that many rural communities were suffering the effects of deteriorating employment opportunities in
many non-agricultural industrial sectors (Bluestone and Harrison, 1986).
Indeed, by mid-decade the focus of research had shifted so dramatically
that it appeared to have returned full circle to that which had prevailed
twenty years earlier, prompting one observer to comment on the problems
of rural America in a paper entitled 'Communities Left Behind—Again'
(Wilkinson, 1986).

Dependency and the cycle of rural instability

These shifts in the focus of rural social science and planning endeavors
reflect the inherent instability of rural communities, and the potential for
recurrent cycles of expansion, stagnation and decline. This cycle of rural
instability results from conditions of underdevelopment commonly
observed in rural areas which are enmeshed in dependency relationships
with regional, national and multinational extralocal organizations (see
Lovejoy and Krannich, 1982).

Dependency relations appear to have a pervasive influence on the vitality
and viability of most rural sectors of advanced industrial societies (Buttel
and Newby, 1980). This is largely traceable to the limited economic diversity of rural areas, and an associated sensitivity to any shifts in the demand
for or profitability of rural-produced goods and services. Indeed, an
unstable economic base has been characterized as one important dimension
of the 'social costs of space' associated with 'sparsity of settlement and
distance from the centers of economic development and power' (Wilkinson, 1986, p. 342; Kraenzel, 1980).

The problems of instability associated with cyclical growth, stagnation
and decline appear to be especially pervasive in communities which are
resource dependent, e.g., where the economic, social and cultural conditions of community life are intertwined with, and ultimately dependent
upon, the production of a natural resource commodity or commodities. As

Table 1.1 *Average unemployment rates in counties specializing in agriculture and natural resources, 1976–85*

Industry	1976	1977	1978	1979	1980	1981	1982	1983	1984	1985
Energy	5.9	5.8	6.2	6.0	7.0	7.4	10.1	13.9	10.7	11.0
Mining	8.3	8.1	7.4	6.1	7.4	7.6	15.8	15.5	10.3	11.7
Forestry and wood products	8.4	8.1	7.1	7.6	9.8	10.7	13.4	12.4	10.6	10.3
Agriculture	5.7	5.8	5.5	5.5	6.9	7.4	9.3	9.6	8.4	8.5
Total labor force (16 years old and over)	7.7	7.0	6.0	5.8	7.1	7.6	9.7	9.6	7.5	7.2

Source: E.H. Weber, E.N. Castle and A.L. Shire, 1988, 'Perfoi nance of natural resource industries', in D.L. Brown *et al.* (eds.), *Rural economic development in the 1980s*, US Department of Agriculture, Economic Research Service, Washington, DC, pp. 103–33

Field and Burch observe, 'Resource-dependent communities may be unique in that the primary production processes and changes therein have direct consequences for community stability' (1988, p. 38). Patterns of resource dependence emerge in a variety of settings, but primarily involve communities in which economic activity revolves around agriculture, forestry, fisheries, mining, petroleum resource development and recreation and tourism attractions capitalizing on features of the local natural environment.

Communities which rely upon these resource-based industries are especially susceptible to cycles of expansion and decline. National data on several types of resource-dependent counties in the USA clearly illustrate the cyclical trends and instability that affect such places. For example, Table 1.1 presents data on unemployment patterns reported by Weber, Castle and Shriver (1988). These data show that unemployment rates in counties specializing in mining and forest-related industries fluctuated sharply during 1976–85, and in all years were higher than for the total labor force. Unemployment in counties specializing in energy resource industries remained below the national average during the late 1970s, but increased dramatically during 1982–5 in conjunction with the world-wide oil glut. Unemployment in agricultural counties also increased to above the national average during 1984–5, a period corresponding to the height of the US farm crisis (Strange, 1988).

In addition to fluctuating and periodically high rates of unemployment, resource dependency is also associated with high levels of economic underemployment. For example, Lichter and Costanzo (1987) reported that the national rate of underemployment for all industries in non-metropolitan areas was 21 per cent in 1980. However, non-metropolitan underemployment in the extractive industries was nearly 28 per cent, a figure that is far higher than for any other industries.

The economic instability of resource dependent rural areas is also reflected in demographic trends. During 1960–70, 1970–80 and 1980–4, non-metropolitan counties with very high percentages of employment in agricultural activities (30 per cent or more) consistently exhibited negative annual growth rates, in sharp contrast to positive and generally substantial growth in counties with little agricultural dependence (Brown, 1988).

During 1984–8, the population of non-metropolitan counties in the USA grew by just 1.2 per cent overall. However, this slow rate of overall growth masks important differences in the growth experiences of different types of rural areas. Non-metropolitan counties dependent on manufacturing grew by nearly 2 per cent during this period, and counties dependent on retirement-related development grew by over 6 per cent. In contrast, farming-dependent counties (with 20 per cent or more of labor and proprietor's income from agriculture) experienced a net loss of population, declining by almost 1 per cent during 1984–8. Mining-dependent counties (with 20 per cent or more of labor and proprietor's income from mining industries) experienced more substantial population losses, with overall declines of about 5 per cent during the same period (USDA-ERS, 1989).

Like other places which rely on one major manufacturing plant for employment and income, resource-dependent communities are often affected by extralocal corporate decisions regarding such things as the profitability of a particular mine or sawmill, or the availability of a substitute location where the resource is more accessible, or where labor and other production costs are lower. In other words, the control of resource extraction and utilization by extralocal interests is a frequent contributor to instability in resource-dependent communities, whether they be farming communities (Vogeler, 1981) or places dependent on minerals, timber, or other natural resources.

Shifts in demand for development of particular resources can occur very rapidly as a result of either global economic and political conditions or technological developments. Mining and forestry employment cycles are doubly impacted, both by national economic climatic changes and international energy resource availability, and by the growing infusion of capital intensive technologies which have displaced large numbers of labor while greatly reducing production costs. Such shifting circumstances can result in the rapid onset of stagnation and decline, as illustrated by declining oil prices during the 1980s and the resulting collapse of oil exploration and processing activities in areas of the western USA. In contrast, rapid expansion of resource-related activity can also arise, as in the case of energy development in the western USA during the late 1970s, or recently renewed gold and silver mining activities in the Black Hills of South Dakota and throughout Nevada that have been stimulated by new technologies for extracting precious metals from low-grade ore bodies.

Resource-dependent communities also experience instability as a result of factors linked more directly to conditions of the natural resource base, which in some cases is itself unstable. Agricultural communities experience fluctuations linked to the periodic occurrence of drought, flooding, insect damage and crop disease. Despite their reliance on a major renewable resource, timber-dependent communities suffer decline both when the harvest of mature trees exceeds the pace of new growth, and as a result of diseases which threaten the long-term sustainability of this resource. Communities dependent on the extraction of non-renewable resources such as minerals or petroleum products face the potential for decline when reserves are exhausted. Fisheries-dependent communities experience instability as a result of fluctuations in fish populations resulting from natural population cycles, overharvesting, persistent environmental contamination, or short-term environmental disasters such as the 1989 *Exxon Valdez* oil spill in Alaska and the *World Prodigy* oil spill in Rhode Island. Recreation-dependent communities experience fluctuations linked to a variety of weather-related events, as illustrated by the major declines in visitation which resulted from the widespread fires in Yellowstone National Park in 1988, declines in the New England ski and foliage-viewing tourist markets as a result of the energy crises of the early 1980s, or the periodic declines in skier visitations at resort areas affected by unusually warm and/or dry winters.

The conditions of resource dependency clearly contribute to a potential for extreme economic, demographic and social instability which can threaten the viability and sustainability of many rural communities. The exploitation of rural areas and their natural resources by extralocal centers of population and power contributes to a pattern of uneven development, and frequently gives rise to persistent underdevelopment. Cycles of growth, stagnation and decline cause a host of problems that strain the adaptive capabilities of rural communities and people. These cycles of growth followed by decline, reflecting the double-edged sword of rural resource dependency, are a major obstacle to effective rural development response efforts.

Obstacles to effective response

The context of instability and cyclical growth and decline which characterizes many resource-dependent rural communities creates some substantial obstacles to effective rural development responses. Whether initiated locally or through extralocal intervention, attempts to enhance community stability and viability often fail because conditions of resource dependency have left the community incapable of acting effectively to pursue legitimate development opportunities (Krannich and Greider, 1990; Humphrey, 1990; Swanson, 1990; Wilkinson, 1990). In fact, the cumulative effects of sustained instability can limit the capability of the local community to even *react* to problems associated with either growth or decline, much less to *act* in an organized, proactive manner to stimulate desirable change (Tilley, 1973; Luloff, 1990b). This incapacity for community action occurs for several reasons. First, residents accustomed to cyclical expansion and decline may see little use in responding to changes, when past experience suggests that such changes are likely to be transitory. Thus, responses to growth pressures tend to be inadequate, due in part to expectations that the growth will not be self-sustaining. Responses to decline are also often all but absent, reflecting perceptions that decline is also a cyclical and inevitable dimension of community change. This pattern of non-response is especially evident in places such as mining towns which have experienced recurrent boom and bust periods during the past 50 to 100 years. Residents of such places frequently exhibit a willingness to do without many community facilities and services even during periods of prosperity, due in part to concerns about the ability to support expanded services during future periods of stagnation or decline. Similarly, periods of stagnation and decline frequently generate little in the way of organized growth-promotion efforts. In some instances this reflects a widespread sense of powerlessness and quiescence, resulting in a tendency for residents of such communities to resign themselves to their fate (Gaventa, 1980). Interestingly, in many places which have experienced cycles of growth and decline, a failure to intervene into the process in order to develop some stability reflects expectations, based on long-term experiences, that growth will inevitably return.

Second, the periods of in-and-out migration which characterize many resource-dependent communities can contribute to the emergence of a more or less 'rootless' population (Williams, Frost and Sibley, 1960). Residents of such places frequently have a limited array of long-term social ties and commitments, which can result from either the presence of relatively large numbers of recent in-migrants or the presence of longer-term residents who have witnessed the outmigration of many family members and friends. In either case, the conditions associated with cycles of instability provide residents with little reason to anticipate the establishment of local commitments in the future. Residents of resource-dependent communities therefore find it difficult to think seriously about or commit effort on behalf of the future of their community.

Third, the draining away of human capital during periods of outmigration can reduce the number of locals who are suitably prepared to address the problems of dependency. As has been widely documented elsewhere, those who migrate away from rural communities during periods of stagnation and decline tend to be younger, and generally more capable with respect to employment skills and educational attainment (Lee, 1966, 1970; Schwarzeller, Brown and Mangalam, 1971; Beale, 1978). This leaves many rural communities with a scarcity of local individuals who are both capable of and willing to devote the effort needed to effectively organize the community in pursuit of rural development opportunities. In short, the community often lacks the human capital needed to seize the moment when rare opportunities for truly beneficial and sustainable development become available.

Another constraint on the response capabilities of such communities is the limited array of development alternatives which are likely to become available. Quite often, new alternatives which arise represent the potential for development of a different type of resource-related industry. As a result, communities often find themselves entangled in a dependency substitution process, whereby a previous or existing form of resource dependency is simply replaced by another. There are numerous examples of one-time mining communities where the development of ski resort facilities has transformed the community from mining-dependent to recreation-dependent; Park City, Utah and Telluride, Colorado are well-known examples of this situation. Similarly, some areas once dependent on agriculture, logging and/or mining have made a transition to dependency on recreation and tourism, as evidenced by the transformation of places like Jackson Hole, Wyoming and Moab, Utah into major tourism centers. In other cases, communities previously dependent on agricultural activities have attracted large-scale mining activities and a resulting dependency substitution, as has occurred in sections of the northern Great Plains (Gold, 1985).

Unfortunately, such shifts often provide little in the way of real opportunities for development and diversification, for one form of resource dependency is frequently incompatible with another. For example, tourism attracted by natural scenic features is generally considered to be incompatible with widespread timber harvesting or surface mining activities. As a result, areas where recreation development becomes extensive often exhibit growing resistance to proposals for new or expanded mining or logging, even though those activities comprise the traditional economic base of the area. In the same vein, places characterized by new and expanding recreation and tourism developments often experience land-use conflicts involving previously established agricultural activities that may retain land targeted for expansion of recreation developments, generate offensive odors, or cause concerns over use of agricultural chemicals. Nor is it surprising that large-scale surface mining can interfere with traditional agricultural land uses, resulting in an erosion of the traditional socio-economic structures based on ranching and farming.

One major consequence of this incompatibility is the potential for widespread community conflict between those who espouse established and traditional resource-dependent activities and those wishing to promote new resource utilization processes and activities. Many resource-dependent communities exhibit social and cultural systems which have evolved over the course of generations that are intricately intertwined with the traditional resource-based economic structures of resource utilization. Such entrenched social and cultural systems can limit local acceptance of

THE LIBRARY
BISHOP BURTON COLLEGE
BEVERLEY HU17 8QG
TEL: 0964 550481 Ex: 227

development options which are perceived to clash with the established resource-based community social organization.

One well-documented example of the emergence of community conflict under such conditions is provided by the case of Delta, Utah, where rancorous conflict (Gamson, 1966) arose over the transfer of water rights from traditional agricultural uses to an industrial one (Greider and Little, 1988; Little and Greider, 1983). Other examples include conflicts in areas of the northern Great Plains where the traditional ranching culture was threatened by surface mining activities (Gold, 1985), places where tourism and recreation developments threatened traditional agricultural activities (Canan and Hennessy, 1989) and places where the subsistence hunting and fishing culture of native Alaskans has been threatened by oil exploration (Robbins and Little, 1988).

Even in situations where there are development alternatives which do not rely directly on natural resource utilization, the range of opportunities available to resource-dependent communities is often severely constrained. Promotion of industrial development and other growth processes is common in non-metropolitan places, despite the fact that successful growth promotion outcomes may be rare (Krannich and Humphrey, 1983). The potential for development of industry or other stability-producing economic activities in remote areas characterized by a history of cyclical growth and stagnation is often especially limited. One possible exception to this situation involves the development of various undesirable or noxious facilities, which are often extremely difficult to site in more populous and/or more politically powerful areas. Facilities such as hazardous waste dumps and incinerators or sludge and solid waste landfills are frequently proposed for rural areas. Not surprisingly, these types of facilities are much more likely to receive local support in communities where a period of decline has created a climate of desperation. Such a climate engenders local support for virtually all new economic development opportunities. It is in such a context that resource-dependent communities are prone to engage in what many others would call bad deals. Even when proposed projects are widely recognized as undesirable in terms of health, safety, lifestyle, or other quality of life dimensions, there is often broad-based local support for project implementation. Such support often reflects a collective willingness to trade off quality of life for new economic opportunities. Often such actions are indicative of the resignations of such communities to a fate which allows that even an undesirable facility is better than nothing.

Two recent illustrations of this situation are provided by the communities of Caliente, Nevada and Green River, Utah. Both have experienced sustained periods of stagnation and decline, reflecting the deterioration of the resource-related economic activities that had once sustained community growth. In Caliente, stagnation and decline have endured since the early 1950s, when a transformation from steam engines to diesel engines initiated a period of substantial and sustained reductions in local railroad-related employment opportunities (Cottrell, 1951). Further, the virtual collapse of once extensive mining in the area coupled with the withering of agricultural activities have compounded this community's economic woes. Green River, Utah has also withered since the 1960s, due largely to the collapse of the uranium mining industry which grew there during the 1950s and early 1960s.

Recently, both of these communities have been proposed as sites for the development of hazardous waste disposal and incineration facilities, to be owned and operated by non-local corporations. In both instances, these facilities were previously proposed for other communities in the region which were not experiencing the persistent stagnation associated with Caliente or Green River. When local opposition to the development of hazardous waste facilities emerged, the project proponents sought alternative sites where local opposition would be less formidable; two places were located—Caliente and Green River.

Both communities have expressed strong support for the development of the proposed hazardous waste facilities, contradicting the 'Not In My Back Yard' (NIMBY) response which typically arises in communities confronted by proposals for development of nearby toxic or hazardous facilities (Edelstein, 1988). Local support for these projects is in fact apparently widespread, despite the potential environmental and health hazards of such facilities and the limited number of new jobs, few of which can be expected to go to local residents.

Such support may in fact reflect little more than frustration with the sustained periods of decline these communities have endured as a result of dependence on non-viable resource-related industries. While others might view such actions as getting in on a 'bad deal', many local residents apparently view such facilities as the only development alternatives available. This is reflected in the words of one county commissioner, who observed that 'it's sad that we're to the point where we have to compete for these kinds of things, but we really don't have any other options'. In essence, such observations reflect an awareness that the pursuit of hazardous, noxious, or otherwise undesirable facilities may represent community participation in a 'bad deal', but that such facilities may also represent the 'only deal' which is likely to be forthcoming.

Implications for rural development

The preceding discussion suggests that resource-dependent rural communities face a staggering array of obstacles to effective rural development. In particular, outside control of resources and resource development decisions, a situation common throughout rural society, restrict the ability of rural communities to take direction of their own destinies. In addition, residents of many rural communities express a degree of quiescence and apathy about rural development goals, due to both a widespread sense of powerlessness and a tendency for past or anticipated residential transiency to restrict levels of community attachment and commitment. The human capital resources of rural communities tend to be constrained as a result of the periodic occurrence of economic decline and outmigration. Finally, the options for economic diversification and development of new employment opportunities are often limited. As a result, resource-dependent rural communities frequently become involved in the substitution of one form of resource dependency for another, or participate in bad deals involving undesirable projects which provide few if any rural development benefits.

In order to address the problems of rural resource-dependent communities in a meaningful way, rural development initiatives need to address these obstacles in a coherent and integrated manner, rather than in a piecemeal fashion. This involves a multifaceted approach which would address both the constraints linked to local community conditions and those linked to extralocal forces.

At the community level, the problems of apathetic local attitudes and pessimism about the ability to effect meaningful community actions need to be addressed through carefully designed community development programs. Programs which foster a sense of collective purpose and build organizational structures and capabilities are required. This approach to community development, while frequently the focus of academic discussions, is often bypassed by policy-makers. The latter tend to place undue emphasis on bricks and mortar programs as the focus of local development efforts. Such programs are largely delivered through grants and loans, which attempt to address rural fiscal and service shortcomings. Although many communities may need physical and fiduciary bolstering, effective efforts to break the cycle of resource dependency and encourage proactive community responses *must* start with efforts to build community leadership and action structures, rather than infrastructure (Israel and Beaulieu, 1990; Sokolow, 1990; Luloff, 1990b). Such efforts could also help ameliorate conflicts which emerge over new development proposals, especially when all segments of the community are involved in collective decision-making efforts.

Such a procedure would address human capital limitations. Often there are capable and competent individuals who, given the opportunity and encouragement, will emerge and become involved in rural development efforts. A comprehensive rural development program must capitalize on the presence of such individuals, often thought of as marginal men (Coleman, 1957), through the provision of effective incentive and training programs. The provision of incentives, perhaps in the form of part-time employment or consultant opportunities, would help to encourage such individuals to commit their time and development efforts. The involvement of such individuals in carefully focused training programs addressing issues such as grantsmanship and organizational skills would enhance their knowledge about rural development programs and opportunities, thereby enabling them to respond to other opportunities as they emerge. Finally, the development of effective information dissemination programs and community education efforts would help to expand the array of informed and capable local residents who could be drawn into participation in rural development efforts.

Addressing the problem of the outside control of resources and decisions is more difficult. However, a starting-point in that process is the development of local community structures and human resource capabilities in a manner that enhances both organizational strength and levels of local participation and commitment. That foundation provides a basis for efforts to build community action responses which would enable local communities to interact more effectively with, negotiate with, and if necessary confront outside agencies and firms whose actions may affect local development opportunities (Little and Krannich, 1982). This component of rural development involves helping local communities learn how to stand up for themselves, how to represent the community better in negotiations with potential developers, how to use available programs, regulations and laws to their best advantage, and when to engage the more urban corporate mentality of worker buyout programs (Russell, 1985). The development of such capabilities would reduce the tendency for rural communities to engage in bad deals, and would help them to pursue more effectively projects and opportunities that would generate maximum social and economic benefits while minimizing the negative impacts potentially associated with some projects.

In addition, the issue of extralocal resource control should become a focus of national rural development policies. New programs need to be developed which provide incentives for resource development projects that are locally owned or controlled, and which will utilize local labor. This could take the form of rural enterprise zone programs, in which local investors would receive subsidized loans and grants to pursue business and industrial ventures. A large element of such a program would be placed on retention and expansion efforts as opposed to industrial capture. By reinforcing efforts here, local firms with ties to the community receive preferential attention and support. This linkage will help deter the footlooseness of many of those industries captured as a result of economic incentives (Bluestone and Harrison, 1982). In addition, programs which might encourage the development of community-owned and employee-owned businesses and industries could benefit rural communities, much as they have benefited urban areas where employees have purchased and operated steel mills closed by multinational corporations.

In summary, the problems of resource-dependent rural communities are multifaceted. Consequently, any realistic effort to implement effective rural development programs to address the problems of resource dependency must also be multifaceted. Anything less than a comprehensive rural development approach that addresses both local and extralocal dimensions of the resource dependency cycle will inevitably fail.

References

Beale, C.L., 1975, *The revival of population growth in nonmetropolitan America*, Economic Research Service, US Department of Agriculture, ERS-605, Washington, DC

Beale, C.L., 1978, 'People on the land' in T.R. Ford (ed.), *Rural USA: persistence and change*, Iowa State University Press, Ames, pp. 37–54

Beale, C.L. and Fuguitt, G.V., 1986, 'Metropolitan and nonmetropolitan population growth in the United States since 1980' in *New dimensions in rural policy: building upon our heritage*, prepared for the Subcommittee on Agriculture and Transportation, Joint Economic Committee, US Congress, US Government Printing Office, Washington, DC, pp. 46–62

Bluestone, B. and Harrison, J., 1982, *The deindustrialization of America*, Basic Books, New York

Bluestone, B. and Harrison, J., 1986, 'Patterns of change in the nonmetro and metro labor force since 1979' in *New dimensions in rural policy: building upon our heritage*, prepared for the Subcommittee on Agriculture and Transportation, Joint Economic Committee, US Congress, US Government Printing Office, Washington, DC, pp. 121–33

Brinkman, G., 1974, 'The conditions and problems of metropolitan America' in G. Brinkman (ed.), *The development of rural America*, University Press of Kansas, Wichita, pp. 51-73

Brown, D.L., 1988, 'Beyond the rural population turnaround: implications for rural economic development' in *Proceedings of the first annual meeting of the national rural studies committee*, Western Rural Development Center, Corvallis, OR, pp. 47–56

Buttel, F. and Newby, H., 1980, *The rural sociology of the advanced societies: critical perspectives*, Allenheld Osman, Montclair, NJ

Canan, P. and Hennessy, M., 1989, 'The growth machine, tourism and the selling of culture', *Sociological Perspectives*, **32** (2): 227–43

Coleman, J., 1957, *Community conflict*, The Free Press, Glencoe, IL

Cottrell, W.F., 1951, 'Death dieselization', *American Sociological Review*, **16** (4): 358–65

Edelstein, M., 1988, *Contaminated communities: the social and psychological impacts of residential toxic exposure*, Westview Press, Boulder, CO

Field, D.R. and Burch, Jr, W.R., 1988, *Rural sociology and the environment*, Greenwood Press, Westport, CN

Gallaher, A. and Padfield, H., 1980, *The dying community*, University of New Mexico Press, Albuquerque

Gamson, W., 1966, 'Rancorous conflict in community politics', *American Sociological Review*, **31** (Feb.): 71–81

Gaventa, J., 1980, *Power and powerlessness: quiescence and rebellion in an Appalachian valley*, University of Illinois Press, Champaign, IL

Gold, R.L., 1985, *Ranching, mining, and human impact of natural resource development*, Transaction Books, New Brunswick, NJ

Greider, T. and Little, R.L., 1988, 'Social action and social impacts: subjective interpretation of environmental change', *Society and Natural Resources*, 1 (1): 45–55

Heffernan, W.D. and Heffernan, J.B., 1986, 'The farm crisis and the rural community' in *New dimensions in rural policy: building upon our heritage*, prepared for the Subcommittee on Agriculture and Transportation, Joint Economic Committee, US Congress, US Government Printing Office, Washington, DC, pp. 273–80

Humphrey, C.R., 1990, 'Timber dependent communities' in A.E. Luloff and L.E. Swanson (eds), *American rural communities*, Westview Press, Boulder, CO, pp. 34–60

Israel, G. and Beaulieu, L., 1990, 'Community leadership' in A.E. Luloff and L.E. Swanson (eds), *American rural communities*, Westview Press, Boulder, CO, pp. 181–202

Kraenzel, C.F., 1980, *The social costs of space in the yonland*, Big Sky Books, Bozeman, MT

Krannich, R.S. and Greider, T., 1990, 'Rapid growth effects on rural community relations' in A.E. Luloff and L.E. Swanson (eds), *American rural communities*, Westview Press, Boulder, CO, pp. 61–73

Krannich, R.S. and Humphrey, C.R., 1983, 'Local mobilization and community growth. Toward an assessment of the growth machine hypothesis', *Rural Sociology*, 48 (Spring): 60–81

Lee, E., 1966, 'A theory of migration', *Demography*, 3: 47–57

Lee, E., 1970, 'Migration in relation to education, intellect and social structure', *Population Index*, 36 (4): 437–44

Lichter, D.T. and Costanzo, J.A., 1987, 'Nonmetropolitan underemployment and labor force composition', *Rural Sociology*, 52 (Fall): 329–44

Little, R.L. and Greider, T., 1983, *Water transfer from agriculture to industry: two Utah examples*, Monograph No. 10, Institute for Social Science Research on Natural Resources, Utah State University, Logan, UT

Little, R.L. and Krannich, R.S., 1982, 'Organizing for local control in rapid growth communities', in B.A. Weber and R.E. Howell (eds), *Coping with rapid growth in rural communities*, Westview Press, Boulder CO, pp. 221–41

Lovejoy, S.B. and Krannich, R.S., 1982, 'Rural industrial development and domestic dependency relations: toward an integrated perspective', *Rural Sociology*, 47 (Fall): 475–95

Luloff, A.E., 1990a, 'Small town demographics: current patterns of community change' in A.E. Luloff and L.E. Swanson (eds), *American rural communities*, Westview Press, Boulder, CO, pp. 7–18

Luloff, A.E., 1990b, 'Community and social change: how do small communities act?' in A.E. Luloff and L.E. Swanson (eds), *American rural communities*, Westview Press, Boulder, CO, pp. 214–27

Morrison, P.A. and Wheeler, J.P., 1976, 'Rural renaissance in America? The revival of population growth in remote areas', *Population Bulletin*, 31 (3): 1–26

Price, M.L. and Clay, D.C., 1980, 'Structural disturbances in rural communities: some repercussions of the migration turnaround in Michigan', *Rural Sociology*, 45 (Winter): 591–607

THE LIBRARY
BISHOP BURTON COLLEGE
BEVERLEY HU17 8QG
TEL: 0964 550481 Ex: 227

Robbins, L.A. and Little, R.L., 1988, 'Subsistence hunting and natural resource extraction: St Lawrence Island, Alaska,', *Society and Natural Resources*, **1** (1): 17–29

Russell, R., 1985, *Sharing ownership in the workplace*, State University of New York Press, Albany

Schwarzeller, H.K., Brown, J.S. and Mangalam, J.J., 1971, *Mountain families in transition: a case study of Appalachian migration*, Pennsylvania State University Press, University Park

Sokolow, A.D., 1990, 'Leadership and implementation in rural economic development' in A.E. Luloff and L.E. Swanson (eds), *American rural communities*, Westview Press, Boulder, CO, pp. 203–13

Strange, M., 1988, *Family farming: a new economic vision*, University of Nebraska Press, Lincoln

Summers, G.F., Evans, S., Clemente, F., Beck, E. and Minkoff, J., 1976, *Industrial invasion of nonmetropolitan America*, Praeger, New York

Swanson, L., 1990, 'Rethinking assumptions about farm and community' in A.E. Luloff and L.E. Swanson (eds), *American rural communities*, Westview Press, Boulder, CO, pp. 19–33

Tilley, C., 1973, 'Do communities act?', *Sociological Inquiry*, **43** (3–4): 209–40

US Department of Agriculture, Economic Research Service, (USDA-ERS), 1989, *Rural America: economic performance, 1989*, Economic Research Service, Washington, DC

Vogeler, I., 1981, *The myth of the family farm: agribusiness dominance of US agriculture*, Westview Press, Boulder, CO

Weber, B.A., Castle, E.N. and Shriver, A.L., 1988, 'Performance of Natural Resource Industries' in D.L. Brown, N. Reid, H. Bluestone, D. McGranahan and S. Mazie (eds), *Rural economic development in the 1980s: prospects for the future*, US Department of Agriculture, Economic Research Service, Washington, DC, pp. 103–33

Weber, B.A. and Howell, R.E. (eds), 1982, *Coping with rapid growth in rural communities*, Westview Press, Boulder, CO

Whiting, L.R., 1974, *Communities left behind: alternatives for development*, Iowa State University Press, Ames.

Wilkinson, K.P., 1986, 'Communities left behind—again' in *New dimensions in rural policy: building upon our heritage*, prepared for the Subcommittee on Agriculture and Transportation, Joint Economic Committee, US Congress, US Government Printing Office, Washington, DC, pp. 341–6

Wilkinson, K.P., 1990, 'Crime and community' in A.E. Luloff and L.E. Swanson (eds), *American rural communities*, Westview Press, Boulder, CO, pp. 151–67

Williams, M.J., Frost, H.H. and Sibley, W.E., 1960, 'Page, Arizona: a rootless community?' *Proceedings of the Utah Academy of Arts and Letters*, **47**: 97–101

Zuiches, J.J. and Brown, D.L., 1978, 'The changing character of the nonmetropolitan population, 1950–1975' in T.R. Ford (ed.), *Rural USA: persistence and change*, Iowa State University Press, Ames, pp. 55–72

2 On the threshold of the 90s: issues in US rural planning and development

Mark B. Lapping and Irene Szedlmayer

As the decade of the 1980s drew to a close a wide range of issues and problems confronted rural America. These included: the national 'no net loss' policy regarding development on non-tidal wetlands; farmland preservation; farm chemicals and pesticides; drought; state plans; and rural economic development. These issues are now considered in turn.

Wetlands

Without doubt growing concern over wetlands has emerged as one of the nation's central rural land-use issues. The National Wetlands Policy Forum, a group of governors, farmers, developers and conservationists convened by the Private Conservation Foundation, at the request of the US Environmental Protection Agency, estimated that the US has lost more than 50 per cent of its wetlands since Europeans began settling in America in the 1600s (Detlefsen, 1989a). The National Wetlands Policy Forum, has set a goal of 'no net loss' of wetlands to development, a goal supported by President Bush. However, an agreement between the US Army Corps of Engineers and the US Environmental Protection Agency, intended to implement the 'no net loss' of non-tidal wetlands expected to become effective in December, 1989, was withdrawn at the last moment, modified, and re-released in February 1990.

This change was brought about largely to meet the demands of the oil industry and the Alaska congressional delegation regarding the impact of 'no net loss' policy upon Alaska, half of which is wetlands, and the North Slope, in particular, virtually all of which is wetlands when not frozen. The modified agreement acknowledges that 'no net loss' might not be feasible in every case. However, the exception, as written, is broad enough to cover other situations where a high proportion of the land is wetlands (Detlefsen, 1990).

In other wetlands matters, the Environmental Protection Agency is now pursuing criminal prosecution of wetlands violators more vigorously. For example, between 1972 and early 1988 there was only one conviction for infilling a wetland under the Clean Water Act, but between early 1988 and early 1989 four convictions were handed down in federal court (Detlefsen, 1989a). In October 1989, a Federal District Court judge in Florida sentenced two men to 21 months in jail, without parole, plus one year of probation, a $5,000 fine and the cost of restoration of the wetlands for knowingly infilling a wetland without a permit and digging a drainage canal on their property (Detlefsen, 1989b).

Numerous other wetlands legislative proposals were made in Congress. Bills were introduced to create private charitable wetlands trusts, conserve and restore coastal wetlands in Louisiana, and to expand the Conservation Reserve Program to 60 million acres by 1995 and establish a 'net gain' policy for wetlands (Detlefsen, 1989c; Detlefsen, 1989a; Detlefsen, 1989d).

Farmland preservation

During the past few years, Federal level interest in farmland preservation has receded, though interest in soil conservation may be said to be higher than ever. Most of the initiatives of relevance are being promulgated and implemented on the state and local levels. Land in the United States devoted to urban use nearly tripled nationwide from 1949 to 1982 while the amount of land used for agriculture in 1982 (1.1 billion acres) was about the same as in 1949 (Detlefsen, 1989e). Controversies about the future of agriculture are most pronounced when urban and rural residents collide at the urban–rural fringe. About 372 of the nation's 640 leading agricultural counties are either within or adjacent to major metropolitan areas.

All states and many local governments have taken some measures to encourage the retention of land in agricultural use (Lapping, Daniels and Keller, 1989). The eight most common techniques used by the states to preserve farmland (followed in parentheses by the number of states that have adopted such a program) are: differential tax assessment (50); and centralized land-use policies (8); transfer/purchase of development rights (16); agricultural zoning (25); agricultural districting (16); right-to-farm laws (47); absentee landownership regulations (27); erosion and sediment control legislation (20) (Klein, 1980). These programs are identified by state in Table 2.1.

Differential tax assessment programs fall into three main categories: (1) preferential assessment in which agricultural land is taxed according to its use as farmland rather than its potential 'highest and best' use; (2) deferred taxation which combines preferential assessment with the requirements that some portion of the tax benefit conferred be repaid if the land is converted to a non-farming use; and (3) restrictive agreements which provide preferential tax treatment for a specified period of time in exchange for a restriction of use to agriculture of said land. Taxation of capital gains from the sale of land can be used to discourage speculation of agricultural lands. In Vermont, the capital tax rates vary according to the amount of the gain and the length of time the land is held (Daniels, Daniels and Lapping, 1986).

Agricultural zoning usually takes the form of minimum lot size restrictions. The minimum lot size must be sufficient to maintain blocks of land large enough to allow profitable farming and also be too expensive for residential uses.

Agricultural districts are formed voluntarily by farmers in an area of some specified minimum size (500 acres, for example, under the New York program). The creation of an agricultural district may confer upon the land within the district preferential tax treatment, protection from nuisance laws restricting farm practices and control on extensions of public sewer and water lines and roads into districts.

Purchase of development rights programs allow a farmer to sell an easement restricting development to the government while retaining ownership of the land. The easement runs with the land and is binding upon all subsequent purchasers. Transfer of development rights (TDR) programs attempt to address the costliness of governmental purchase of development rights. Under a TDR program owners of land within a designated agricultural preservation zone may sell the development rights of their land to owners of land within development zones. When development rights are transferred from preservation zones land within development zones may be developed to a greater density than otherwise allowed.

Right-to-farm legislation protects agriculture when suburban and urban residents in the vicinity of farmland, while relishing the bucolic setting provided by agriculture, object to the noise of farm machinery, the smell of livestock and manure, traffic congestion aggravated by slow-moving farm vehicles and the use of toxic herbicides and pesticides. Non-farmers have pushed to enact nuisance laws that restrict or ban certain farm practices. Right-to-farm laws favor agricultural uses and supersede local nuisance ordinances. The laws usually require that agriculture predate the other uses, that a farm be managed according to 'good' or 'standard' farming practices and that farmers comply with applicable environmental and land-use controls (Lapping and Leutwiler, 1988).

Though not yet much used in the United States, land banking and land trusts offer some promise for preserving agricultural land. A land trust can be a private, non-profit corporation that accepts philanthropic gifts with the objective of holding land in its natural state or agricultural use. A land trust can also be formed between a local government and a farmer, when the farmer is allowed to concentrate the development potential of all the land, on a certain portion of the property, if the remainder is dedicated to the land trust for continued agricultural use. Land banking involves the actual acquisition of farmland by government for future sale or lease back to farmers.

Table 2.1 *State programs for farmland preservation*

	Differential tax assessment	Centralized land use policies	Transfer/ purchase of development rights	Agricultural zoning	Agricultural districting	Right-to-farm laws	Absentee landownership reg./rest.	Erosion and sediment control legislation
Alabama	X		X			X		
Alaska	X		X			X		
Arizona	X				X	X		
Arkansas	X					X		
California	X	X	X	X	X	X	X	
Colorado	X			X		X		
Connecticut	X		X			X	X	
Delaware	X					X		X
Florida	X	X				X	X	
Georgia	X					X		X
Hawaii	X	X		X	X	X	X	X
Idaho	X			X	X	X	X	X
Illinois	X			X	X	X	X	
Indiana	X			X		X	X	
Iowa	X			X	X	X	X	X
Kansas	X			X		X	X	
Kentucky	X				X	X	X	
Louisiana	X				X	X	X	
Maine	X	X	X	X		X		X
Maryland	X		X	X	X	X		X
Massachusetts	X		X			X		
Michigan	X			X	X	X		X
Minnesota	X			X	X	X	X	X
Mississippi	X					X	X	
Missouri	X					X	X	
Montana	X					X	X	X

State	1	2	3	4	5	6	7
Nebraska	X					X	X
Nevada	X					X	X
New Hampshire	X		X		X		X
New Jersey	X	X	X	X			
New Mexico	X				X		
New York	X	X	X	X	X		X
North Carolina	X		X		X	X	X
North Dakota	X	X			X	X	
Ohio	X			X	X	X	X
Oklahoma	X				X	X	
Oregon	X	X	X		X	X	X
Pennsylvania	X	X		X	X	X	X
Rhode Island	X	X			X		
South Carolina	X		X		X	X	X
South Dakota	X		X		X	X	X
Tennessee	X		X		X		
Texas	X				X		
Utah	X		X		X		
Vermont	X	X	X		X	X	X
Virginia	X		X	X	X	X	
Washington	X	X	X	X	X		
West Virginia	X		X			X	
Wisconsin	X	X	X		X	X	
Wyoming	X					X	

Note: The data are from National Association of State Department of Agriculture Research Foundation (1985); Klein (1980, p. 12); Lapping, Penfold, and MacPherson (1983, p. 466); and Authan (1988, p. 53)

Most of these agricultural preservation techniques have serious limitations related to cost and in preserving land most at risk for conversion to other uses, that is, agricultural land close to urbanized areas. Differential tax assessments have not been able to dampen the increasing monetary value of farmland for non-farm uses. 'Roll-back' penalties are usually insufficient to discourage conversion. In many cases, speculators holding agricultural land have been the primary beneficiaries of the tax breaks. The most serious obstacle to preservation of farmland is the declining profitability of farming which these land preservation techniques can only marginally address.

Farm chemicals and pesticides

The safety of American farm products and practices has increasingly been brought into question. Decisions were made by the US Environmental Protection Agency (EPA) in 1989 to bar the application of the widely used fungicide captan on a broad range of fruits and vegetables because it posed a significant cancer risk and to phase out the use of daminozide (traded as Alar) on apples because of significant risk of cancer, especially in children (Shafecoff, 1989). The Environmental Protection Agency also proposed to ban for most uses a broad class of chemicals—EDBC (ethylene bisdithiocarbamate)—widely applied to fruits and vegetables because of concerns of cancer risk (Gold, 1989). These decisions provided some support for the concerns raised by consumer and environmental activists about chemicals approved for use before the EPA was established in 1972. The testing that these chemicals underwent was less rigorous than contemporary standards would require and modern evaluation of their risks and benefits has not yet been completed (Mott and Snyder, 1987).

Two calculations—(1) the estimate of health risk that a certain amount of pesticide would impose and (2) a measure of how much chemical residual remains on food sold to consumers—are the basis of state and federal regulations of agricultural chemicals. Representatives of the agricultural community and agricultural chemical producers assert that pesticide residues are so small as to constitute absolutely no threat. Virtually no one advocates that people refrain from eating fresh fruits and vegetables. However, there is little doubt that growing public concerns over food safety, fertilizer-based soil and water pollution and degradation, and farmer and farmworker health and safety have combined to make these issues among the most significant for US agriculture in the years to come.

At the same time that states have been moving to retain farmlands, enhance the viability of farming—often seen as the creation of a more entrepreneurial agriculture—and guarantee safety of the food system, a massive drought affected much of American agriculture in the closing years of the decade, as shown in Figure 2.1.

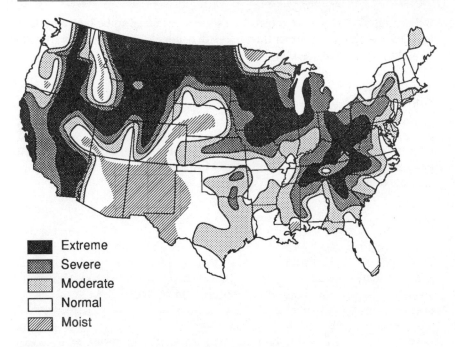

Extreme
Severe
Moderate
Normal
Moist

Figure 2.1 *US drought severity, August 1988*

Source: National Oceanic and Atmospheric Administration, US Department of Agriculture Joint Agricultural Weather Facility (1988)

Drought

By the fall of 1988, 1,531 counties in 24 states were declared eligible for Federal drought assistance. Eighteen states were entirely covered by this major agriculture relief program. These states were: Alabama, Delaware, Illinois, Indiana, Iowa, Kentucky, Maryland, Michigan, Minnesota, Mississippi, Missouri, New Jersey, North Dakota, Ohio, Pennsylvania, South Dakota, Wisconsin, and West Virginia (News Division, 1988). Even with such emergency loan support available, farm incomes took another hit just as they were on the upswing. One USDA study put the loss to direct income for farmers from between 12 per cent in North Dakota to less than 0.5 per cent in Ohio (Petrulius, Sommer and Hines, 1989; Sanberg and Taylor, 1988). Generally speaking, the impact of drought on the local economy increased as the importance of agriculture to the county/region's overall domestic product increased. Where non-farm economic inputs were stronger, the drought's impact declined in relative importance. Another study, which focused specifically on Kansas, estimated the total loss to the state's economy at $1.61 billion in 1988/89, or 3 per cent of the total Kansas 1989 gross product (Tierney, Darling and

Willard, 1989). The most severe losses were estimated to be borne by farm families and the Main Street businesses dependent upon them. Clearly, the drought constituted another blow to rural America.

State plans

Several states altered existing or initiated planning systems which dealt with rural land-use issues generally and the subdivision of rural lands into more intensive uses more specifically. Most prominent among these efforts are those of New Jersey and Vermont.

New Jersey

New Jersey's State Planning Act (NJSA 52:18A-19b *et seq.*) adopted in 1986 mandates the adoption of a plan which promotes beneficial economic growth; conserves natural resources including agricultural land, environmentally sensitive areas, historic sites and scenic and recreational open space; facilitates the revitalization of the cities; encourages the development of affordable housing; and allows the provision of necessary infrastructure in an economic and efficient manner (Lawrence, 1988).

At the close of 1989 the Preliminary State Development and Redevelopment Plan was undergoing an innovative 'cross-acceptance' process whereby New Jersey's 21 counties and 565 municipalities compare the plan with their own county and municipal plans and regulations (Office of State Planning, 1989). The process is expected to result in a written document specifying the consistencies and inconsistencies, compatibilities and incompatibilities among the county and municipal plans and regulations compared with the Preliminary State Plan. Following the comparison phase, the three governmental entities will enter a negotiation phase in an attempt to reconcile the inconsistencies and incompatibilities. The State Planning Commission will use the results of these negotiations to formulate an Interim Plan. A state-wide impact assessment will be conducted upon the Interim Plan. Then, following a series of public hearings on the Interim Plan, the State Planning Commission will adopt a State Plan.

New Jersey's Preliminary State Development and Redevelopment Plan (hereinafter the PSDRP) encompasses three major components: state-wide strategies, a regional design system and a tier system. The six state-wide strategies include (1) the strengthening of planning capabilities at all levels of government; (2) the provision of carefully planned and prudently financed infrastructure; (3) fostering beneficial economic development; (4) ensuring a variety of housing affordable to varying income groups in a choice of locations; (5) better integration of land-use planning with the highways, roadways and public transportation systems; and (6) improved coordination, management and protection of natural and cultural resources. The second major component of the PSDRP is a regional design system. The regional design system, which aims to redistribute growth from sprawling settlement patterns into relatively compact, mixed-use communities, has three essential parts: (1) a hierarchy of central places—cities, corridor centers, towns, villages and hamlets; (2) transportation corridors which connect the central places into regional networks; and (3) the land surrounding the regional network which should remain sparsely settled (Office of State Planning, 1989). The third major component of the PSDRP involves the geographic and functional division of the state into seven tiers: (1) redeveloping cities and suburbs; (2) stable cities and suburbs; (3) suburban and rural towns; (4) suburbanizing areas; (5) exurban reserve; (6) agricultural areas; and (7) environmentally sensitive areas.

The PSDRP's state-wide strategies, regional design system and tier system all have significant ramifications for New Jersey's rural and agricultural areas. The State Planning Act specifically requires the State Planning Commission to identify agricultural areas and to coordinate planning activities and establish state-wide planning objectives with respect to agricultural and farmland retention. Tier Six contains New Jersey's most productive farmlands, those with longterm economic viability for the production of crops, timber, livestock, poultry, dairy or nursery products, determined in cooperation with County Agricultural Development Boards.

In Tier Six the PSDRP calls for the promotion of a land development pattern that directs development into communities of central place, preserves the rural character by managing growth according to carrying capacity analysis and retains large, contiguous and economically viable areas of farmland which are buffered from incompatible uses. The PSDRP calls for adequate levels of public investment in infrastructure to sustain agricultural activities, support the rural economy and protect public health and safety. Capital facilities and services should not be provided when they conflict with the goal of farmland retention. In Tier Six economic development should be pursued in a manner which retains agriculture, ensures the fiscal viability of rural municipalities, provides off-farm employment opportunities and expands the market for farm products. Housing development in Tier Six should be centered in rural communities, in a wide range of tenure and cost choices, consistent with the primary objective of farmland retention.

Tiers Five, Six and Seven are all rural areas, but it is Tier Six—agricultural areas—that has proven to be the most controversial element of the PSDRP. A primary concern raised during cross-acceptance is the protection of farmland equity. In many parts of New Jersey the market value of farmland for non-agricultural development purposes far exceeds its value for agricultural uses. The persistent problem of eroding agricultural profitability has resulted in farmers relying on these rising land values as collateral for farm and non-farm loans and retirement income. The PSDRP states that farmland equity issues must be addressed through a number of mechanisms including land acquisition, easement purchase and easement transfer. The Commission has supported transfer of development rights legislation. The State Planning Commission believes it has already taken an accommodating stance by rejecting agricultural zoning as a recommendation, but farmer interests coupled with developer interests want the Planning Commission to demonstrate that there will be financing to compensate for any loss in land value once the plan is implemented (Bierbaum, 20 April 1990). At this time it is uncertain what additional compromises will be written into the plan as a result of the negotiation phase of cross-acceptance.

Vermont

Among the most famous state planning strategies has been Vermont's, known generally as Act 250. Operational for well over a decade, Act 250 has largely been credited with helping to preserve much of the bucolic flavor and beauty of America's most rural state. Still, the program has proved less than satisfactory in controlling small developments which escaped review, and large-lot subdivisions of farming and forest lands. On the one hand the cumulative effect of so many non-regulated small developments has amounted to the nickel-and-diming of Vermont, while large-lot developments have reduced the critical masses of land necessary to maintain and promote economically viable farming and forest products operations (Daniels and Lapping, 1984; Porter, 1989). To respond to these and other problems, in 1988 the state passed Act 200, which sets out a more elaborate process of municipal and regional planning. Act 200 specifies a large number of state-wide planning goals with which local plans must be in compliance. Locally and regionally significant agricultural and forest resource lands are given specific protection. Where municipalities do not comply, or fail to adopt either a municipal or regional plan, they are prevented from levying impact fees to pay for development, no longer receive planning assistance from state agencies and are subject to state-derived regional plans. In an effort to tie capital and infrastructure investments to land-use goals, state agencies are now required to have their spending plans consistent with Act 200's goals. A new council of regional planning boards has also been created to review, approve and hear appeals on local and regional plans. To provide the necessary funding for the program the Vermont property transfer tax has been significantly increased with the majority of funds raised being returned to those municipalities complying with the system. Some communities have found compliance 'not in any way a difficult or onerous task' (Vermont Department of Housing and Community Affairs, 1990). Still, other communities, especially in the Northeast Kingdom—the state's most heavily forested and poorest region—have mounted substantial opposition to the plan (Braithwaite, 1990).

Rural economic development

The long record of neglect of land-use and environmental programs during the Reagan years shows little sign of turning around in the early years of the Bush administration, rhetoric notwithstanding. The rural economy, too, has been allowed to deteriorate further. Indeed, poor performance of the basic commodities sectors—agriculture, forest products, minerals, energy and fisheries—as well as in manufacturing, together with federal reductions in spending through the demise of revenue sharing, deregulation and privatization and outright indifference have left scores of rural Americans in a far more precarious position than they have been in many years. One recent USDA assessment has pointed out that among the most severe contemporary rural problems are: job growth rates less than a third as fast as urban areas; unemployment well above national rates; rural poverty rates far higher than urban levels; continuing out-migration and slow population growth; and higher rates of illiteracy and lower levels of educational attainment than in other areas (Rural Revitalization Task Force, 1989, p. 25). It is no wonder, then, that much of the rural planning efforts has focused upon rural and economic development. Perhaps nowhere else has there been a greater emphasis in the last several years than in 'rural revitalization'. In the last year of the Reagan administration, Secretary of Agriculture Richard Lyng issued a rather optimistic view of rural conditions, entitled *Signs of Progress* (Vautour, 1989). A department and agency-by-agency assessment of Federal activities to promote rural economic strength and development, the report concludes with a strong call for the restructuring of rural economics away from dependence upon traditional sectors in the economy. 'Rural economic revitalization' is the goal with growing emphasis upon manufacturing, services and value-added production. By utilizing enterprise zones, nurturing rural leadership, creating private–public partnerships and stimulating volunteerism, rural economies could be renewed, so it is argued. Yet, the record of the Federal government was very much the opposite of its stated strategies. Cut-backs in nearly all areas occurred, and some agencies, like regional planning authorities, the Small Business Administration and categorical grants to small communities and rural areas, were very often the target for extinction by the government. The record was, at the least, one of negligence if not outright hostility. The result was very largely the same: a worsening in the quality of life of rural Americans and the growing peripheralization of whole regions, especially those not located in proximity to growing metropolitan areas. The hollowness and poverty of Reagan policy and rhetoric was underscored in the final report of the Economic Policy Council headed by Clayton Yeutter, a multi-agency task force on rural economic development, when it noted that 'today, the bulk of federal spending in rural areas can be classified as either income transfers or income subsidies. Only about six per cent goes into economic development' (Economic Policy Council, 1990, p. 5). This critical assessment argues that 'rural development efforts must look beyond agriculture', that rural development 'is, at the heart, an economic issue', and that the stresses rural areas are witnessing are, in the main, 'global in scope' (Economic Policy Council, 1990, pp. 4–5). The Federal government could make a great contribution to stimulating 'a vibrant rural economy, not a subsidized rural economy', by 'tighter federal coordination' of programs, building infrastructure, like the Rural Electrification Administration (REA), and creating a more cooperative relationship between different levels of government which serve rural and small town constituencies. To achieve this the Working Group called for the encouragement of regional planning and coordination to better allocate scarce resources; greater support and training for local leadership; an emphasis upon improving rural job skills through greater access to advanced courses in maths, science and foreign languages; attacking illiteracy; assisting local governments with the necessary infrastructure for expanding local business enterprises as well as attracting new economic activity; and better targeting of Federal rural development programs to support state and local efforts, many of which were generating some success (Economic Policy Council, 1990, pp. 10–17). Many of these suggestions reflect Secretary of Agriculture Yeutter's previous post as chief US trade negotiator and his larger concern over US competitiveness in an increasingly globalized market-place. These strategies followed closely upon the analysis and recommendations of another Bush administration study, *A Hard Look at USDA's Rural Development Programs* (Rural Revitalization Task Force, 1989). This sought to focus attention on the lack of adequate venture capital pools in rural areas, the need to create more non-farm income generating opportunities and numerous other educationally-related vulnerabilities. What is most noteworthy in this analysis, what marks it as truly significant, is the recognition that barriers to a more effective federal role in rural development are often to be found within the USDA itself. The programs of the USDA are not as well coordinated with other levels of government, and even within USDA, as they might be; continue to be based on nationally standardized policies that limit their ability to support local innovation; tend to focus far too much on existing economic activities when adjustments and diversification would be more appropriate; and prevent the redirection of existing resources to better uses (Rural Revitalization Task Force, 1989, p. 74). These problems underscore even greater problems in the structure of the federal system. The Task Force, which represented all USDA constituent programs and agencies, concluded that, quite simply, there is no 'long-term strategy for rural development'; a lack of 'policy coordination within USDA'; no clear 'USDA mission statement for rural development'; and little public recognition of USDA's central role in rural policy and programming (Rural Revitalization Task Force, 1989, p. 10).

The efforts of USDA's Task Force on Rural Revitalization and the Working Group on Rural Development, as well as others in the new Bush administration, found substantial support in the Democratic Party controlled Congress. Both the House of Representatives and the Senate came forward with versions of a rural economic development act in 1989. Still tied up in committee hearings, and placed on the 'back burner' by the huge federal budget deficit problem, as well as the Savings-and-Loan bank failure crisis, key provisions in the bills include the following: support for rural school enhancement; medical and business telecommunications linkages; creation of a natural rural data information clearing-house; business and extension service program support; water and wastewater facility funding; loan programs; business incubator monies; and other such initiatives. Perhaps the greatest potential consequence, and closely tied to internal USDA debate and analysis, is the designation of the Rural Electrification Administration (REA), within the USDA, as the 'lead agency' for rural economic development. To give greater urgency to such efforts a new position is proposed, Assistant Administrator of REA, to provide coordination, leadership and responsibility. Indeed, the entire scope of the REA is altered and a genuine focus within the sprawling USDA bureaucracy has been provided.

While the focus of Federal rural economic development has been late in coming, many state level programs have been in operation for a number of years as shown in Table 2.2. Eisinger (1990) has astutely noted that state economic development programs have now matured from an almost purely supply side orientation toward more balanced approaches, which include demand side packages. Locational incentives, tax write-offs, etc., have now been joined by strategies to nurture entrepreneurial talents, venture capital pools, loan funds and a wide range of human resource enhancement programs. More balanced planning leads away from the old 'smokestack chasing' formula to more longer-term investment strategies. The day of the quick fix is gone, though how communities and regions may actually stimulate economic diversification and growth still alludes easy and facile description. Perhaps it is, as Rubin (1988) has argued, that those engaged in such activities must, ultimately, 'shoot anything that flies; claim anything that falls'.

Table 2.2 State rural development programs

	I. Agriculture-related development	II. Transition tools	III. Rural business assistance	IV. Rural community assistance
Alabama	C,F	H,J,K	P,R,T,U,W	Z,CC,EE,GG
Alaska	A,C,D,E,F,G		M,N,O,R,S,T,W,X	Z,AA,CC,DD,EE,FF,GG
Arizona	A		M,N,O,P,T,U,X	Z,AA,BB,CC,DD,EE,FF,GG, HH
Arkansas	A,B,F		P,T,U,V	CC,EE,GG
California	B,F	H	M,N,T,R,U,V,W	Z,AA,BB,CC,EE,GG
Colorado	D		N,O,P,Q,T,U,V,X	
Connecticut	F			DD,HH
Delaware			M	AA,BB,CC
Florida	A,B,E,F	I,K	M	Z,BB
Georgia	A,B,F,D	K	N,Q,S,T	
Hawaii	A,B,C,D,E,F	H,I,J	P,V	Z,CC,GG,HH
Idaho	A,E,F,G	H,J,K	T,U	AA,CC
Illinois	A,B,C,D,E,F	H,J,K	M,N,O,P,Q,R,S,T,U,V,W,X	Z,AA,CC,DD,EE,FF,GG,HH
Indiana	A,B,C,D,F	J,K	N,P,T,U,W	CC
Iowa	A,B,C,D,E,F	H,I,J,K	M,N,O,P,Q,R,S,T,U,V	Z,AA,CC,DD,EE,FF,GG
Kansas		H,J,K	M,P,R,T,U,V,W	CC,GG
Kentucky	B,C	I,K	M,N,Q,P,T,U,V,W	Z,BB,CC,EE
Louisiana	A,B,C,D,E,F	H,J	N,P,Q,T,U,V,W	Z,AA,BB,CC,EE,GG
Maine	A,B,C,D,E,F	H,I,J,K		GG,HH
Maryland			T,U,V	Z,CC,EE,GG
Masschusetts			M,P,Q,T,U	BB,CC,EE,HH
Michigan	A,B,C,D,E,F	J,K	M,N,P,R,T,U,V,W	Z,CC,EE,GG,HH
Minnesota	D,E,F	H,J	M,N,Q,P,R,T,U,V,W	AA,CC,EE,GG,HH
Mississippi	A,E,F	H	P,Q,T,U,V,X,W	AA,CC,DD,GG,HH
Missouri	A,B,E,F	J,K	V,T,Q	CC,EE
Montana	B,C,D,E,F,G	H,J,K,L	M,P,T,U,W	AA,BB,CC,DD,GG,HH
Nebraska	A,B,C,D,E	J,K	M,N,O,P,T,U,W,X	GG,HH
Nevada			M,N,O,P,R,T,U,W	Z,BB,CC,DD,EE,GG
New Hampshire			M,U	DD,EE,GG,HH

State	Ag-related dev.	Tools	Programs	Other
New Jersey	A,B,C,F	I,J,K	P,Q,T,U,V,W	CC,GG,HH
New Mexico	A,B,D,E,F		M,P,R,T,U,W,X	Z,AA,CC,EE,GG
New York	D,F	H,I,J,K	M,N,O,P,T,U,V,W,X	AA,BB,CC,GG
North Carolina	D	H	M,P,T,U	CC,DD
North Dakota	A,B,C,D,E,F	H,I,J,K	M,N,P,T,U,V,Y	Z,CC,DD,GG,HH,EE
Ohio	C,F		P,R,T,W	CC,DD,GG
Oklahoma			U,V,W	EE,GG
Oregon	D,F	H	N,P,R,T,U,V,W	Z,CC,EE,GG
Pennsylvania			M,N,O,P,R,T,U,V,W,X	
Rhode Island	F		R,T,U	CC,DD,GG
South Carolina	C,F	H,J	M,N,P,U	EE,GG
South Dakota	C	H,J,K	O,U,X	
Tennessee	A,B,C,D,E,F	H,I,J,K	N,P,R,T,U,V	Z,CC,DD,EE,GG
Texas		H	M,T,U	AA,CC
Utah	D,E,F	H,K	Q,T,U,X	Z,AA,BB,EE,GG
Vermont	A,D,F	H	M,N,P,Q,T,U,V,X	AA,CC,GG,HH
Virginia	A,B,C,D,E,F	H,J,K	M,N,P,T,U,V,X	AA,DD,EE,GG,HH
Washington	A,B,D,E,F	I	N,O,P,T,U,W	Z,CC,GG
West Virginia			P,T,U,W	CC
Wisconsin	A,B,D,E,F	H,I,J,K	P,O,R,T,U,W	Z,DD,EE,GG
Wyoming	A,B,C,D,E,F	H,J,K	M,N,O,P,Q,T,U	Z,GG

Notes: I. Agriculture-related development: A. Agriculture Export Development; B. Attracting Value-added Business; C. Beginning Farmer Programs; D. Biotechnology & Technology Transfer; E. Crop Diversification; F. Marketing Ag/Rural Products; G. Other. II. Transition tools: H. Ag & Rural Development Commissions, Agencies, etc.; I. Assessing Competitive Advantages; J. Farmer & Agribusiness Financial; K. Farmer Retraining and Counseling; L. Other. III. Rural business assistance: M. Economic Development; N. Entrepreneurship, Business Incubators, etc.; O. Job Creation/Training; P. Location of New Business/Industry; Q. Marketing and Export; R. Plant/Military Base Closing; S. Procurement Assistance; T. Retention and Expansion of Existing Business; U. Small Business Assistance; V. Rural Enterprise Zones; W. Tax Incentives for Private Investments; X. Technology Transfer; Y. Other. IV. Rural community assistance: Z. Culture and Arts; AA. Financial; BB. Housing; CC. Infrastructure; DD. Land Use; EE. Parks and Recreation; FF. Quality of Life; GG. Tourism; HH. Other.

Source: The Book of the States 1988–89, 1988, Vol. 27 (Lexington, KY: Council of State Governments, 1989 editions), p. 434. Copyright 1989 by the Council of State Governments. Reprinted by permission.)

THE LIBRARY
BISHOP BURTON COLLEGE
BEVERLEY HU17 8QG
TEL: 0964 550481 Ex: 227

References

Authan, G., 1988, 'A grass-roots movement to save farmland', *Governing*, **1**: 52–4

Bierbaum, M.A., 1990, *Interview*, Office of State Planning, State of New Jersey, 20 April

Braithwaite, C., 1990, 'How the voters voted in 1990', *Orleans County (VT) Chronicle*, **17**: 10 (17 March)

Daniels, T., Daniels, J. and Lapping, M., 1986, 'The Vermont land gains tax: a lesson in land policy design', *American Journal of Economics and Sociology*, **45** (4): 441–56

Daniels, T. and Lapping, M., 1984, 'Has Vermont's land use control program failed? Evaluating Act 250', *Journal of the American Planning Association*, **50** (4): 502–9

Detlefsen, B. (ed.), 1989a, 'Federal, state efforts mount to stem huge loss of wetlands', *Land Use Planning Reports*, **17** (8): 59

Detlefsen, B. (ed.), 1989b, 'Warning: wetlands violations can land you in jail', *Land Use Planning Reports*, **17** (21): 173

Detlefsen, B. (ed.), 1989c, 'Wetlands are not wastelands', *Land Use Planning Reports*, **17** (8): 59

Detlefsen, B. (ed.), 1989d, 'Washington watch', *Land Use Planning Reports*, **17** (9): 74

Detlefsen, B. (ed.), 1989e, 'Report shows big jump in land devoted to urban use', *Land Use Planning Reports*, **17** (17): 139

Detlefsen, B. (ed.), 1990, 'Corps of engineers and EPA announce modified wetlands agreement', *Land Use Planning Reports*, **18** (4): 27

Economic Policy Council, 1990, *Rural development for the 90s: a presidential initiative*, US Department of Agriculture, Washington, DC

Eisinger, P., 1990, *The rise of the entrepreneurial state: state and local economic development policy*, University of Wisconsin Press, Madison

Gold, A.R., 1989, 'Tight limits proposed for popular farm chemical', *New York Times*, 5 December, p. A20

Klein, S.B., 1980, *State soil erosion and sediment control laws*, National Conference of State Legislatures, Washington, DC

Lapping, M., Daniels, T. and Keller, J. 1989, *Rural planning and development in the United States*, Guilford Press, New York

Lapping, M. and Leutwiler, A.N. 1988, 'Agriculture in conflict: right-to-farm laws and the peri-urban milieu of farming' in W. Lockeretz (ed.), *Sustaining agriculture near cities*, Soil Conservation Society of American, Ankeny, IA, pp. 209–18

Lapping, M., Penfold. G. and MacPherson, S., 1983, 'Right to farm laws: do they reduce land use conflicts?', *Journal of Soil and Water Conservation*, **38**: 465–6

Lawrence, B.L., 1988, 'New Jersey's controversial growth plan', *Urban Land*, **47** (1): 18–21

Mott, L. and Snyder, K., 1987, *Pesticide alert: a guide to pesticides in fruits and vegetables*, Sierra Club Books, San Francisco, CA

National Association of State Departments of Agriculture Research Foundation, 1985, *Farmland Project*, Washington, DC, January

National Oceanic and Atmospheric Administration and US Department of

Agriculture, 1988, *Weekly Weather and Crop Bulletin*, Climatic Analysis Center, Washington, DC

News Division, 1988, *USDA Backgrounder*, USDA Washington, DC, pp. 1–12

Office of State Planning, 1989, *Cross acceptance manual, preliminary state development and redevelopment plan for New Jersey*, Vol. II, Office of State Planning, Trenton, NJ

Petrulius, M., Sommer, J. and Hines, F., 1989, 'Drought effects on rural communities vary by strength of local nonfarm economy', *Rural Development Perspectives*, **6** (1): 2–7

Porter, D., 1989, 'The states are coming, the states are coming!', *Urban Land*, **48** (9): 16–20

Rubin, H.J., 1988, 'Shoot anything that flies; claim anything that falls', *Economic Development Quarterly*, **2** (3): 236–51

Rural Revitalization Task Force, 1989, *Report of the rural revitalization task force*, USDA Washington, DC

Sanberg, K. and Taylor, T., 1988, 'The 1988 drought assistance act', US Congress, Northeast Midwest Senate Coalition, Washington, DC

Shafecoff, P., 1989, 'EPA restricts fungicide's use on 42 products, *New York Times*, 17 February, p. A14

Tierney, W., Darling, D. and Willard, M., 1989, *The effects of the drought on the Kansas economy*, Department of Agricultural Economics, Kansas State University, Manhattan, KS

Vautour, R. 1989, *Signs of progress: a report on rural America's revitalization efforts*, USDA Washington, DC

Vermont Department of Housing and Community Affairs, 1990, 'Town plan approval: one town's experience' in *Vermont's future: an update on Act 200 and planning*, Department of Housing and Community Affairs, Montpelier, VT

3 Book review 1

Reviewed by Owen Furuseth

Dealing with change in the Connecticut River Valley: a design manual for conservation and development by Robert D. Yaro, Randall G. Arendt, Harry L. Dobson and Elizabeth A. Brabee. 1989, The Lincoln Institute of Land Policy, Cambridge Massachusetts, $25.00 (paperback), 182 pages, illustrated.

Rarely are books genuinely deserving of the title 'seminal'. In environmental planning Ian McHarg's 1969 work, *Design with Nature*, has had such a profound affect on planners and designers for two decades that the term 'seminal' is well applied. Many of the basic tenets and innovations set forth by McHarg have been carried forward in a new rural planning design text, *Dealing with Change in the Connecticut River Valley: A Design Manual for Conservation and Development*. Given the response that this book has received it too may eventually be considered seminal.

Written by a team of researchers from the University of Massachusetts' Center for Rural Massachusetts in conjunction with the state's Department of Environmental Management, *Dealing with Change* was originally intended for use by 19 towns and cities bordering along the scenic and environmentally sensitive portion of the Connecticut River which cuts through central Massachusetts. Drawing on traditional New England design features and modern environmental conservation standards, the text presents creative and implementable solutions for maintaining environmental, scenic and historical rural resources while accommodating economic and land-use change. A central theme is that rural areas can maintain their special character and resources while accepting urban-related growth.

Although *Dealing with Change* is specifically centered around the environmental conditions and cultural precedents of the Connecticut River Valley, its approach and strategies are applicable throughout the industrial world. The universality of this text is based on the authors' concern and attention to fundamental design and environmental issues. Thus, a site planning strategy which works well to minimize the visual impact of vacation cottages along a narrow waterway in rural Massachusetts would be similarly effective in rural portions of Scotland, New Zealand, or California.

The book is structured around hypothetical planning scenarios based on real world settings. Using this approach the authors first present the

the existing environmental, land-use and design setting, and then lay out a probable development option for the area. Having set the stage, a conventional development scenario is offered. These conventional alternatives are not overly offensive nor economically unrealistic, rather they reflect common strategies to rural development. Having presented the norm, the authors then posit a progressive scenario, one which allows the same amount of economic gain but without destroying the rural character of the site. The authors make heavy use of graphic aids, including multicolored maps and renderings. The differences between 'normal' and 'creative' development is stark and powerful. In particular, the aerial renderings illustrating how careful development can be positioned into a rural landscape without wholesale destruction of the area are valuable tools. Planners can employ these materials to help 'sell' creative planning options to elected officials and citizens.

Ten hypothetical planning scenarios are presented. Eight of these are exclusively rural and deal with settings varying from steep, upland terrain to river and lake frontage. The development alternatives considered are equally wide, ranging from high intensity resort-recreational and shopping center scenarios to low intensity residential estates. The remaining planning scenarios focus on two rural towns, Hadley and Gill. The emphasis in these presentations is upon the protection of the existing town character and the linkages to the surrounding countryside while accepting growth. Land-use planning strategies and administrative structures are the primary concerns in these sections.

In addition, *Dealing with Change* provides the reader with a set of tools and guidelines to help communities and governing bodies implement the alternative rural planning state which they recommend. Specific guidance on site plan review, including a model local ordinance and individual guidelines and performance standards; signage control; protective strategies for waterfront areas; farmland alienation, including policies and model local regulations; and roadway growth management tools and alternatives are all addressed. Again, each of these sections is well illustrated.

Although there are a number of rural design and planning texts available, none matches *Dealing with Change* for its depth nor innovation. It is one of those few books which rural planning professionals, public officials and concerned citizens will want for their personal libraries.

4 Book review 2
Reviewed by Frederick Steiner

Saving America's countryside: a guide to rural conservation by Samuel N. Stokes, A. Elizabeth Watson, Genevieve P. Keller, and J. Timothy Keller. 1989, The John Hopkins University Press, Baltimore, $42.50 (hardcover), $16.95 (paperback), 306 pages, illustrated.

This book took a while to write and to be published. Good books often do. I first heard about it from two of its authors in 1982 at a Council of Educators in Landscape Architecture meeting in Blacksburg, Virginia. The theme of the conference was 'The Rural Landscape'. The authors reported then that the book was about complete and ready for publication.

Because I had not only read several chapters in manuscript and found them interesting but also because I needed a text for my 'Planning in Rural Environments' course, I waited each year in anticipation for the arrival of this book. The resultant *Saving America's Countryside* is worth the wait. It is directed at rural citizens, but students and practitioners of rural planning will find it useful, too. The book was prepared under the auspices of the National Trust for Historic Preservation, which sponsored several of the case studies that are nicely described by the authors.

In his foreword, Stewart Udall calls for 'a new wave of conservation action in rural America'. Action is necessary because 'each generation has its own rendezvous with the land, its own opportunity to make history by creating life giving environments for its children' (p. xviii). Mr Udall's plea reflects the grass-roots approach advocated by Samuel Stokes and his colleagues.

Many rural concerns and issues are addressed, including the importance of visual quality, the preservation of historic resources, the maintenance of a healthy environment, the retention of prime farmlands and the need for a vibrant community. The authors are sensitive to local cultures and recognize the need for strong regional economies, but are unabashedly for the preservation of beauty, history and the environment. In fact, they view the preservation of the local culture and ecological integrity as a prerequisite for true economic development and substantive individual fulfillment.

Planning principles and techniques are illustrated through a series of case studies. The topics addressed include how to initiate and manage a rural conservation program, ways to analyze rural communities, the land-protection techniques that can be used in rural settings, where local residents can find outside help and community education devices. The authors emphasize the 'how to' aspects of these topics. Twenty-eight case studies are drawn from twenty-one states from every region of the United States. The case studies where the authors were involved themselves are the most detailed. In particular, the Oley, Pennsylvania and Cazenovia, New York examples exhibit considerable depth and are used in several sections of the book.

The authors explain several rather technical procedures, such as environmental impact assessment and the US Soil Conservation Service's agricultural land evaluation and site assessment (LESA) system, in clear, straightforward prose. The LESA system is explained, then illustrated in two case studies. In McHenry County, Illinois, LESA is used as a part of its ambitious agricultural zoning ordinance, while in Hardin County, Kentucky, the system is applied as a means for 'unzoning'.

McHenry County is one of the original pilot jurisdictions where LESA was developed and tested during the early 1980s. The county was selected because of its previous agricultural land protection efforts, because of its excellent soils and because of the growth pressures from Chicago, 55 miles to the south-east. Its late planner, Stephen Aradas, helped the county develop a strong land-use control ordinance. A 160-acre minimum lot size is required for residential development in the agricultural zone. The LESA system is applied when local officials consider rezoning cases, that is, when landowners wish to change the use of property from farming. The local government 'has approved several rezonings of land adjacent to existing municipalities but has held firm on more remote prime farmland' (p. 141).

In Hardin County, a performance-based approach to land-use regulation was adopted by local officials. After 'tumultuous' opposition to traditional land-use planning, a development guidance system was designed instead of zoning districts in this fast growing county near Louisville. Three steps are involved: a growth guidance assessment, a compatibility assessment and a plan assessment. LESA-based criteria for the point system are employed to review new development. The LESA-derived system helps to ensure that the growth guidance assessment standards are clear and consistent. In the second step, neighboring landowners are involved in public assessments of the compatibility of a proposed development with its surroundings. 'The compatibility assessment involves a required meeting of the developer and neighboring property owners, guided by the planning staff' (p. 148). The final step involves the preparation of a detailed plan that meets specified subdivision requirements.

Other case studies provide links between planning principles and application. One of the most successful aspects of this book is that the authors enliven rural planning. Real places are described, often using the words of real people. The authors are experienced enough to realize that rural planning is not a simple and neat affair. There are no uniform prescriptions. They note that 'such complexities as personalities, culture or custom, government, and changes in land uses mean that the [planning] process is never-ending and constantly open to adjustment to account for new factors' (p. 264).

Still, they offer some ideas that should be helpful to many rural conservation efforts. Think broadly, think about building coalitions, think about the long term, and think and act positively, the authors advise. Such thinking allows the rural conservationist, either citizen or professional, to be a problem-solver and a risk taker. The issues facing rural America demand creative solutions. *Saving America's Countryside* is a wellspring of good ideas.

Section II:
United Kingdom

edited by
Andrew W. Gilg

Introduction
Andrew W. Gilg

Because PIRPAP is a new venture a few words are needed to explain the format of the UK section, to invite comments from readers and to solicit proposals from potential authors. There are three parts to the UK section: a long-term review; a review of the years 1987 to 1989; and a review of current research and events.

In the first part, the editor provides an overall *aide-mémoire* for the 1980s. It is hoped that this will be followed by subject reviews of the 1980s, in subsequent volumes, especially now that the period of Thatcherism is over. Potential authors are requested to contact the author.

In the second part, the so-called Annual Review actually covers the period 1 September 1987 to 31 August 1989. For those many fans of the *Yearbooks'* Annual Review, this will provide continuity and a complete record from 1979 onwards. In Volume Two the period from 1 September 1989 to 31 August 1991 will be covered and in Volume Three a return to an annual review will be accomplished with a review of the year from 1 September 1991 to 31 August 1992. Because PIRPAP has fewer UK words than the *Yearbooks*, and because two years are initially being covered, the Annual Review has had to be modified as follows. First, the most important material is presented as a linked essay, while less important material is, for the first two volumes only, presented as a list. Second, reviews of publications have had to be suspended, in favour of a list. It is hoped this provides a compromise between comprehensiveness and full-blown reviews. In more detail the contents of the Annual Review are as follows:

1. *Legislative review*
Parliamentary Acts and Bills: commentary on individual items
Statutory Instruments: linked essay by topic followed by list
Circulars: commentary by Circular number
Command Papers: linked essay
House of Commons papers: linked essay by topic/committee
House of Lords papers: linked essay by topic/committee

2. *Review of events*
Essay on four major issues: land-use planning; extensification–set-aside; forestry; and agricultural prices
Diary of events
List of new protected areas and designations

3. *Literature list*
150 publications and 150 articles by topic
Annual Reports published by HMSO/Rural planning organisations
Statistical series published by HMSO/Rural planning organisations

The Annual Review is followed by the third part which contains three short articles. Two are by Munton and Willis reporting on the progress of the countryside change initiative, and one is by Brotherton on the debate about the reorganisation of the NCC and Countryside Commission.

THE LIBRARY
BISHOP BURTON COLLEGE
BEVERLEY HU17 8QG
TEL: 0964 550481 Ex: 227

5 Rural planning policies in the 1980s: an *aide-mémoire*

Andrew W. Gilg

It is, I suppose, highly appropriate that this article is being edited just one day after Mrs Thatcher resigned as Prime Minister, since the 1980s were dominated by her policies and her election in 1979 also marked the period covered by the first *Countryside Planning Yearbook* in 1980. Because the purpose of this review is to provide a context for the launch of its successor, this review is based on the events covered by the nine *Yearbooks* published between 1980 and 1988. The events from late 1987 to late 1989 are covered elsewhere in PIRPAP and so collectively the UK section of PIRPAP provides an *aide-mémoire* for the Thatcher decade of 1979–89. For the sake of convenience the material is structured as follows: International influences; General UK legislation; Agriculture; Forestry; Land-use planning; Social and economic policies; and Conservation and recreation. Please note at this stage that references in the text are made only to parliamentary papers: HC (House of Commons); HL (House of Lords); Command (White Papers and Reports) DOE Circulars and so on; for a full reference readers are referred to the *Yearbooks*.

International changes over the whole countryside

There were very few major international agreements affecting the countryside in the 1980s, but the importance of the European Community was further strengthened by the agreement in 1986 to move to a single European market in 1992. The European Community continued to be dominated by agriculture. For example, in 1989 the EC budget broke down as follows: CAP Guarantee payments £17,043 million; Regional Development Fund payments £2,498 million; Social Fund payments £1,880 million; and CAP Guidance Fund payments £989 million, giving these four funds, and agriculture in particular, the lion's share of the total expenditure of £27,206 million (HC 15-xxxvii (88–89)).

Other European or international agreements did however make an impact. For example, agreements on wildlife protection via various conventions and directives forced the passage of the Wildlife and Countryside Act 1981 (see the Conservation section for further details).

The most important agreement, however, was over EC Directive 85/337 on Environmental Assessment (EA). The UK government had resisted the introduction of this directive throughout the 1980s claiming that existing legislation provided for EA procedures via the public inquiry system. The directive did however introduce new methods to the UK. (For more detail see the Statutory Instruments section.)

General UK legislation

There were two main changes in general rural planning powers in the 1980s. First, there was an attack on planning organisations, and second, growing controls over pollution in contradiction to the anti-regulatory stance of the Thatcher administration.

In the first case a very early White Paper (Cmnd 7746, 1979) correctly forecast the demise in the 1980s of the Advisory Council for Agriculture and Horticulture; Regional Economic Planning Councils; the Environment Board; the Inland Waterways Amenity Advisory Council; the Recreation Management Training Committee; the Centre for Environmental Studies; the National Water Council; and the Water Space Amenity Commission. Other bodies changed their status, for example, the Countryside Commission and the Development Commission (for more details see the relevant sections).

The attack on pollution began with the belated implementation of the Control of Pollution Act 1974 between 1984 and 1986 (DOE Circular 17/84), making the very important point that Acts do not always operate immediately. The Act which was largely based on voluntary codes of practice also showed that such an approach is often the precursor to mandatory controls, e.g. straw burning, which after a voluntary code of practice had failed has been banned from the end of 1992. In the case of water pollution by farmers a 13 per cent rise to 3,890 cases in 1987 forced the government to introduce mandatory controls (HC 543 (87–88)) since voluntary exhortation and advice had failed.

In addition to the changes that were made, a number of proposals have been made which have not been accepted. For example, despite numerous calls for a White Paper on the countryside, notably from both chairmen of the NCC and the Countryside Commission in 1984, none has been forthcoming.

Agricultural policy

The 1980s were a decade which continued to heap the by-products of production success at the door of policy-makers in the form of increasingly complex social, environmental and economic issues. Their response, as this section will show, was unfortunately often piecemeal, panic-stricken or inactive, with the result that at the end of the decade many of the problems of 1980 were still in place. The main change of the decade, however, was the realisation that policies for expansion were no longer tenable, although putting this in to practice has been very difficult to achieve. Ironically, the last UK White Paper on agriculture, published just 3 months before the Thatcher period, argued that an increase in production was desirable because of the cost and insecurity of foreign supplies (Cmnd 7458, 1979).

The European and international dimension

In 1980 a European Community paper on the CAP (HL 126-I and II (80–81)) began the decade by considering the many types of ways in which farm policies could be moved away from the single goal of production to wider social and environmental goals while at the same time meeting four objectives: first, to control production and expenditure; second, to reduce stocks; third to preserve the European pattern of agriculture; and fourth, to preserve Europe's position as the world's largest exporter of farm produce. Like all succeeding proposals, this document however rejected price cuts as the main weapon, in favour of co-responsibility levies, and aid targeted at specific farms or regions.

These ideas were carried forward in a 1985 European Commission Green Paper on the future of the CAP ((7872) 8480/85) which placed much emphasis on relating support prices to target levels of production via so-called stabilisers with a drop in price if target levels were exceeded. The use of stabilisers was endorsed again in 1987 by the Commission ((9662) 8250/87 COM (87) 410) and by the Agriculture Committee of the House of Commons (HC 43-iii (86–87)).

The UK dimension

While the European Commission was grappling with the intricacies of reforming the CAP and by and large failing, the UK government passed the Agriculture Act 1986. This Act marked a major change away from a unilateral farm policy towards a multi-purpose policy with Section 17 imposing on Agriculture Ministers a duty to:

have regard to and endeavour to achieve a reasonable balance between the following considerations: (a) the promotion and maintenance of a stable and efficient agricultural industry; (b) the economic and social interests of rural areas; (c) the conservation and enhancement of natural beauty and amenity of the countryside . . .; and (d) the promotion of the enjoyment of the countryside by the public.

The Act also included measures to introduce Environmentally Sensitive Areas (see a later section), extended the range of grant aid subject to management agreements and extended the possibilities of charging for ADAS services.

Having considered the general background to policy change in agriculture it is now time to turn to six detailed aspects of farm policy: support prices; grant aid; quotas; guidance and socio-structural policies; and environmental programmes.

Support prices Throughout the 1980s there were three main areas in which support prices were changed. First, in the first half of the decade support prices were raised at a rate generally below the inflation rate, and then in the second half of the decade prices were generally frozen giving even greater real cuts in prices. Second, selling into intervention was made more difficult for farmers by delaying payments; by restricting the period for sales; by imposing stricter quality controls; and by paying less than the intervention price. Third, in the UK the effects of these changes were cushioned or exacerbated by using the green pound (monetary compensatory amount) mechanism.

Grant aid The 1980s witnessed two significant changes in grant aid. First, as shown in Table 5.1, there were major cuts in overall expenditure taking account of inflation, and second, there was a gradual shift—via the three major schemes—away from production centred aid, initially to better management of farmland, and then gradually towards conservation expenditure. At the same time grants for drainage and hedgerow removal were taken away. Another change was the dropping of prior approval in the early 1980s, except in National Parks and SSSIs, thus removing one opening for MAFF officials to advise on environmental matters.

Quotas Neither price controls nor reductions in grant aid have managed to solve the two main problems of the CAP, surpluses and excessive expenditure. In 1984 milk production threatened to bankrupt finally the CAP in spite of the attempts by various outgoer schemes to encourage dairy farmers to leave the industry. In a panic response in 1984 the Commission imposed quotas on milk production almost overnight, setting Community output at 1981 levels plus 1 per cent, and national output at 1983 levels minus 6 per cent. For the UK this translated into a 9 per cent reduction in 1984–5 on 1983 output. There was a further reduction of 8.5 per cent in 1987 and the scheme was extended in 1988 to 1992. After initial criticism of the scheme (HC 274 (84–84)) dairy farmers found that it offered the chance to increase real profits by staying within the industry or by taking up revised outgoer schemes which offered the average dairy farmer £107,000 over 7 years for leaving and staying out of milk production (HL 84 (85–86)).

Table 5.1 *Expenditure on agricultural grants in the UK, 1979–90*

£ million	Awarded from	1979–80	1984–5	1986–7	1989–90
Community Schemes					
FHDS	1973 to 1980 ⎱	73.9	100.8	51.3	12.2
AHDS	1980 to 1985 ⎰				
AIRS	1985 to 1988	0.0	0.0	9.4	24.9
FCGS	1989 onwards	0.0	0.0	0.0	2.9
Western Isles IDP	1982 to 1987	0.0	4.3	2.4	0.0
ESAs	1986 onwards	0.0	0.0	0.0	9.9
Set-Aside	1989 onwards	0.0	0.0	0.0	11.6
Total		73.9	105.1	63.1	68.9
UK schemes					
Crofting	1912/49 onwards	3.9	6.4	6.2	7.2
FHGS	1977 to 1980 ⎱	72.5	96.3	37.8	2.2
AHGS	1980 to 1985 ⎰				
AIS	1985 to 1988	0.0	0.0	13.7	4.1
FCGS	1989 onwards	0.0	0.0	0.0	10.3
FDGS	1988 onwards	0.0	0.0	0.0	0.5
FWS	1989 onwards	0.0	0.0	0.0	5.0
Total		76.7	102.7	57.7	28.8
Overall total		150.8	207.8	120.8	97.7
At 1988 prices		321	272	138	69

Notes: Acronyms: AHDS/FHDS—Agricultural/Farm and Horticulture Development Scheme; AIR/AIS—Agriculture Improvement Regulations/Scheme; FCGS—Farm and Conservation Grant Scheme; IDP—Integrated Development Programme; ESA—Environmentally Sensitive Area; FHGS/AHGS—Farm/Agriculture and Horticulture Grant Scheme; FDGS—Farm Diversification Grant Scheme; FWS—Farm Woodland Scheme.
Source: National Audit Office, 1990: *Grants to aid the structure of agriculture*, London, HMSO (HC 105 (89–90))

The success of milk quotas in restructuring the dairy industry by providing a stable situation for stayers and reasonably attractive terms for goers, in spite of its *ad hoc* and panic-stricken introduction, obviously raises the question of whether quotas should be introduced for the other main area of surplus production, i.e. cereals. These have, however, been resisted in favour of not only changes in support prices and grant aid as outlined above but also changes in guidance as outlined below.

Guidance and socio-structural policies In 1985 the EC agreed to a new agricultural structures policy (797/85) which up till then had been concentrated on the Less Favoured Areas and on retirement schemes. The new policy covered six areas: investment aids to diversify agricultural holdings and give help for young farmers; specific measures for mountain and hill farming; allowing national funds to help set up Environmentally Sensitive

Areas (ESAs) (see a later section for more detail); encouraging forestry on agricultural holdings; vocational training; and other measures. In 1986 further proposals included a pre-pension scheme; measures to encourage less extensive farming (extensification); greater flexibility for setting Compensatory Allowances; Community Premia for ESAs; and help with training and marketing for diversification into tourism and craft industries.

The main aims of the new structures policy were to help farmers to adapt to the new market situation, to achieve a better balance between supply and demand, to support farming and to contribute to the conservation of the environment and preservation of the countryside. Initial reactions were that the new policy tried to do too much with too little resources and without enough integration (HL 242 (85–86)).

Other structural changes in the 1980s included an extension of the UK's Less Favoured Areas by 1.2 million hectares in 1984 to 8 million hectares. Finally, in a move to cut government expenditure on agriculture, ADAS were increasingly able to charge for their services from 1986 onwards, except for diversification and conservation advice.

Environmental programmes During the debate of the draft socio-structural regulations in the early 1980s much emphasis was placed on the need for them to contain environmental measures as well as socio-economic measures (HC 247 (83–84)). At the same time a crisis over the proposed draining and possible ploughing up of the Halvergate marshes in the Norfolk Broads led to the introduction of the Broads Livestock Grant Scheme in 1985. In return for maintaining low input farming farmers were paid a flat payment of around £120 per hectare. This scheme was used as a model by the UK government when it successfully proposed that Environmentally Sensitive Areas (ESAs) should be included in the new structures regulation.

Eleven ESAs have subsequently been designated in England and Wales and five in Scotland. Typical payments range from £35 to £200 per hectare for agreeing to comply with the management programme set out for each ESA. These include keeping to low grazing rates, only applying limited amounts of fertiliser, or not cutting key meadows till wild flowers have set their seeds. The ESAs however so far designated only cover a fraction of those originally proposed by the NCC and Countryside Commission in 1985. Within the existing ESAs the take-up has been good with around 110,000 hectares now covered by agreements.

Forestry policy

In 1981 the Forestry Act 1981 set in motion a policy to sell off state forests in order to raise cash for the Treasury. In 1984, however, the programme was scaled down after much criticism of the policy (HC 233

Table 5.2 *Forestry Grant Scheme*

Area of wood £/hectare	Conifers	Broadleaved
0.25–0.9	600 (630)	850 (890)
1.0–2.9	480 (505)	700 (735)
3.0–9.9	400 (420)	600 (630)
10.0 and over	230 (240)	450 (470)

(84–85)), and its aim was revised to one of rationalising the Forestry Commission's estate. During the decade, 140,000 hectares of both forested (72,000 hectare) and bare land was sold.

Other changes in the decade included several changes to grant schemes and taxation policy. In 1981 the Basis II Dedication Scheme was closed to new entrants and a new scheme, the Forestry Grant Scheme was introduced, with payments as shown in Table 5.2.

In 1985 the payments were increased as shown by the number in parentheses, and a new scheme designed to maintain and create broadleaved woods, the Broadleaved Woodland Grant Scheme, was instituted with the payments, payable by instalment, varying from £1,200 per hectare for small woodlands below 1 hectare down to £600 per hectare for woodlands above 10 hectares. Both schemes were however replaced in 1988 (see pp. 65 and 80).

In 1986 the abolition of Capital Transfer Tax and the introduction of Inheritance Tax meant that lifetime transfers of farmland or forestry were taxed on a sliding scale depending on how long the donor survived. The full rate of tax is paid in the first 3 years, but then reduces in stages to no tax being paid if the donor survives 7 years.

Land-use planning

For land-use planning the *Zeitgeiste* of the 1980s were deregulation, simplification and relaxation. However, the rhetoric never really matched the reality and at the end of the decade land-use planning looked remarkably similar in its essential principles to what it had been in 1980.

Rhetoric was provided aplenty in no less than four White Papers. At the outset Command 7634 in 1979 promised to remove a mass of minor central government controls over planning. This theme was continued in both Command 9501 (1985) and Command 9794 (1986). These two papers with their tell-tale titles of 'Lifting the Burden' and 'Building Businesses not Barriers' outlined proposals for reducing planning control, simplifying procedures, striving for greater efficiency and speed in decision-making and taking a positive approach.

Although many of the minor proposals were enacted by the two main planning Acts of the decade, most of the changes were relatively minor. In more detail, the only really major Act of the decade, the Local Government Planning and Land Act 1980, removed from County Councils virtually all controls over District Councils' local plans and development control. Other changes were largely procedural in nature, transferring planning functions from one organisation to another. Similarly, the Housing and Planning Act 1986 provided legislation for the introduction of Simplified Planning Zones as the only major change, but otherwise transferred controls again, for example, control over open-cast coal-mining to mineral planning authorities.

Apart from legislation, the end of the decade also saw the DOE adopt the Scottish system of planning guidelines with a series of 15 Planning Policy Guidance Notes published between 1988–90. The most relevant for rural areas were: (1) *General Policy and Principles*; (2) *Green Belts*; (3) *Land for Housing*; (7) *Rural enterprise and development*; (12) *Local Plans*; and (15) *Regional planning guidance, structure plans and development plans*. A series of notes on minerals planning was also issued. For further details on both these series and notes see this volume and Volume Two.

Plan making   The 1980s saw virtually no real changes in plan making. A series of DOE Circulars, 23/81, 22/84 and 24/87 updated and modified advice, and in particular reduced the role of structure plans and enhanced the role of strategic planning. In Scotland the demise of the statutory regional report came in 1982. In England dissatisfaction with overlong and complex structure plans led the government in 1986 to issue a consultation paper proposing their end.

Development control   The mood of relaxation also permeated development control throughout the 1980s. At the outset DOE Circular 22/80 asked local authorities to pay a greater regard to time and efficiency and always to grant planning permission unless there were sound and clear-cut reasons for refusal. However, these reasons still included the need to protect landscapes and good agricultural land. In 1981 a revision to the General Development Order (GDO) (SIs 245 and 246/81) continued the theme by relaxing controls in a minor way, but not in the National Parks, AONBs and Conservation Areas, introducing to some extent a two-tier planning system. This was reinforced in 1986 with a special order (SI 1176/86) which allowed planners in all the National Parks and some adjoining land to have a limited form of control over the design, siting and appearance of farm and forestry roads and buildings, elsewhere exempted from control. It did not, however, include a power to prevent a construction, only power over its details.

Other changes in the 1980s included a simplification of the planning inquiry system and more devolution of decision-making to inspectors. In a move which could pave the way to privatised development control, fees

for planning applications were imposed in 1981, with fees initially set at
£40 per house.

Another change was provided by the introduction of Simplified Planning
Zones in the Housing and Planning Act 1986. In these zones, permission
can be granted in advance for a wide range of developments, but they
cannot be used in National Parks, green belts, SSSIs or in conservation
areas. Any individual in an ordinary rural area can however request an
authority to declare a zone.

Specific planning issues The most controversial planning issue of the
decade concerned land for housing, and several times, specifically twice,
the government made proposals for a major relaxation of planning controls
only to be defeated by an alliance of its own supporters and other groups.
At the beginning of the decade, DOE Circular 9/80 set the tone by calling
on local authorities to maintain a 5-year supply of housing land in their
plans. This advice was continued in Circular 15/84 and expanded to
include proposals for limited extensions to villages and provision for new
settlements in structure plans. But this was a much watered down version
of a previous draft circular.

A second attempt at providing a more relaxed regime was made in 1986
and 1987 when a draft circular proposed removing the need to protect
agricultural land from planning advice. However after much lobbying,
mainly from Tories resident in rural areas, the advice in Circular 16/87 on
'Development involving agricultural land', although it began by arguing
that because of farm surpluses and the need to diversify the rural economy
there was no longer such a need to protect farmland, then argued that the
quality of land and the need to control the rate at which land is developed
remained factors for planners to consider. In a subtle but important
change the Circular advised on the need to protect the countryside for its
own sake rather than primarily for the productive value of the land. Thus
rural land continued to be protected from development but for wider
reasons than before.

Related to the land for housing issue was the future of green belts,
whose area had grown enormously via the process of structure plan
preparation in the 1970s and 1980s. In 1984 after a draft circular had
attempted to weaken green belt control, a new Circular 14/84, the first
since 1957, reaffirmed a strong commitment to their preservation and a
new commitment to their improvement via land management.

The green belts in the absence of major regional policies, however, only
serve to divert development pressures a little further afield, and in the 1980s
an alliance of builders loosely titled Consortium Developments announced
plans to apply for planning permission for a series of 12 small new towns
in the South-East. At the time of writing, three of these had reached the
public inquiry state and all had been turned down, Tillingham Hill, Essex
(1987), Stone Bassett, Oxon (1989) and Foxley Wood, Hants (1989).

In conclusion, to some extent the period of the 1980s was like a phoney war in which various attempts to allow more development in the countryside were frustrated by an alliance of existing residents and rural campaigners, replacing the traditional agricultural lobby, who gradually shifted their view away from food production to diversification. At the same time there was also a polarisation between those who argued for a planning system designed to protect the environment and those who argued for a planning system designed to plan for people, notably the disadvantaged people increasingly being priced out of rural housing by restrictive planning policies. It is to these topics that attention is now turned.

Social and economic policies in the 1980s

There were significant changes in each of the three main socio-economic areas, housing, transport and employment, in the 1980s.

Housing

In the housing field two main issues dominated the decade, council house sales and homes for locals. At the outset the Housing Act 1980 gave tenants the right to buy council houses at a substantial discount. In 'Designated Rural Areas', however, restrictions are imposed restricting subsequent resale to either local people or back to the local authority. Subsequent Acts, for example, the Housing and Building Control Act 1984, extended and enhanced the right-to-buy provisions for tenants, but critics remained sceptical that the provisions would do anything more than gentrify the countryside and produce an underclass of poorly housed rural people (HC 366-I, II and III (80–81)).

In a move to shift the remaining rented tenure from the public to the private sector a series of Acts, culminating with the Housing Act 1988, provided powers to make private renting more attractive for landlords, notably by introducing an assured shorthold tenancy for short lets.

The net effect of the changes was to create three types of rental. These were a small healthy private sector for the mobile employed, a heavily regulated housing association sector dependent on public subsidy and a residual local authority sector for the worst off.

The second main issue of the 1980s was the one of local need for this residual population. Attempts to provide for local need via plan making were effectively scotched by the DOE's refusal in 1981 to accept a 'locals only' policy in the Lake District Structure Plan, arguing that planning is concerned with land use not the identity or merits of people.

However, in a series of attempts to ameliorate growing hardship, the government issued a number of statements and policy proposals in the late 1980s, proposing the use of covenants or conditions on planning permissions for housing of locals which would not otherwise be given permission, but at the same time would not count against planned housing provisions in approved plans. (See Annual Review for more detail.)

Transport

Some radical changes to rural transport were made during the 1980s but only in the methods of control and subsidy. The underlying problem of providing transport for a scattered low density population remained as intractable as ever. Controls over public transport were first relaxed in the Transport Act 1980 which abolished the need for licences for express services (inter-city) and also provided for the designation of trial areas in which local stage services would also be deregulated. There followed a series of White Papers and reports on the issue (Cmnd 9300 and 9561, 1984 and 1985 and HC 38-I, II and III (84–85)). The Transport Act 1985 abolished the licensing of all bus services from 1986, and also further deregulated the use of minibuses and taxis. Transitional grants were made available in order to fund rural buses for a few years, and also powers were given to County Councils to subsidise rural services where no services were provided by the private sector. In spite of much doom and gloom at the time little change has apparently occurred in the provision of rural transport though little research has been done on the subject.

Employment

One of the severest attacks on central planning by the Thatcher government was mounted on employment planning. At the outset the Regional Economic Planning Councils were abolished, swiftly followed by a reduction in the Assisted Areas from 40 per cent to 25 per cent of the country between 1979 and 1982. Many of the remaining areas in a further change in November 1984 were rural regions in South-West England, Wales and Scotland. A further change was the suspension of Industrial Development Certificates in 1981.

In the mid-1980s the remaining regional policies were revised to be more selective and targeted on jobs provision and social factors (Cmnd 9111, 1983). Planning advice was also reshaped in three Circulars (16/84, 1/85 and 14/85), urging planners to be as flexible as possible in granting planning permission for employment-generating projects in rural areas.

Conversely, while general aid for employment was being severely restricted in the 1980s, the Development Commission and COSIRA were given a new lease of life. In 1982 they were given greater freedom to carry out their work and in 1984 they were given grant-in-aid body status. Also in 1984 they replaced the Special Investment Areas with Rural Development Areas, albeit covering both a smaller area and population. In 1988 the two bodies were merged to form a stronger Rural Development Commission. Throughout the decade a stream of innovative grant and other schemes emerged from the Commission in a bid to help the restructuring of the rural economy.

A further aid to the rural economy was provided in 1987 when the European Commission proposed a doubling of all three Structural Funds from 7,400 million ECU to 13,000 million ECU between 1987 and 1992 ((9805) 8251 (87) COM (87) 376). The main aim of this increased funding was to help not only the less developed (usually rural) regions but also the adjustment of agriculture structures, and also to remind everyone that the EC was more than the CAP (HL 82 (87–88)). Unfortunately, most of the aid is restricted to the Assisted Areas which the government had much reduced in size earlier in the decade, thus shooting itself in the foot. None the less, this new source of support was therefore added to the support already available under the 1982 EC's Integrated Development Programme for the Western Isles.

Conservation and recreation

Without doubt the most important piece of legislation in the decade was the Wildlife and Countryside Act 1981 which signalled not only the use of the voluntary approach backed up by compensation or acquisition but also a move away from negative protection in island type reserves towards positive management in the wider countryside.

Conservation

Many of the measures of the 1981 Act were included in a Labour bill of 1978, the Countryside Bill, but when this bill was lost in 1979 at the general election, the Tories added all the provisions needed to implement EC Directive 79/409 on the conservation of wild birds. More significantly, the Tories changed the thrust of the bill from control to persuasion. Conservation therefore ceased to be a matter of consensus but became one of party politics.

The crucial sections of the Act are those (sections 28 to 42) which deal with the measures which can be taken if conservation values are threatened by changes in land use, normally occasioned by the offer of a farm grant. In these cases, various public authorities can offer farmers compensation via management agreements for not proceeding with the proposals backed up by the threat of compulsory purchase as a last resort

(DOE Circular 24/82 and 4/83). Most of these provisions relate to designated areas such as National Parks and in particular SSSIs.

Management agreements were also introduced into Scotland, as well as Regional Parks, a Scottish concept, in the Countryside (Scotland) Act 1981.

Various loopholes in the main Act were closed in 1985 by two Acts—an Amendment and a Service of Notices Act—but the key issue of debate concerned the efficiency and morality of financial management agreements. Despite many calls for major revisions to this procedure (HC 6-I and II (84–85)), the government remained firmly committed to both the voluntary and financial principle (Cmnd 9522, 1985). To some extent their resolve was made easier by the dismantling of farm capital grants throughout the 1980s, as already outlined, and a general slowdown in farm activity. However, although 5,283 SSSIs had been declared by 30 April 1990, representing a major advance from the 3,329 in existence in 1981, claims by the government that the 1981 Act had been a success still seemed largely hollow in the face of constant evidence from the NCC showing a continued decline in habitat and species.

Elsewhere it was a fairly quiet decade on the conservation scene. The National Parks passed a scrutiny of their economic efficiency in 1984 and gradually acquired more independence, notably in plan making from local authorities (Circular 27/85), and their funding increased above inflation.

AONBs also acquired new members in the 1980s including Cranbourne Chase, the Howardian Hills and the High Weald. The designation of the 38th, the North Pennines, in 1988 made history by being the largest and the first to be subjected to a public inquiry. In Scotland, the National Scenic Areas were given more status with greater central control over certain planning applications, for example, those involving the development of more than five dwelling units.

At the beginning of the decade, the Ancient Monuments and Archaeological Areas Act 1979 and the National Heritage Act 1980 increased powers over the listing and protection of ancient monuments, and set up a National Heritage Fund with powers and money to buy land for the nation, including beautiful scenery or land with a high nature conservation value. However, proposals made in 1986 to set up Landscape Conservation Orders, in which harmful operations would have had to be submitted to National Park Authorities in key areas, who could then have forbidden them in return for compensation, were dropped in 1988.

Recreation

The decade saw very few developments in recreation policy. Initially the 1981 Act downgraded local authority powers to provide access to the countryside via footpaths, and a series of private members' bills in the

Table 5.3 *Central government spending on countryside planning: actual and planned, 1984–93*

£ million	1984–5 Actual	1988–9 Actual	1992–3 Planned
Agriculture and forestry			
Net UK expenditure on EC schemes			
including intervention	1,282	1,050	1,340
Net domestic expenditure	542	500	680
Forestry Commission	54	53	90
Total	1,905	1,632	2,140
Environment and employment			
Rural Development Commission	19.8	24.3	26.9
Countryside Commission	12.7	21.1	26.8
Nature Conservancy Council	15.0	39.0	48.6
Broads Authority	0	0	1.1
Groundwork	n.a.	1.5	2.9
Total	47.5	85.9	106.3

Note: In 1989–90 the DOE provided £9.06 million to cover 75% of the cost of National Parks

Source: Command 1003 and 1008, 1990, *The Government's expenditure plans*, London, HMSO

1980s calling for improved access to the countryside (HC 64 (81–82), HC 63 (83–84)) all failed to win approval, continuing the downbeat theme.

Conclusion

In conclusion, the 1980s promised to be a radical decade for rural planning and in some ways it was, but ultimately the rhetoric was more apparent than real, and in spite of calls for an even more radical fourth post-Thatcher term of office the latest expenditure plans for the main countryside planning agencies as shown in Table 5.3 for 1992–3 look remarkably similar to those for 1984–5. Agriculture retains the lion's share, and until there is a radical reform of the CAP, maybe via GATT, it is hard to see any fundamental change.

It is far more likely that the soft underbelly of rural planning, namely the small sums of money and minor controls that have grown up over the years like Topsy, will continue to undergo change, while the skeleton and the body go marching on. It is hoped that PIRPAP will be able to chart these changes for the 1990s as effectively as did the *Yearbook* for the 1980s. Authors are invited to contribute ideas for this space.

6 'Annual Review' rural planning in the United Kingdom, 1987-89

Andrew W. Gilg

The purpose of this Annual Review is to provide a survey of the following items: legislative change; changes in grant aid and other support for rural areas (e.g. farm support prices, forestry grants); major policy statements; land-use designations (e.g. new National Parks, Nature Reserves etc.); and a list of major books, reports, articles and statistical sources published in the year. The style is intended to be mainly factual, short and snappy, to give coverage in breadth but not in depth or detail. Its main purpose is to provide a check-list, for all those academics/planners/pressure group personnel and other people employed in rural organisations, who feel that the world is passing them by as they are submerged under the weight of new material which day-to-day demands of the job prevent them from reading. The review is thus an *aide-mémoire* rather than a discursive piece. Where possible, further reading is listed so that the reader can follow up a topic.

In order to classify matters the Review is broken up into three major sections: Legislative review; Review of events and news stories; and Literature list. This broadly follows the previous pattern of the *Countryside Planning Yearbook* (1980–6) and the *International Yearbook of Rural Planning* (1987–8). In order thus to provide continuity with the Yearbook, Volume One of PIRPAP covers the period from 1 September 1987–31 August 1989, Volume Two will cover the period 1 September 1989–31 August 1991 and Volume Three will resume the annual period by covering the period 1 September 1991–31 August 1992.

Legislative review

Again to ensure continuity with the *Yearbooks*, this section is divided in the same way, namely: Acts; Bills; Statutory Instruments; Circulars; Command Papers; House of Commons Papers; and House of Lords Papers. Annual Reports are not however now covered in this section but mainly in the Literature section.

Acts of Parliament

The Water Act 1989 (published as Chapter 15 on 14/7/89 at £20.00) privatised the supply of water in England and Wales by setting up new limited companies to provide water and sewerage services. At the same time, the regulatory functions of the former Water Authorities were taken over by a new public body, the National Rivers Authority (NRA) including water pollution; water resource management; flood defence; fisheries; and, in some areas, navigation. In the government's view, this division of responsibilities removed the poacher/gamekeeper conflict inherent in the previous situation, but critics of the Act argued that the NRA had too few powers and resources to do more than dip its toe into the waters of setting standards of water quality, which anyway will be set by the Secretary of State rather than the NRA.

The Act also introduced a new designation, Nitrate Sensitive Areas, in which controls can be introduced over agricultural activity in order to reduce the amount of nitrate leaking into the ground and thus into water sources.

One of the most contentious features of the Act, however, was the debate about the future of the 180,000 hectares of surplus land owned by the water companies around their reservoirs. After many amendments and counter-amendments the Act included discretionary powers for the Secretary of State to require that such land—if put on the market—should either be offered first to conservation groups at the market price or that it be protected indefinitely by management agreements or covenants before being put up for sale. However, this power only relates to the 110,000 hectares of such land in National Parks, AONBs and SSSIs, leaving 70,000 hectares of other rural land often in prize sites for recreational demand subject only to the control of normal planning procedures. The future of such land will clearly be a major issue in the 1990s as to whether it remains open to the general public or is converted to expensive private facilities for boating or other sporting activities. On 6 July 1989 a code of general practice was issued by the DOE to help solve the matter.

Background to the Act is provided by the proceedings of Standing Committee D, which amended the original bill (HC 1 (88–89)) and transferred it into HC 33 (88–89). The Lords made a number of amendments (HC 166 (88–89)) which were disputed by the Commons in HL 72 (88–89). Commentary is provided by (1) DOE press notices for 24/11/88; 24/1/89; 31/3/89; 27/4/89; 31/5/89; 30/6/89; 21/6/89; 6/7/89; 7/7/89; 2/8/89; and 16/8/89; (2) Countryside Commission press notices for 10/1/89 and 1/6/89; (3) NFU press notices for 7/2/89; 30/3/89; and 13/6/89; (4) articles in *Planning* 9/12/88 p. 11; 3/2/89 pp. 16–17; 7/4/89 p. 3; 14/4/89 p. 10; 9/6/89 p. 3; 21/7/89 p. 32; (5) *Farmers Weekly* 12/5/89 p. 15; 14/7/89 p. 14; (6) *The Planner* 7/7/89 p. 7; and (7) *Environment Digest* August 1989 No. 2 pp. 9–11. Further reading may be found in the Literature section.

The Farm Land and Rural Development Act 1988 (published as Chapter 16 on 16/5/88 at £1.60) provided the necessary legislative framework for the introduction of two new schemes: (a) farm diversification; and (b) farm woodlands. The purpose of the scheme was twofold, first to help farmers adapt to changing rural economies, and second, to cut surpluses. More details of the schemes are given in the Statutory Instruments section (SIs 1948, 1949, 1950/87 and 1125/88). The crucial aspect of the Act was that for the first time discretionary farm grants became available for non-capital expenditure, notably to cover the cost of market research and feasibility studies incurred in the establishment, expansion or promotion of farm-based businesses, or the marketing of anything supplied or produced by such businesses.

For a commentary on the Act, see the consultation documents issued by MAFF in 1987 (*International Yearbook of Rural Planning*, Vol. 2, 1988, pp. 4–5 and 12) and MAFF press notices for 22/10/87, 5/11/87 and 10/5/88; and *Scottish Planning Law and Practice 1988*, 25, p. 74. The non-controversial bill was debated by Standing Committee B and amended by the House of Lords in HL 11 and 36 (87–88).

The Norfolk and Suffolk Broads Act 1988 (published as Chapter 4 on 31/3/88 at £5.50) created Britain's 11th National Park to be managed by the Broads Authority which began work on 6 June 1988. Under the Act the Broads Authority is responsible for nature conservation, public enjoyment, planning and controls over navigation and boating. In more detail, the Authority is the planning authority for the area; is required to produce a plan setting out its policies; is required to draw up a map of areas of natural beauty which it is particularly important to conserve; and must produce a list of specific areas where prior notification must be given to the Authority of specified operations which might affect the character of these areas. Commentary on the Act is provided by DOE and Countryside Commission press notices of 16/3/88 and by M. Shaw, the Norfolk Country Planning Officer, in the *Journal of Planning and Environmental Law*, April 1989, pp. 241–6.

The Act was fairly controversial and was debated by Standing Committee B which amended the original bill HC 6 (87–88) into HC 18 (87–88). The House of Lords made further amendments in HL 27, 30 and 42 (87–88) which were summarised in HC 101 (87–88). A previous bill was also published in the 1986–7 session and amended by HC 129 (86–87).

The Housing Act 1988 (published as Chapter 50 at £11.80) made major changes to the rental sector. In the public sector, it breaks up the near monopoly of local authority provision by allowing tenants to vote for the transfer of the housing stock to other owners. The Act could thus mark the gradual rundown of council estates already diluted by right-to-buy provisions. In the voluntary sector, Housing Associations are given greater freedoms but subject to a number of constraints, namely overall cash limits on schemes and a 75 per cent upper limit in government subsidy. This means that Associations will have to act less like social agencies and more like commercial businesses.

The Housing Act also introduced two types of lease in the private sector: an assured tenancy or an assured shorthold tenancy. Assured tenancies provide security of tenure, but assured shorthold tenancies are for a fixed term. In both cases rents are agreed freely between tenant and landlord in order to encourage more lettings. Also to encourage more lettings the Act makes it easier for landlords to regain possession.

In summary, the Act presupposes a threefold rental sector for the 1990s. First, there is a small healthy private sector for the mobile employed, second, a heavily regulated housing association movement dependent on public subsidy and third, a residual local authority sector mainly limited to catering for the worst off. It does not augur well for the rural poor or for the disadvantaged tied tenant.

The Act was debated by Standing Committee G in 21 sittings and in the House of Lords; see HL 109 (122, 130 and 136 (87–88)). A commentary is provided in *Development and Planning*, 1989, p. 12–13.

The Electricity Act 1989 which provided powers to privatise electricity supplies also imposed a series of duties on the new companies to minimise the effects of their operations on natural beauty. These duties are to be backed up by a set of environmental guidelines to be prepared both by the new companies and by various countryside groups including the NCC and Countryside Commission. Commentary is provided by *Environmental Digest*, No. 28. 1989, pp. 5–7; press notices from the NFU for 6 and 18 July; the Countryside Commission, 9/6/89; and the NCC, 16/2/89. Also see *Planning*, 14/7/89, p. 3.

The Local Government and Housing Act 1989 simplified powers for local authorities to promote the economic development of their areas.

The Finance Act 1988 allowed forestry tax breaks for schemes approved before 15 March 1988 to continue until 1993.

The Local Government Act 1988 is outlined in the Circulars section.

The Public Utility Transfers and Water Charges Act 1988 provided powers to transfer the powers and properties of water authorities and electricity boards to new bodies in the run up to privatisation.

The Regional Development Grants (Termination) Act 1988 ended grants under Part II of the Industrial Development Act 1982 as from 31/3/88.

In contrast, the Scottish Development Agency Act 1987 and the Welsh Development Agency Act 1988 raised the financial borrowing limits of the two agencies from £700 million to £1,200 million and £450 million to £700 million respectively.

Finally, the Common Land (Rectification of Registers) Act 1989 will allow land to be removed from the Common Land Register from 1992 if it is part of the land attached to a dwelling house.

Failed bills

Two attempts were made to bring the demolition of houses under planning control, first by the Planning Permission (Demolition of Houses) Bill 1988 (HC 42 (87–88)), and second, by the Planning Permissions (Demolitions of Houses) Bill 1989 (HC 46 (88–89)).

The Planning Notification of Development Proposals Bill 1989 (HC 59 (88–89)) would have called on planning authorities in England and Wales to prepare a code of practice for neighbour notification of planning applications.

Another attempt to widen planning controls was made by the Hedgerow Bill 1989 (HC 41 (88–89)) which would have made it an offence to uproot or remove a hedge without planning permission or other good cause.

A more comprehensive bill, the Environmental Charter Bill 1989 (HC 147 (88–89)), would have made it a duty for every local authority to protect and enhance the environment and establish an ecology working group. These groups would have had to produce an environmental charter for local authorities which would have had to be the subject of an annual report in its implementation.

An attempt to open up the meetings of the Forestry Commission's Regional Advisory Committees to the public, and make their documents open to public scrutiny, was made by the Forestry Commission Advisory Committees (Public Access to Information) Bill 1988 (HC 112 (87–88)).

Finally, the Definitive Map Modification Bill 1989 (HC 27 (88–89)) sought to modify the working of the 1981 Wildlife and Countryside Act to make the slow review of Definitive Maps less of a problem by inserting past facts or future intentions into sections 53 (3)(c)(iii) and 53 (3)(c)(ii).1 (see Circular 21/88).

Statutory Instruments

The period under review saw a major restructuring of farm grants and the introduction of a new range of grants. On 1 January 1988 Capital Grants covering 25 per cent of the cost of capital investments of up to £35,000 became available for *farm diversification schemes* including tourism, sport and recreation, food and timber processing, farmshops and restaurants, nature trails and interpretation centres (1948, 1949 and 1950/87 and 1938/88). Later in the year, non-Capital Grants for up to £10,000 became available from 1 August 1988 for feasibility studies and marketing costs associated with diversifying a farm business, including the processing of farm produce; the provision of holiday accommodation; recreational activities; and pick-your-own (1125/88). The rate of grant varies from 20 per cent to 50 per cent depending on the project.

In mainstream farming the Agriculture Improvement Scheme (AIS) was closed in November 1988 and replaced by the Farm and Conservation Grant Scheme in 1989 (128/89 and 219/89). This scheme includes a budgetary target of £50 million to be spent between 1989 and 1992 on grants to farmers towards the cost of installing facilities for the storage, treatment and disposal of slurry and silage effluent.

Three new grants at a rate of between 35 per cent and 50 per cent were also introduced for the regeneration of native woodlands and heather moors, and to assist in the cost of repairing farm buildings. In contrast, grants for new farm buildings and roads were discontinued. These changes therefore marked a major step in the move away from farm grants for production towards grants for conservation. They are only available under an approved improvement plan allowing the further imposition of possible conservation aims if necessary.

Another change was the introduction of Set-Aside in 1988 (1352/88 and 1042/89). Under this scheme farmers must take at least 20 per cent of their land out of production for five years in return for certain payments, as shown in Table 6.1.

The final new scheme was the Farm Woodland Scheme which came into operation on 1 October 1988 (1291/88). The scheme is experimental and limited to 36.000 hectares in its first 3 years, at an initial cost of around £10 million per year. The payments are additional to the planning grant available under the Woodland Grant Scheme (see p. 80) and are designed to bridge the gap between planting and the first receipt of income from the wood in about 20 or 40 years. For example, payments will extend to 40 years for oak woodland, 20 years for conifers and 10 years for coppice. The rates of payment are as shown in Table 6.2.

Table 6.1 *Set-Aside Scheme*

Type of Set-Aside	Non LFA Land	LFA Land
	£ per hectare	
Permanent fallow	200	180
Rotational fallow	180	160
Woodlands	200	180
Woodlands with Farm Woodland Scheme	190	150
Non-agricultural use excluding		
residential, industrial, or retail use	150	130

Table 6.2 *Farm Woodland Scheme*

	Lowlands	Less Favoured Areas	
		Disadvantaged	Severely disadvantaged
		£ per hectare	
Arable land and improved grassland	190	150	100
Unimproved grassland or rough grazing	—	30	30

The other major change during the period brought about by Statutory Instrument was the introduction of Environmental Assessment on 3 July 1988. This implemented EC Directive 85/337 which identifies two types of project for Assessment. Annex I projects have to be subjected to Assessment. These projects include major developments, for example: oil refineries; power stations, airports and motorways. Annex II projects may be subjected to an Assessment depending on whether the national government considers it necessary or not. Although Annex II includes forestry, the Statutory Instruments make it clear that forestry proposals will not normally be assessed unless they involve significant planting in areas subject to national designation on ecological grounds. In other areas, the government advised that only a few Annex II proposals would pass the basic test of having 'significant' environmental effects. These would probably be major projects having a more than local impact, and were proposed to take place on particularly sensitive or vulnerable locations. Examples of this are large pig and poultry rearing units, new salmon rearing installations, new flood relief works, land reclamation from the sea and major mineral or sand and gravel workings. The general tenor of the Statutory Instrument was to use the existing planning system wherever possible. The following Instruments are relevant (1199, 1207, 1217, 1218, 1221, 1241, 1249 and 1272/88).

At the other end of the planning scale the period under review also saw several amendments of the General Development Order in both Scotland

and south of the Border (97/88, 1249/88, 1272/88, 2091/88, 148/89, 603/89). In between these amendments a totally new Order for England and Wales came into force on 5 December 1988 (1813/88). It replaced the 1977 Order and 12 other Orders and amendments. The main changes included: (1) restricting the requirements to consult MAFF to developments only involving the loss of 20 hectares or more of farmland of grades 1, 2 or 3a; (2) introducing control over the development of livestock units and associated buildings, e.g. slurry tanks within 400 metres of non-agricultural buildings; (3) removing the power of highway authorities to direct planning decisions on classified roads and replacing it with a right to be consulted; (4) introducing planning controls over clay pigeon shooting taking place more than 14 days in a year; (5) introducing a requirement to consult waste disposal authorities of development of new landfill sites; (6) bringing 'stone cladding' under control in areas such as National Parks, AONBs and Conservation Areas; and (7) new controls over loft extensions. In essence, however, the new GDO was a revamp rather than the badly needed simplification and total rewrite required by rural planners.

In Scotland, a new Use Classes Order was also introduced (147/89) but unlike the 1987 English Order it used 16 Classes rather than the five used in England and Wales.

Finally, Statutory Instruments 1146/89 and 1152/89 brought most of the provisions of the Water Act 1989 into operation as from 1 September 1989 including the code of practice on access and recreation issued by the DOE on 6 July 1989.

The following areas were also covered by Statutory Instruments during the period:

Advertisements 2227/87, 670/89
Agricultural Development (Improvement) 491/88, 1056/88, 1201/88, 1982/88, 1983/88, 2065/88, 2066/88
Areas of Special Protection under 1981 Wildlife Act 324/88, 1479/88
Beef Special Premium 574/89, 575/89
Broads Act 1988 955/88, 277/89
Cereals co-responsibility levy 1001/88, 1267/88, 576/89
Conservation Areas 1529/87
Control of Pollution Act 1974 818/88
Crofting 559/88
Dutch Elm Disease 604/88
Environmental Assessment 1199/88, 1221/88
Environmentally Sensitive Areas; Lleyn Peninsula 2027/87, Cumbrian Mountains 2026/87, Breckland 2029/87 and 1645/88, North Peak

2030/87, Shropshire Borders 2031/87, South Downs 2032/87, Suffolk River Valleys 2033/87 and 1645/88, Test Valley 2034/87, General (England) 174/88, General (Wales) 173/88, the Broads 175/88, Somerset Levels 176/88, Breadalbane 491/88, Loch Lomond 492/88, Stewarty 493/88, Whitlaw and Eildon 494/88, Machair of the Uists, Benbecula, Barra and Vatersay 495/88
Fees for Planning Applications 193/89
Fish farming 1134/87
Forestry 970/88, 971/88
Hill Livestock 2129/87
Housing Act 1988 2056/88, 2152/88, 203/89, 404/89, 430/89
Housing and Planning Act 1986 1554/87, 1607/87, 1759/87, 1939/87, 283/88, 1787/88
Listed Buildings 1529/87
Local Plans 1760/87
Milk 132/88, 182/88, 534/88, 653/88, 714/88, 1803/88, 1814/88, 16/89
Mining 1936/87, 1937/87, 2002/87, 726/88
Planning Applications 1812/88, 1087/89
Planning Inquiries 1522/87, 1531/87, 944/88, 945/88, 577/89
Right to Buy 1732/87, 1810/87, 944/88, 1726/88, 2057/88, 174/89, 512/89, 513/89
Simplified Planning Zones 1532/87, 1750/87, 1849/87
Structure Plans 1760/87
Tree Preservation Orders 963/88
Wildlife and Countryside Act 1981 288/88, 906/89

DOE Circulars

24/87, Local Plans: Housing and Planning Act 1986. Draws attention to changes made to Local Plan procedures by the 1986 Act including a new set of provisions for Local Plan Schemes. Much of the advice contained in Circular 22/84 remains valid however.

25/87, Simplified Planning Zones. Draws attention to the Statutory Instruments (1750/87, 1759 and 1760/87) implementing the power to declare such zones under the 1986 Housing and Planning Act. However zones are expected to be declared almost entirely in urban areas and cannot by law be designated in protected areas such as SSSIs, green belts and conservation areas and National Parks. In other rural areas individuals can none the less request an authority to declare a zone, thus potentially providing a route for relaxing planning controls.

27/87, Nature Conservation. Outlines the relevant legislative changes since the last circular in 1977. Most of the circular deals with the 1981 Act.

However it also stresses the role local authorities could play in nature conservation by a greater use of all sorts of existing legislation and by imposing conditions on planning permissions.

28/87, Open-cast Coal-Mining. Supersedes Circular 3/84 which sets out transitional procedures for the new procedure under which British Coal still needs to obtain planning permission for open-cast coal-mining from mineral planning authorities but no longer requires the authorisation of the Secretary of State.

10/88, The Town and Country Planning (Inquiries Procedures) Rules 1988 etc. Gives detailed advice on the new inquiry and appeal procedures laid down by Statutory Instruments 944/88 and 945/88. These are designed to speed up the process and make it more efficient. The main changes involve pre-inquiry processes designed to streamline the actual inquiry or appeal. To this end the circular contains idealised flow charts and codes of practice for both inquiries and appeals.

12/88, Local Government Act 1988. Outlines the provisions of the Act which contains a number of measures to encourage the expansion of the private rented housing sector. These include a power for local authorities to provide financial assistance for any private schemes including housing associations, for example, by selling land on concessionary terms, or by making a capital grant. The Act also allows the building of houses catering for local need to be subsidised by local authorities up to 30 per cent of the cost of the scheme, and the subsidisation of private rents to keep them within affordable levels.

15/88, Environmental Assessment. Gives advice on the series of Statutory Instruments outlined in the previous section. The core advice is that an Assessment should only be required in those very few cases where 'significant' environmental effects are expected.

18/88, Painting of Listed Buildings. Draws attention to a 1987 legal case where it was held that changing the colour of a listed building by painting could affect its character and that if a significant change in colour were contemplated it would need planning consent.

21/88, Modifications to the Definitive Map. A 1987 court case has drawn attention to an error in the 1981 Wildlife and Countryside Act. This means that a modification order even when a mistake was made in the first place cannot be used to delete a right of way shown on a definitive map. Even though the government intends to rectify this anomaly as soon as possible, a private members' bill failed to do so. (see Failed Bills section).

22/88, General Development Order Consolidation. Draws attention to and gives advice on the new GDO (see Statutory Instrument 1813/88 for more details).

7/89, Water and the environment. A very detailed set of advice about the discharge of dangerous substances into the aquatic environment.

12/89, The Housing (Right to Buy) (Maximum Discount) Order 1989 and Regulations. Draws attention to two Statutory Instruments (512/89 and 513/89) which increased the maximum discount from £35,000 to £50,000 in April 1989.

18/89, Publication of Information about unused and underused land. Draws attention to a bid by the Secretary of State to make better use of unused and underused land owned by local authorities by the use of powers invoked in 1989—under the Local Government Planning and Land Act 1980—forcing local authorities to publish registers of such land on an annual basis.

Other relevant DOE Circulars published during the period include: 23/87, The Housing (Extension of Right to Buy) Order 1987; 1/88, Planning policy guidance and Minerals planning guidance; 2/88, Town and Country Planning (Control of Advertisements) Regulations 1987; 24/88, Environmental Assessment of projects in Simplified Planning Zones and Enterprise Zones; 5/89, The Town and Country Planning (Fees for Applications and Deemed Applications) Regulations 1989; 14/89, Caravan Sites and Control of Development Act 1960. Model Standards; 15/89, Town and Country Planning Control of Advertisement Regulations 1989; and 17/89, Landfill Sites: Development Control.

Department of Transport Circulars were also published on: 1/88, Transport Policies and Programmes. Submissions for 1989/90; 1/89 As for 1/88 but for 1990/91.

Scottish Development Department Circulars During the period these included 18/1987 Development Involving Agricultural Land which cancelled and amended Circulars 77/1975 and 24/1981 respectively. It advised that rather less weight should be given to retaining agricultural land in production, but that the need to protect the countryside from inappropriate development remains as strong as ever. In more detail, DAFS only need to be consulted if an application involves either two or more hectares of farmland of Classes 1, 2 and 3.1 under the Macauly Institute classification, or 10 hectares of other land. In crofting areas a lower threshold may be necessary.

22/1987, Town and Country Planning (Minerals) Act 1981. Draws attention to the provisions of the Act which came into force on 1 January 1988, notably, the need to monitor sites where work recently ended or work has yet to begin.

23/1987, Open-cast coal-mining. (See DOE Circular 28/87)

1/1988, EC Directive on the conservation of wild birds. Reminds planning authorities of their duties under the 1979 directive (the Ramsar Convention) notably with regard to Special Protection Areas.

13/1988, Environment Assessment. Draws attention to the Statutory Instrument (see p. 65) involved with the introduction of Assessment from 1988 and reminds planning authorities that the basic question to be asked is whether a proposal will have 'significant' environmental effects.

29/1988, Notification of applications. Explains the provisions of a number of Statutory Instruments which collectively set out ten categories of proposed development which need to be notified to the Secretary of State for his possible call in if planning permission is going to be granted by the local authority. The ten categories include: development of prime agricultural land; development contrary to approved plans; and development involving nature conservation sites.

6/1989, The Town and Country Planning (Use Classes) (Scotland) Order 1989. Draws attention to the new Order, see p. 66.

The SDD also produced Circulars on: Simplified Planning Zones (16/1987 and 26/1988) and Appeals (2/1989 and 14/1989).

Command Papers (Cm.)

The most important White Paper of the period was Cm. 569/1989, *The future of development plans*, which contained the key proposal to replace the two-tier system of plan making with a one-tier district-based system. Structure Plans would be replaced by statements of country planning policies prepared by County Councils, dealing with key issues, but excluding agriculture. The main feature of the proposed system would, however, be single-tier development plans at the district level. All District Councils would be required to prepare such a plan for the whole of their areas consistent with national and regional guidance with 'Planning Policy Guidance Notes' and 'County Statements'. The National Parks would replace both county type statements and area-wide development plans [NB The proposals were suspended in the Autumn of 1990.]

Other White Papers dealt with a continued reform of development control.

For example, Cm. 512, 1988, *Releasing Enterprise*, floated the idea of giving permitted development rights for a number of environmentally acceptable uses of open land and existing buildings compatible with rural areas, as an aid to diversifying the rural economy. From the other direction Cm. 433, 1988, *The Conduct of Local Authority Business*, promised to provide local authorities with a specific power to carry out economic development in their areas at their discretion subject to certain provisos, in order to clarify the existing confused situation over such issues.

The need for local authority aid was increased by Cm. 278, 1988 DTI, *The Department for Enterprise*, which took away the automatic right to a grant in Assisted Areas and replaced it with a selective system under which companies have to show that they genuinely need grant aid to set up new employment creating projects.

With reference to infrastructure Cm. 693, 1989, *Roads for Prosperity*, proposed a £7 billion increase on roads spending and Cm. 698, 1989 *New Roads by new means* proposed the possibility of allowing private developers to build roads and pay for them by tolls.

Cm. 214, 1987, *Housing—The Government's Proposals*, set out the government's four principal aims for housing. These were first, to reverse the decline of the private sector; second, to given council tenants the right to transfer to other landlords; third, to target money on the most acute problems; and fourth, to continue to encourage the growth of home ownership. Many of these aims found expression in the Housing Act 1988 (see earlier sections), but the White Paper also set out a longer-term strategy for achieving the four aims.

In Scotland Cm. 242, 1987, *Housing—The Government's Proposals for Scotland*, set out the government's plans in a framework designed to: give people a wider choice; improve the supply and quality of housing; encourage greater individual responsibility and control; and deal with the residual problems of homelessness. In detail the White Paper proposed setting up a new agency, 'Scottish Homes'. Rural areas were singled out as having special difficulties but it was envisaged that the proposals would deal with these on a national basis.

Three White Papers also set out *The Government's Expenditure Plans*, Cm. 288 (1988), 604 and 609 (1989) as shown in Table 6.3.

Other White Papers set out the details of the 1991 Census (Cm. 430, 1988), and the report of the Royal Commission on Environmental Pollution on the 'Best Practicable Environmental Option' (Cm. 310, 1988).

Table 6.3 *Expenditure plans for rural planning*

Agriculture	1986–87 out turn	1990–91 plans (Cm 288)	(Cm 604)	1991–92 plans (Cm 604)
		£ million		
Intervention Board for Agricultural Produce and EC expenditure	1,189	1,840	1,450	1,620
Domestic agriculture	864	970	980	1,000
Forestry Commission	51	70	80	80
Total*	2,190	2,980	2,620	2,820
EC receipts	1,509	1,300	1,500	1,570
Other spending				
Rural Development Commission	23.6	30.1	30.6	30.8
Countryside Commission	17.9	19.5	23.4	24.6
Nature Conservancy Council	32.1	40.1	41.6	43.3

Note: * Totals do not exactly add up due to differences in allocating expenditure between countries in the UK

House of Commons Papers

These remain a most useful series of information. One of the most useful are the papers produced by the House of Commons Select Committee on European Legislation. The 1987–8 session produced 39 reports on Europe (HC 43-i to xxxix (87–88)). Out of these iii examined CAP reforms; v and xxxvi looked at the reform of the Structural Funds; xiii considered Set-Aside and Extensification; xix examined the Regional Development Fund, Stabilisers, Set-Aside and the Cessation of farming; xxi commented on the farm price proposals for 1988–9; xxxii looked at the control of biotechnology; and xxxviii looked at milk quotas (compensation for outgoers) and the report on the 'Future of Rural Society' produced by the EC in 1988 (COM (88) 501).

In the 1988–9 session the same Select Committee in the period under review produced 33 reports (HC 15-i to xxxiii (88–89)). Out of these i looked at the GATT negotiations on agriculture, the reform of the Structural Funds and the review of the beef regime (also in vii); ii looked at the review of the sheep meat and goat meat regimes and the draft EC budget for 1989; viii looked at forestry; xi, xii, xiii and xiv looked at agricultural price proposals for 1989–90; xxxii looked at milk quotas and the proposed European Environment Agency; and xiv looked at water pollution by nitrates.

Useful data on past, present and planned future government spending on rural affairs is also provided by: HC 107-III and VI (87–88), 123 (87–88), 339-IV and X (87–88); 231-IV and X (88–89) for agriculture, forestry and environmental services; 707-III (87–88) for agriculture and forestry; and 17-VI (88–89) for environmental services.

Within agriculture HC 121 (87–88), a report by the Committee of Public Accounts on the 'Measurement of Farm Incomes' recommended that MAFF institute more widespread surveys of farm income, notably for off-farm incomes and should also monitor the impact of farm support policies more closely. HC 230 (87–88) contains the government's response to the Agriculture Committee's report on the December 1986 agreement to cut back CAP support, notably in the dairy sector. HC 275 (87–88) contains a report by the Comptroller and Auditor General on the way in which import levies and export refunds for agricultural produce are operated by the UK. In a report on this report the Committee of Public Accounts (HC 342 (87–88)) concurred that the main problem lay in possible fraud since there are insufficient checks by Customs and Excise and the Intervention Board for Agricultural Produce.

In addition to these reports by non-agricultural committees the subject specific Agriculture Committee also produced a number of reports and conducted a number of enquiries. The biggest of these was into Land Use and Forestry but its report was not published until after the period covered by this review, and so it will be covered in Volume Two. In the mean time, the enquiry received evidence from the Forestry Commission (HC 678-i (87–88)), the UK agriculture departments (ii), the NCC and RSPB (iii), various Scottish organisations (HC 23-i (88–89)), the Countryside Commission and County Councils Associations (ii), the forestry industry (iii), Ramblers and Field Sports Organisations (iv), the Forestry Commission again (v), DOE, SDD and TGWU (vi), nature conservation groups (vii), five farmers' organisations (viii) and University foresters (ix).

In two reports on the 'Implementation of the CAP in Great Britain' the Comptroller and Auditor General (HC 31 (88–89)) and the Committee of Public Accounts (HC 66 and 66-i (88–89)) made a mass of detailed comments about implementation, for example, mistakes by the MMB costing £44 million. In general, however, they found that the administration of the CAP was carried out efficiently. However, both reports stressed the need for MAFF to produce a clearer statement of how much the CAP costs Britain, either via setting up an Annual Report or via the annual expenditure White Paper.

However, expenditure on agriculture is expected to drop by 12 per cent between 1988 and 1991-2 according to Cm. 288, the 1989 public

THE LIBRARY
BISHOP BURTON COLLEGE
BEVERLEY HU17 8QG
TEL: 0964 550481 Ex: 227

expenditure White Paper which is examined by the Agriculture Committee in HC 335 (88–89).

Finally, the Agriculture Committee (HC 402 (88–89)) conducted a report into the Beef Special Premium Scheme which replaced the Beef Variable Scheme in 1989. The effectiveness of this scheme is according to the Committee limited by the low payment of £29.19 per animal and the maximum upper limit of 90 cattle per year.

With reference to employment creation, both the Comptroller and the Auditor General and the Committee of Public Accounts produced reports on Regional Incentives (HC 346 (87–88)) and Regional Assistance (HC 406 (87–88)) respectively. The former report considered that the changes of the late 1980s were too recent to have had much effect but the latter report expressed concern that the new system allowed greater room for fraud and wondered why better monitoring schemes had not been implemented for regional aid over the last 40 or so years.

The Comptroller and Auditor General also cast his eye over road planning (HC 688 (87–88)) and concluded that although schemes were often over or under-generous the overall benefit to cost ratio of new roads is 1.9:1. The Transport Committee in their review of the Comptroller's report (HC 101 (88–89)) endorsed the view that the evaluation of road schemes is poorly developed and concluded that in future it was better to err on the side of over rather than underprovision. This theme of roads for the future was also examined in advance of a report in a collection of evidence submitted to the Committee by a wide variety of transport and environmental organisations (HC 62-i to xi (88–89)). Finally the Committee in a report (HC 238 (88–89)) on bus fund grants argued that an inquiry should be conducted into whether £15 million a year spent on such grants was really needed and if so how its use could be monitored.

In the continuing debate over Historic Buildings the government in their two replies (HC 263 (87–88) and HC 563 (88–89)) to the Environment Committee's 1987 report on the topic (see IYRP, Vol. 2, p. 67) accepted over half of the recommendations and pointed out that spending on the heritage had increased by 75 per cent in real terms since 1979.

In another reply to a previous Environment Committee report this time on water pollution (see IYRP, Vol. 2, p. 68) the government (HC 543 (87–88)) noting a 13 per cent increase between 1986 and 1987 in farm pollution incidents to 3,890 announced that more controls would have to be introduced over farmers in order to reinforce the 'Code of Good Agricultural Practice', already backed up by new and more generous grants to deal with slurry.

In terms of new reports, the Environment Committee in a report on the British Waterways Board (HC 237 (88–89)) noted that the canal network could be seen as a country park, two thousand miles long and ten yards wide. However, there is a conflict of interest over its use for leisure and/or conservation and the Committee argued that the Board should be forced to give nature conservation a higher priority. In a report on the proposed European Environmental Agency (HC 612 (88–89)) the Committee clearly welcomed the proposal but expressed concern that its remit should not extend to more than an advisory agency.

Finally, the following papers which are of some interest to rural planning were produced during the period: HC 444 (87–88), the government's response to the Welsh Affairs Committee report on 'Tourism in Wales'; HC 650 (87–88) and a special report on the Hampshire (Lyndhurst By-Pass) Bill.

House of Lords Papers

The House of Lords Select Committee on the European Communities produced ten relevant reports during the period under review. Central to their deliberations were EC proposals for restructuring Community Finances. In HL 14 (87–88) the Committee pointed out that agricultural spending needed to be brought under control if other EC schemes were to be increased, but that support for agriculture would have to be transferred to support for rural areas if rural depopulation and dereliction were not to occur at an unacceptable level. The preferred method of control via stabilisers was further considered by the Committee in HL 43 (87–88) which concluded that by themselves they might not make a major impact and that they should be seen as an *ad hoc* back up to other measures, for example, long-term price planning or set-aside.

Set-Aside was considered by the Committee in more detail in HL 65 (87–88). This concluded that the current scheme is only a 'toe in the water' but since it was a good idea they made a number of suggestions for improving the scheme. These included: replacing the fixed compensation paid with a system of bidding, or increasing the rate to around £260–285 per hectare; reducing the minimum amount of land from 20 per cent to 10 per cent and increasing the element of land management in the scheme.

An adventitious form of set-aside might be achieved by controlling nitrogen use which has increasingly been implicated in unacceptable levels of nitrates in water. In a major report on this issue (HL 73 (88–89)) the Committee argued that nitrogen was an indirect factor in increasing nitrates by increasing organic material in the soil. Measures to limit nitrogen use proposed by the EC were however conceived by the

Committee as too draconian since they could lead to at least a 59–73 per cent drop in the arable area of the drier parts of the UK . Given the scientific uncertainty surrounding nitrates the Committee thus recommended the more cautious approach advocated by the UK in the Nitrate Sensitive Areas policy adopted under the Water Act 1989.

Long-term price policy must however remain the key plank in CAP reform according to the Committee and so they welcomed the farm price proposals for 1988–9 and 1989–90 in HL 85 (87–88) and HL 34 (88–89). Both these sets of proposals marked time while the effects of stabilisers and the ceiling on CAP overall spending imposed in February 1988 began to take effect. The basic policy of a price freeze (cuts in real terms) is however undermined according to the Committee by the continuation of MCAs which allowed the UK to experience only a 9.7 per cent increase in farm incomes compared to a 12.8 per cent rise in Germany. In spite of the problems of MCAs, the Committee do not expect them to be abolished by the time of the Single Market in 1992.

With reference to specific products EC proposals to phase out the sheep meat regime were accepted by the Committee in HL 98 (87–88). In the Beef and Veal sectors however while the Committee (HL 22 (88–89)) broadly agreed with the objectives of a new regime for the sector, they felt that restricting payments to only 90 cattle per holding would discriminate against the UK and could possibly destabilise the market.

Moving away from agriculture, the Committee in their reports on the draft EC directive on the protection of natural habitats (HL 72 (88–89)) endorsed the key proposal to create a network of at least 100 protected areas to be known as 'Natura 2000' by the year 2000. However, the Committee noted a lack of enthusiasm in the UK for this and other EC conservation proposals, partly because the proposals themselves are flawed. They therefore recommended the full implementation of the Berne Convention on conservation, followed by a commitment to a degree of absolute protection for conservation sites, allied to an extension of conservation programmes to the wider countryside.

Finally, the Committee in HL 82 (87–88) examined EC proposals to double the money available to the three Structural Funds, the EAGGF, ESF and ERDF, from 7,400 million ECU in 1987 to 13,400 million in 1992, in order to promote the development of less developed regions and to aid the restructuring of agriculture arising from reforms in the CAP. The Committee welcomed the proposals as a reminder that the CAP is not the only active part of the Community, but noted that a major reorientation of the EAGGF to aid the growth of farm employment should be a necessary part of the changes.

The Select Committee on Science and Technology produced reports on Agricultural and Food Research in HL 13-I and II (88–89) and HL 104 (87–88). The earlier report (104) called for the creation of a new research body, the Natural Resources Research Council, to be created by merging NERC and AFRC. The main report (13) stressed that agriculture would have to move from quantity to quality and towards an environmentally benign type of farming. Food surpluses do not therefore lead to a need to cut research, but a continued commitment to it, especially with regard to forestry which is needed not only to fill the import gap but also to use up surplus farmland. There is also a need for research to develop ways in which environmental and agricultural interests can be more closely merged in the years to come.

Review of events and news stories in rural planning, November 1987 to October 1989

This review is structured into three sections. First, there is a set of four short reviews of four major issues: Land-use planning; Extensification and Set-Aside; Forestry; and the farm price debate. This is followed by a diary of events, and finally, a list of new protected sites.

Four major issues

Land-use planning During the period under review there were four big issues. These were low-cost rural housing; housing needs in the South-East; proposals to increase permitted use rights in the countryside; and proposals to increase the efficiency of the planning system.

In the area of low-cost rural housing the then Secretary of State for the Environment, Nicholas Ridley, announced a major change in February 1989 in a written answer to the House of Commons. Under a new policy, sites in the countryside that would not normally be given permission for housing could exceptionally be released for low-cost housing schemes, if the planning authority is satisfied that there is a need for such housing, and that arrangements can be made to reserve it for local people. This could include the involvement of Housing Associations, or Village Trusts, or the use of covenants or Section 52 agreements. Such planning permissions would be extra to housing allocations already made in plans.

In a further move it was also announced in February 1989 that the Housing Corporation's target for low-cost village housing had been increased from 450 to 600 for 1989/90 and that new targets for 1990/91 and 1991/92 had been set of 900 and 1,100 respectively. Finally, in the March 1989 budget capital gains tax rules were relaxed so that landowners giving land away or selling it off cheaply would no longer be liable to tax on the notional profits they could have made if they had sold the land at full market value. In theory, this could increase the amount of low-cost land available for social housing.

In the mean time, at the other end of the housing spectrum there was much debate during the summer of 1988 over the need for new housing in the South-East. The focus of the debate was the series of proposals for new towns/villages in or beyond the green belt, and between the growth and conservation wings of the Tory Party, notably Ridley versus Heseltine. The arguments centred over the amount of genuine new need over and above migration, the enormous effect of occupancy rates (with 80 per cent of demand coming from single households) and whether the high rate of building in the 1980s would need to be sustained or had satisfied demand. At the start of the debate the House Builders Federation wanted 660,000 new houses in the 1990s, the DOE 610,000 while existing plans provided for only 460,000. In the end, a compromise target of between 560,000 and 580,000 was reached.

A year later in May 1989, the DOE issued a consultation paper on 'Permitted Use Rights in the Countryside' in a bid to deregulate planning further, and to aid farm diversification. Among the activities which it proposed to free from control were: equestrian activities; the display and sale of farm produce; outdoor sport and recreation; and educational uses related to farming. The proposals met with a barrage of opposition notably from the CPRE, the Countryside Commission, the Ramblers' Association, Friends of the Earth, the RTPI, the Town and Country Planning Association, the Association of District Councils and the County Planning Officers Society. The NFU provided a rare message of support. Indeed, out of 279 responses, the DOE had to admit that most were critical, and in October 1989 the proposals were withdrawn.

Finally, in July 1989, another consultation paper 'Efficient Planning' proposed giving general planning permission for specified developments, a power to turn away repetitive applications and fees of between £100 and £4,000 for planning appeals. In line with the previous paper most reaction was unfavourable even for normally anti-planning bodies such as the RIBA and the House Builders Federation.

Extensification and Set-Aside In 1987 European Community Council Regulation 1760/87 sought to achieve in each member state a reduction of at least 20 per cent in the production of all surplus products for at least a five-year period. The Regulation is mandatory for each state but not for each farmer. In December 1987 MAFF published a consultation paper setting out extensification schemes for cereals and beef. For cereals, the proposals included flat rate payments, tendering by farmers and a move to organic farming. In the event, the flat rate system was adopted. For beef, detailed proposals were set out in a second consultation paper in June 1989 which proposed two schemes. First, it proposed limiting beef production on extensified farms to animals reared on the farm, and prohibiting the purchase of calves. Second, it wished to reduce sales by 20 per cent. The paper also proposed for sheep a system based on cutting flock size by 20 per cent.

The only extensification scheme actually to get off the ground however was cereals set-aside. The details of the scheme were published in June and July of 1988 (see the Statutory Instruments section for details). In essence, the scheme offers payments of up to £200 per hectare for not farming land, although uses such as woodland are allowed. Just what is and is not allowed has however been a bone of contention and a good deal of fine tuning has had to be made to the detailed regulations. In March 1989 the DOE announced a system to allow conservation uses to be funded by a top-up scheme, and details of this were announced by the Countryside Commission in June 1989. Under this scheme, payments of between £45 and £120 per hectare can be made on top of set-aside money for creating new meadowland for example. The top-up grants were only made available however, in seven counties in eastern England.

In the first year of the basic scheme only 1,800 farmers took up the offer, and only 58,000 hectares were set aside by May 1989. In the second cycle, by September 1989, the take-up rate had risen to 110,000 hectares, but was still enormously short of the target by about a factor of 10. Permanent fallow accounted for 80 per cent of the take-up, followed by non-agricultural use (11 per cent), rotational fallow (7 per cent), and woodland only accounted for 2 per cent. This poor uptake is not surprising since the UK has chosen a rate of compensation at the lower end of the scale allowed by the EC and about half the rate paid in Germany. The NFU also points out that the rates paid are far less than the fixed costs that the farmer has to bear. Not surprisingly, a *Farmers Weekly* poll in June 1989 found that diversification was far more popular than set-aside, with no less than 26 per cent of the poll of 800 farmers having diversified. In terms of policy alternatives to set-aside, quotas, with 42 per cent support, and a return to the free market, with 28 per cent support, were the two most favoured options.

Set-aside is also not popular with rural planners. Critics point out that it is wrong in principle to pay farmers for doing nothing, and in practice alienates them. Economists using the experience of the USA since the 1930s point out that the most marginal land will be set aside and that increased inputs elsewhere will not only offset lost production but also increase pollution. Other concerns centre around the short-term nature of the system, and the limited input allowed for conservation. All the signs are that set-aside is so far just a toe in the water of a very big pond.

Forestry For forestry the period under review saw a series of policy changes and the introduction of several new grants. Most of these changes occurred in 1988. First in March the budget abolished tax relief (schedule B) on commercial woodland, thus ending the tax incentives for rich individuals to plant up land. It was hoped that this move would stop the cynical 'tax' motivated afforestation of the 'Flow Country' of northern Scotland (see below). Profits from the sale of mature timber remained

Table 6.4 *Woodland Grant Scheme*

Area approved for planting or regeneration	Conifer }/ha.	Broadleaved }/ha.
0.25 to 0.9	1,005	1,575
1.0 to 2.9	880	1,375
3.0 to 9.9	795	1,175
10.0 and over	615	975

exempt from taxation in order to encourage genuine long-term forestry. At the same time, however, a general decrease in the top rate of tax from 60 per cent to 40 per cent reduced the attraction of any form of forestry as long-term tax avoidance since there was now less tax to pay.

Within forestry policy the government announced in March and October 1988 that the target rate of new planting would be 33,000 hectares a year, to be provided mainly by the private sector and almost exclusively in Scotland and Wales. In October 1988 it was made clear that approval for forestry above 800 feet would no longer be given in England, except in those small areas where it would be environmentally acceptable such as in the industrial Pennines. Afforestation of surplus land would, however, be acceptable, and in October 1989 the threshold for consultation with agricultural ministers over the afforestation of good agricultural land was raised to 40 hectares.

As a further aid for the afforestation of surplus farmland a new grant scheme, the Woodland Grant Scheme (WGS), was announced in March 1988 to replace both the Forestry Grant Scheme and the Broadleaved Woodland Grant Scheme. The objectives of the WGS are: to encourage timber production; to provide jobs and economic potential in areas of declining agriculture; to assist in the reduction of farm surpluses; to enhance the landscape, create new habitats and to provide recreation; and to encourage the conservation and regeneration of existing woods. Rates of grants for the 1988 scheme are set out in Table 6.4.

The new rates were much higher than for the schemes replaced, generally £375 higher and for broadleaves even higher. Many commentators argued that the increases were so great that they more than offset the tax losses in the 1988 budget. Early evidence from the uptake of the scheme would seem to confirm this, for in March 1989 it was announced that in the first nine months of the scheme 5,479 applications had been made to plant 34,278 hectares, 30,215 in Scotland, and 3,104 in England. Environmental sensitivity was added to the scheme in December 1988 with the announcement of a 'Native Pinewoods Planting Scheme' for specified areas of Scotland.

Another supplement to the WGS is provided by the Farm Woodland Scheme (FWS) more fully described in the Statutory Instruments section. In essence, grants under this scheme are intended to bridge the gap between planting and harvesting. Unlike the WGS, however, take-up of the FWS has been slow, and in the first ten months of the scheme up till 31 July 1989 nearly 1,000 applications had been made to plant 6,925 hectares. England accounted for 4,383 hectares and Scotland 2,108 hectares, with about 75 per cent of planting schedules to be broadleaves.

In May 1989 the European Community agreed the European Community Forestry Action Programme under which up to £6 million a year will be made available to the UK for the FWS and the WGS.

Finally, many of the changes outlined above stemmed from the furore over tax evasion planting in the 'Flow Country' of northern Scotland. In January 1988, the Secretary of State for Scotland announced his preliminary decisions over the area. First, around half of the total unafforested area, some 350,000 hectares, should be SSSIs, thus implying a substantial increase in the area of existing SSSIs. Second, the target for afforestation should be 100,000 hectares. Third, out of the seven applications for forestry before him he supported four, giving a further 2,318 hectares of forestry. In June 1988 four more applications out of five were supported on 1,059 hectares, and in January 1989 565 further hectares were approved, but 479 hectares refused for grant aid.

In January 1989 the Highland Regional Council published a report setting out a land-use strategy for the area, confirming the need to conserve the peatlands, but at the same time increasing the area acceptable for forestry from the existing afforested area of 61,000 hectares, by 39,000 hectares to 100,000 hectares. In March 1989 the Secretary of State confirmed the policies of the report, and, in line with the new target, approved aid for a further 315 hectares in July 1989. Although an apparent compromise appears to have been achieved, many conservationists still argue that too much ground has been conceded to the forestry lobby in a unique European habitat. In the meantime, as the diary section of this review shows, attention will now shift to proposals to afforest very different land in the Midlands and the urban fringes.

Agricultural prices The period under review saw a further erosion of support for agriculture and the introduction of several new schemes. Most of these are now covered either in the legislative review or in this section, for example Set-Aside. In this section a brief outline is given of general agreements by the EC and of specific changes in individual commodities.

In February 1988 a special summit of EC heads of government was necessitated by a failure to agree on methods for curbing CAP costs in December 1987. This crisis meeting produced two new schemes to curb costs, firstly, stabilisers or, in Eurospeak, guaranteed thresholds, and secondly, set-aside. Under the stabiliser schemes, a guarantee threshold of 160 million tonnes for cereals was set for the four years 1988–91. Overproduction above that level within the EC leads to a 3 per cent rise in coresponsibility levy and a 3 per cent cut in the intervention price.

Underproduction, within the year, of only 3 per cent leads to the levy being repaid in full or part. In common with milk quotas, however, the threshold was set well above the estimated demand of 135–140 million tonnes and also above the 1987 harvest of 155 million tonnes. Another problem is that the system is retrospective, with as much as an 18-month time-lag, which means that farmers can be asked to pay a levy in one month and then be repaid it in full or part a couple of months later.

The stabiliser scheme was, however, enforced in June 1988 when the EC froze the support prices for most farm products. For the UK a cut of 3.2 per cent in MCAs as from 1 January 1989 meant a small rise for some prices, at least before inflation. In the 1989 price agreement made in April 1989 for 1989/90, prices were again frozen. For the UK, a further 3.9 per cent cut in MCAs was almost entirely offset by a 3 per cent price cut for cereals triggered by the stabiliser system, and then more than offset by a 6 per cent rise in co-responsibility levy to £7.32/tonne caused by stabilisers and the devaluation of the green pound. The changes left a system in which intervention for cereals only operated between November 1989 and May 1990, rising from £109.94 to £115.46 per tonne.

Dairy prices for 1988/89 were frozen at a meeting of the agricultural ministers in December 1988 but for the UK a devaluation in the green pound of 2.84 per cent slightly offset this, giving a rise for the target milk price from 19.08p/litre to 19.64p as from 1 January 1989. In April 1989, a further devaluation of 3.1 per cent increased the price as from 30 April 1989 to 20.26p, with an average producer price of 17.8p. In October 1989, an extra quota of 155 million litres was given to those farmers who had been out of dairying when quotas were set in 1984 as a result of being in previous schemes designed to take producers out of dairying.

In January 1989 the open-ended subsidy to British beef farmers, known as the Variable Beef Premium, was severely cut back by limiting payments to 90 male animals per year, and at a flat rate of £28.42 per head, instead of flexible payments which before could be set as high as £50 per head. In May 1989, however, the rate was increased to £29.19, and the Suckler Cow Premium was increased from £33.40 to £47.43. Elsewhere livestock support remained unaltered and in December 1988 it was announced that Hill Livestock Compensatory Amounts for 1989 would stay the same at £54.50 per cow and £4.50 per ewe in the severely disadvantaged areas, and £27.25 and £2.25 in the disadvantaged areas.

With reference to sheep meat the July 1988 price agreement lifted prices by 2.8 per cent but only because of a green pound devaluation, not enough to offset an earlier fall of 3 per cent due to stabilisers, and another fall of 1 per cent in December 1988, for 1989, again due to stabilisers. In May 1989 a further devaluation of the green pound, however, led to an increase of 4.2 per cent in UK prices for 1990, but once again this was offset by another fall due to stabilisers, this time by 7 per cent. Retrospectively in April 1989 the Sheep Annual Premium for 1988 was set at £6.108 per ewe, at a cost of £120 million to FEOGA. However, in July 1989 the EC agreed measures to phase out the Sheep Variable Premium, starting with a reduction of 75 per cent of the forecast support throughout 1990, and the introduction of a community-wide premium by 1 January 1993 to replace the UK variable premium, unique to the UK since the regime began in 1980. As in the beef scheme, upper limits were expected to be imposed of 500 ewes in the lowlands and 1,000 in the uplands, with 50 per cent payments above these.

In conclusion, the gradual reform of the CAP continued during the period under review, but became if anything more complex and cumbersome. Most commentators, while welcoming stabilisers as bringing rigour to price freezes, none the less queried the uncertainty they would bring, and most people called either for really big price cuts (economists), supply control-code for quotas—(farmers), or a diversion of farm support to land management (environmentalists).

Diary of events 1 November 1987 to 31 October 1989

November 1987
Compensation payments announced for farmers affected by October gales.
Proposed South Warwickshire Coalfield called in by DOE.

December 1987
Disputed forestry appeals referred to Regional Advisory Committees to be advertised.
Approval sought for 6,000-home Stone Bassett, Oxon, and given for 3,500 houses on interim green belt land at Brenthall Park in Essex.

January 1988
Ministry of Defence undertakes to maintain conservation on its 276k hectares.

February 1988
Timothy Hornsby of DOE becomes Director General of NCC.
Consultation paper on GDO proposes more control over livestock units and relaxation of requirement to consult MAFF.
DOE asks NCC to consider the NNR network and possible sale of some sites.

March 1988
MAFF claim budget contains seven items of good news for farmers.
Ridley and Heseltine clash in correspondence over need for S-E housing.

April 1988
COSIRA and Development Commission merge into Rural Development Commission.
Convention of Scottish Local Authorities call for controls on fish farms.

May 1988
Average increase of 11.5 per cent in National Parks grant exceeds inflational rises to £12.18 million for 1989/90.

June 1988
85 per cent of suitable land taken up by farmers in first ten ESAs by closing date.
£3.5 million grant announced to replace trees lost in 1987 gales.
Forestry Commission appoints its first Archaeological Consultant.

July 1988
English Tourist Board launch rural tourism strategy, 20 per cent growth target for 1988–92.

August 1988
Countryside Commission urges more farmers to follow the ploughing code.

September 1988
DOE drops proposals for Landscape Conservation Orders in National Parks.
UK harvest at 21.4 million tonnes, down 0.25 million tonnes on 1987, and 5.0 million on 1985.

October 1988
Countryside Commission appoints team to look at new forest in Midlands.
DOE announces plan for National Parks to top up farm capital grants.

November 1988
North York Moors Environmentally Friendly Farming Scheme launched.

December 1988
DOE publishes provisional scheme for the National Rivers Authority.
Lake District National Park Officer proposes radical bill to withstand development and visitor pressures and to raise money from visitor tax.

February 1989
Scottish Development Department announces 20-year, £2.5 million Central Scotland Woodland Project to promote tree planting in the region.

March 1989

Countryside Commission laments end of Community Programme and proposes a Countryside Task Force with places for 10,000 young people.

MAFF consults over Nitrate Sensitive Zones. Consultation paper out in May.

April 1989

Government gives £180,000 over three years to Farming and Wildlife Trust.

May 1989

EC announces that 24 per cent of UK eligible for Structural Fund aid under objective 5b (rural areas) which came into effect on 1 January 1989.

MAFF announces savings of £379 million on farm support costs in 1988 due to lower intervention purchases ($-£147$ million for cereals and $-£107$ million for butter).

DOE announce that forestry grants will no longer be included in estimates of profits foregone in SSSI negotiations by NCC.

DOE responds to NCC report on NNRs and confirms need for some to be publicly owned (see February 1988).

31 Environmental Assessments prepared in the first nine months of the EC system. The majority are under Schedule 2.

June 1989

Government sets target of 100,000 hectares of forest land to be disposed of by the Forestry Commission between 1990 and 2000.

In the year to 31 March 1989 private owners plant 25,000 hectares of new forest to 4,000 hectares planted by the Forestry Commission.

DOE awards grants of £964,000 to 49 environmental and heritage groups.

ESA uptake reaches 110,000 hectares with 2,708 agreements.

MAFF submits application to extend LFAs by 95,000 hectares to EC.

July 1989

Dramatic falls in surplus farm produce in store since 1985. Butter down by 94 per cent, cereals by 89 per cent, beef by 79 per cent and skimmed milk completely gone.

DOE turns down Stone Bassett (see December 1987) but is minded to accept Foxley Wood (Hants), a 4,800-house new town in open countryside.

DOE issue code of practice on Conservation, Access and Recreation under Section 10 of the Water Act for the new water companies and the NRA.

DOE issues consultation paper on amending planning gain under Section 52.

Table 6.5 *List of new protected areas and designations (not including areas set up by Statutory Instruments, e.g. ESAs)*

Date	Name and area	Area and/or type of protection	Type of habitat
February 1988	Coed-Y-Cerrig North Gwent	10.9 ha NNR	Semi-natural woodland
February 1988	Abernethy Forest Grampian	30 sq. miles for RSPB using DOE funds	Caledonian pine forest
April 1988	The Wash	Special Protection Area	Wetland
June 1988	North Pennines	722 sq. miles AONB	Upland
July 1988	Land around Haweswater	10,000 ha. RSPB wardening agreement	Fell and woodland
Summer 1988	Brecon Beacons	9,060 ha of common land for NPA	Woodland
December 1988	Ashdown Forest	2,560 ha acquired by E. Sussex CC	Winnie-the-Pooh land
January 1989	North Norfolk Coast	Special Protection Area (since 1986 SSSI)	Marshland Inter-tidal
February 1989	Westhay Moor Somerset	NCC compulsory purchase order on SSSI	Somerset Levels
February 1989	Severn Estuary	Over 100 miles made SSSI and possible SPA	Saltmarsh sand/mud flat
May 1989	Throughout Britain	46 Forest Nature Reserves	Forests
May 1989	Duich Moss Islay	£270,794 to extract peat elsewhere	Peatland already SPA
May 1989	Kenfig Mid Glamorgan	494 ha National Nature Reserve	Sand dunes Freshwater
October 1989	Kielder Forest	Over 1,000 ha subject to management plan	Border Mires

MAFF selects twelve candidate areas as Nitrate Sensitive Areas covering 17,000 hectares and eight candidate areas for advisory campaigns over 24,000 hectares.

Countryside and Forestry Commissions announce plans for twelve community forests in the urban fringe covering up to 50 sq. miles each.

August 1989
DOE announces that holiday cottages let for more than 140 days a year
will be subject to higher business rate rather than poll tax.

September 1989
National Rivers Authority (NRA) launched as new water watch dog.
Countryside Commission and English Tourist Board agree on six prin-
ciples to protect the distinctive landscape of National Parks.

October 1989
New DOE boss, Chris Patten, overrules decision to give Foxley Wood go
ahead (see July 1989).
Chris Patten also reverses six years of policy in draft of new PPG Note
3 on housing land, emphasising infill but leaves new small village
option.
MAFF sets out restrictions over farming in Nitrate Sensitive Areas.
Countryside Commission survey shows that 25,000 miles of the 140,000
mile footpath network are obstructed.
UK harvest estimated at 22.5 million tonnes, up 1.4 million tonnes on
1988.
MAFF announces first national study of the economics of organic farming.

Literature list, 1987–9 (compiled by Andrew W. Gilg)

About 600 pieces of writing relevant to rural planning appears in the
period under review. Space precludes the inclusion of each item, but
although half have been selected the list still gives a more comprehensive
bibliography of the period than found in any other publication. The
material is divided into two main sections: publication and articles; it is
subdivided by subject matter.

150 selected publications

Format: Author, *Title*, Publisher, Date. If title is unclear a subtitle is
provided in parentheses.

General publications
Agriculture and Food Research Council, *Science, agriculture and the environment*,
the Council, 1987
Blunden, J. and Curry, N., *A future for the countryside*, Blackwell, 1988
Bracewell-Milnes, B., *Caring for the countryside*, Social Affairs Unit, 1988
Bunce, R. and Barr, C., *Rural information for forward planning*, HMSO, 1988
Cloke, P. (ed.), *Rural land-use planning in developed nations*, Unwin Hyman, 1988

—— *Policies and plans for rural people*, Unwin Hyman, 1988

Countryside Commission, *Planning tools*, the Commission, CCD27, 1989

—— *Training for tomorrow's countryside*, the Commission, CCP269, 1989

Environment, Department of, *Our common future: a perspective by the UK on the report of the World Commission on Environment and Development*, HMSO, 1988

Friends of the Earth, *The environment: the government's record*, Friends, 1989

Green, R., Holliday, J. and Arden-Clarke, C., *The future planning of the countryside*, Town and Country Planning Association, 1989

Hart, P. and Atherden, M. (eds), *The role of institutions in countryside management*, College of Ripon and York St John, 1988

Irvine, S. and Ponton, A., *A green manifesto*, Macdonald-Optima, 1988

Little, B., *Green Party Countryside Policy*, Green Party, 1988

Miller, F. and Tranter, R., *Public perception of the countryside*, Centre for Agricultural Strategy, 1988

Newby, H., *The countryside in question*, Hutchinson, 1988

Pearce, D., Markandya, A. and Barbier, E., *Blueprint for a green economy*, Earthscan, 1989

Rural Voice, *Rural strategy*, Voice, 1987

Selman, P. (ed.), *Countryside planning in practice: the Scottish experience*, Stirling University Press, 1988

Social and Liberal Democrats, *Green and pleasant land*, the Party, 1988

Wathern, P. (ed.), *Environmental impact assessment*, Unwin Hyman, 1988

Agriculture

Agriculture, Fisheries and Food, Ministry of, *Loaves and fishes: an illustrated history of the Ministry 1888–1988*, HMSO, 1989

—— *Agricultural land classification: revised guidelines*, the Ministry, Lion House, Willowburn Trading Estate, Alnwick, NE66 2PF, 1988

—— *Milk production before and after quotas*, HMSO, 1988

Bell, M. and Bunce, R. (eds), *Agriculture and conservation in the hills and uplands*, Institute of Terrestrial Ecology, 1987

Boyd, R., *Red or green for farmers*, Broad Leys, 1987

Burnham, C., Green, B. and Potter, C., *Set-aside as an environmental and agricultural policy instrument: Summary Report*, Wye College, 1988

Centre for Rural Studies, *Cereal extensification: the wildlife benefits. Report to NCC*, the Centre, Cirencester, 1988

Council for the Protection of Rural England, *Removing land from agriculture: the implications for farming and the environment*, CPRE, 1988

Countryside Commission, *Broads Grazing Marshes conservation scheme 1985–8*, the Commission, CCD20, 1988

—— *Occupancy change and the farmed landscape: a report*, by R. Munton, T. Marsden and J. Eldon, the Commission, CCD33, 1989

—— *Incentives for a new direction for farming*, the Commission, CCP262, 1989

—— *The Countryside premium for set-aside land*, the Commission, CCP267, 1989

Harrison, A. and Tranter, R., *The changing financial structure of farming*, Centre for Agricultural Strategy, University of Reading, 1989

Jenkins, N. and Bell, M. (eds), *Farm extensification: implications of Regulation 1760/87*, Institute of Terrestrial Ecology, Merlewood, 1987

Labour Party, *Towards a new agriculture: a Labour view*, the Party, 1987

National Economic Development Council, *Directions for change: land use in the 1990s: Report* and *Conference Proceedings*, the Council, 1987

National Farmers Union, *Farm support policies: the reasons why*, the Union, 1988

North, J., *Future land-use patterns in the UK*, Department of Land Economy, University of Cambridge, 1988

Robinson, G., *Agricultural change: geographical studies of British agriculture*, North British Publishing, 1988

Soil Association, *The case for organic agriculture*, the Association, Elm Farm Research Centre, Berkshire, 1988

Tracy, M., *Structural policy under the CAP*, Arkleton Trust, 1988

Worldwide Fund For Nature and Institute for European Environmental Policy, *Reform of the structural funds: an environmental briefing*, the Fund, 1989

Conservation

Association of National Park Officers, *National Parks—environmentally favoured areas*, the Association, 1988

Council for the Protection of Rural England, *Paradise protection*, CPRE, 1989

Countryside Commission, *Landscape assessment: a Countryside Commission approach*, the Commission, CCD18, 1987

—— *Conservation monitoring and management*, the Commission, CCP231, 1987

—— *Declarations of commitment to the National Parks*, the Commission, CCP247, 1987

—— *Landscape assessment of farmland*, the Commission, CCP255, 1988

—— *Employment and training opportunities in countryside conservation and recreation*, the Commission, CCP256, 1988

—— *Grants for landscape conservation*, the Commission, CCP207, 1989

Countryside Commission for Scotland, *An inventory of gardens and designated landscapes in Scotland*, the Commission, 1988

Dartington Institute, *Employment and nature conservation: a report to the NCC*, Nature Conservancy Council, 1987

Market and Opinion Research International (MORI), *Farmers' attitudes towards nature conservation*, MORI, 1987

—— *Public attitudes towards nature conservation*, MORI, 1987

Micklewright, S. (ed.), *Sites for science or places for heritage: problems with the SSSI designation and possible solutions*, Ecology and Conservation Unit, Gower Square, London, WC1E 6NT, 1988

Mowle, A., *Nature conservation in rural development: the need for new thinking about rural sector policies*, NCC, 1986

National Farmers Union, *EC Agenda for Agriculture—what we want—why we want it*, the Union, 1988

Nature Conservancy Council, *Changing nature*, NCC, 1988

—— *Site management plans for nature conservation: a working guide*, NCC, 1988

Royal Society for the Conservation of Nature, *A future for commons*, RSNC, 1988

Royal Society for the Protection of Birds, *The reform of the CAP: new opportunities for wildlife and the environment*, RSPB, 1988

Town and Country Planning, Department of, University of Newcastle upon Tyne, *Resource costs of agricultural intensification and wildlife conservation*, by C. Saunders, K. Willis and J. Benson, the Department, 1989

—— *Social costs and benefits of agricultural intensification at three sites of special*

scientific interest, by same authors, the Department, 1989
—— *Estimating wildlife conservation site benefits using a travel cost method,* by K. Willis, J. Benson and L. Mitchell, the Department, 1989

Extractive industries
Agriculture, Fisheries and Food, Ministry of, and Environment, Department of, *Conservation guidelines for drainage authorities,* MAFF and DOE, 1988
Bowers, J., O'Donnell, K. and Whatmore, S., *Liquid assets: the likely effects of privatisation of the Water Authorities on wildlife habitats and landscape,* CPRE, 1989
Council for the Protection of Rural England, *The hidden depths of water privatisation,* CPRE, 1989
Countryside Commission, *Changing river landscapes,* the Commission, CCP238, 1988
—— *The water industry in the countryside,* the Commission, CCP239, 1988
Environment, Department of, *Minerals Planning Guidance Notes*: MPG1: *General considerations and the development plan system*; MPG2: *Applications, permissions and conditions*; MPG3: *Open-cast coal-mining*; MPG4: *The review of mineral working sites*; MPG5: *Minerals planning and the GDO*; MPG6: *Guidelines for aggregates provision in England and Wales,* HMSO, 1988 and 1989
—— *The National Rivers Authority: the government's policy for a public regulatory body in a privatised water industry,* HMSO, 1987
—— *The nitrates issue,* HMSO, 1988
—— *Water Bill: Draft code of practice on conservation, access and recreation,* DOE, 1989
Friends of the Earth, *Water privatisation and the environment: an overview of the issues,* FOE, 1989
McDonald, A. and Kay, D., *Water resources: issues and strategies,* Longmans, 1988
Purseglove, J., *Taming the flood: a history and natural history of rivers and wetlands,* Oxford University Press, 1988

Forestry
Adam Smith Institute, *Pining for Profit,* the Institute, 1988
Convention of Scottish Local Authorities, *Forestry in Scotland: planning the way ahead,* COSLA, 1987
Council for the Protection of Rural England, *Land use and forestry,* CPRE, 1989
Countryside Commission, *Forestry and the countryside,* the Commission, CCP245, 1987
—— *Forestry for the community,* the Commission, CCP270, 1989
—— *The community forest: planning, design and implementation,* the Commission, CCP271, 1989
Forestry Commission, *Forestry Capability Maps of Scotland,* the Commission, 1989
—— *Forest landscape design guidelines,* the Commission, 1989
—— *Farm woodland practice,* the Commission, 1988
—— *Farm woodland planning,* the Commission, 1988
—— *Environmental assessment of afforestation projects,* the Planning Commission, 1988
Forestry Institute, University of Oxford, *Report on implementation of Broadleaved policy,* Forestry Commission, 1989

PIEDA, *Budgeting for British forestry: recommendations for reform of forestry taxation policy*, CPRE, 1987

Price, C., *The theory and application of forest economics*, Blackwell, 1989

Land-use planning

Adam Smith Institute, *An environment for growth*, the Institute, 1987

────── *The green quadratic*, the Institute, 1988

Agriculture, Fisheries and Food, Ministry of, and Environment, Department of, *Planning permission and the farmer*, MAFF and DOE, 1989

BSL Business Strategies, *The costs of the Green Belt*, ARC Properties, 1989

Buckley, M., *Farm output loss in land-use planning decisions*, Department of Town Planning, South Bank Polytechnic, 1987

Centre for Policy Studies, *Planning planning: clearer strategies and environmental controls*, the Centre, 8 Wilfred Street, London, SW1E 6PL, 1988

Clark, M. and Herrington, J. (eds), *The role of environmental impact assessment in the planning process*, Mansell, 1988

CoENCO, *The future of the planning system*, London Ecology Centre, 80 York Way, London, N1 9AG, 1988

Council for the Protection of Rural England, *Concrete objections—the Ministry of Agriculture's response to applications for development of agricultural land*, by A. Wilson, CPRE, 1988

Countryside Commission, *Planning for change: development in a green countryside: a discussion paper*, the Commission, CCD24, 1988

────── *Planning for a greener countryside*, the Commission, CCP264, 1989

Environment, Department of, *The Green Belts*, HMSO, 1988

────── *Planning Policy Guidance Notes: PPG1: General policy and principles; PPG2: Green Belts; PPG3: Land for housing; PPG7: Rural enterprise and development; PPG12: Local Plans; PPG13: Highways considerations*, HMSO, 1988

Evans, A., *No room! No room! The costs of the British town and country planning system*, Institute of Economic Affairs, 2 Lord North Street, London, SW1P 3LB, 1988

Garbutt, J. *Green belt renegotiation in the outer metropolitan area*, School of Planning, Oxford Polytechnic, 1989

Healey, P., McNamara, P., Elson, M. and Doak, A., *Land-use planning and the mediation of urban change*, Cambridge University Press, 1989

Lock, D., *Riding the Tiger. Planning in the South of England: a discussion paper*, Town and Country Planning Association, 1989

Steen, A., *PLUMS: Public Land Utilisation Management Scheme*, Conservative Political Centre, 32 Smith Square, London, SW1P 3HH, 1988

Recreation

Council for National Parks, *Large-scale tourist facilities in the Parks*, the Council, 1988

Countryside Commission, *Rights of Way Survey Manual*, the Commission, CCP250, 1988

────── *Paths, routes and trails: a consultation paper*, CCP253, 1988

────── *Changing the rights-of-way network: a discussion paper*, CCP254, 1988

────── *Paths, routes and trails: policies and priorities*, CCP266, 1989

Countryside Recreation Research Advisory Group, *Recreation and wildlife—working in partnership*, School for Advanced Urban Studies, University of Bristol, 1988

English Tourist Board, *Rural tourism*, the Board, 1988

Hoggarth, J. and Gregory, R. (eds), *Ranger 2000: a view of the future*, Association of Countryside Rangers, 4 Park Cottages, Drury Lane, Knutsford, 1989

Royal Institution of Chartered Surveyors, *Managing the countryside. Access, recreation and tourism—the policy framework*, RICS, 1988

Sports Council and Countryside Commission, *Sport, recreation and nature conservation*, Sports Council, 1989

Socio-economic issues

Acre and Planning Exchange, *Country Work*, Acre, 1989

Association of Countryside Rangers, *The impact of the Manpower Services Commission in the countryside*, the Association, 6 Victoria Terrace, Longstone, Bakewell, Derbyshire, DE4 1TA, 1988

Association of County Councils, *Homes we can afford*, the Association, 1989

Association of District Councils, *The future for rural communities: the district council view*, the Association, 1988

Bell, P. and Cloke, P., *Bus deregulation in the Powys/Clwyd study area: an interim report*, Transport and Road Research Laboratory, 1988

Black, J., *Reducing isolation: telecommunications and rural development*, Arkleton Trust, 1988

Breakell, M. (ed.), *New opportunities for rural employment*, School of Planning, Oxford Polytechnic, 1987

Bryden, J. and Fuller, A., *Pluriactivity as a rural development option*, Arkleton Trust, 1988

Business in the Community, *Work for the Countryside*, as Authors, 227a City Road, London, EC1V 1LX, 1988

Champion, A. (ed.), *Counterurbanisation*, Edward Arnold, 1989

Clark, D., *Affordable homes in the countryside*, Acre, 1988

Council for the Protection of Rural England, *Welcome homes—housing supply from unallocated land*, CPRE, 1988

Country Landowners Association, *Enterprise in the rural environment*, CLA, 1989

Countryside Commission, *Public transport to the countryside: a marketing handbook for operators and local authorities*, the Commission, 1987,

County Planning Officers Society, *County Planning and the local economy*, Director of Planning, Cleveland CC, Middlesborough, TS1 1QT, 1987

——— *Structure plans and housing land*, County Planning Department, Hertfordshire CC, Hertford, SG13 8DN, 1988

Environment, Department of, *Housing in rural areas—village housing and new villages*: Two Volumes: *A statement by the DOE*; and *A discussion paper*, the Department, 1988

Greenwood, J., *Planning for low-cost rural housing*, School of Planning, Oxford Polytechnic, 1989

Grigg, A., *An evaluation of the East Sussex transport broker*, Transport and Road Research Laboratory, 1989

Joint Unit for Research on the Urban Environment, *Developing the rural economy: an assessment of the Development Commission's economic activities*, the Unit, University of Aston, 1987

Midwinter, A., Mair, C. and Moxen, J., *Rural deprivation in Scotland*, Department of Administration, Strathclyde University, 1988

Minay, C. and Weston, J., *The future of work: jobs in the environment*, School of Planning, Oxford Polytechnic, 1987

Moyes, A., *The need for public transport in Mid-Wales*, Department of Geography, University of Wales at Aberystwyth, 1989

National Agriculture Centre Rural Trust, *A practical guide to providing affordable village housing*, the Trust, 1989

National Economic Development Council, *Work in the countryside*, NEDO Books, 1989

Rural Development Commission, *Promoting transport in rural communities*, the Commission, 1989

Watkins, C. and Winter, M., *Superb conversions?* (Barn conversions), CPRE, 1988

Williams, G. and Banister, C., *Monitoring housing policies in local plans*, Department of Town Planning, University of Manchester, 1988

Winter, M. and Rogers, A., *Who can afford to live in the countryside? Access to housing land*, Centre for Rural Studies, Cirencester, 1988

Bibliographies

Countryside Commission, *National Parks*, CCP200; *Broadleaved woodlands*, CCP212; *The Uplands*, CCP176 and CCP240; *Agricultural Landscapes*, CCP241, the Commission, 1987 and 1989

Environment Council, *Who's who in the environment*, Scotland, Countryside Commission for Scotland, 1988

Environment, Department of, *Annual list of publications 1987*, DOE, 1988

Peters, G., Agriculture: *Reviews of UK Statistical Sources*, Chapman and Hall, 1988

Lambert, G., *Green Belts 1980–7*, DOE Library, 1987

Robinson, G.A., *A register of research in rural geography*, Department of Geography, University of Edinburgh, 1988

Rural Economy and Society Study Group, *Register of members*, the Group, 1988

150 selected articles

Format: Author, Title, *Journal*, Vol. no. (if one), Issue no. (if one), Year, Pages. If title is unclear, a subtitle is provided in parentheses.

General publications

Barlow, J., 'The politics of land into the 1990s', *Policy and Politics*, 16, 2, 1988, pp. 111–21

Bell, P. and Cloke, P., 'The changing relationship between the private and public sectors: privatisation and rural Britain', *Journal of Rural Studies*, 5, 1, 1989, pp. 1–5

Bichard, E. and Frost, S., 'EIA in the UK planning system', *Land Use Policy*, 5, 4, 1988, pp. 362–4

Blowers, A., 'Transition or transformation? Environmental policy under Thatcher', *Public Administration*, 65, 3, 1987, pp. 277–94

Breakell, M., 'Current issues in rural areas', *The Planner*, 75, 2, 1989, pp. 83–5

Brotherton, I., 'What voluntary approach?', *Ecos*, 10, 2, 1989, pp. 36–40

Brown, D. and Taylor, K., 'The future of Britain's rural land', *Geographical Journal*, 154, 3, 1988, pp. 406–11

Clark, B., 'Environmental impact assessment: on the eve of legal implementation', *The Planner*, 74, 2, 1988, pp. 18–22

Clark, R., 'Shaping a new countryside', *The Planner*, 74, 1, 1988, pp. 33–4

Cloke, P., 'Understanding rural policy and planning: the importance of concepts of the State', *Planning Quarterly*, 89, 1988, pp. 12–15

Cloke, P. and Little, J., 'Policy planning and the state in rural localities', *Journal of Rural Studies*, 3, 4, 1987, pp. 343–52

Cloke, P. and Little, J., 'Public sector agency influence in rural policy making', *Tijdschrift voor Economische en Sociale Geografie*, 79, 4, 1988, pp. 278–89

Cloke, P. and Thrift, N., 'Intra-class conflict in rural areas', *Journal of Rural Studies*, 3, 4, 1987, pp. 321–34

Cocklin, C., Lonergan, S. and Smit, B., 'Assessing conflicts in the use of rural resources', *Journal of Rural Studies*, 4, 1, 1988, pp. 9–20

Copeland, S., 'The role of the planner in rural Britain', *The Planner*, 74, 2, 1988, pp. 73–7

Cox, G., 'Reading nature: reflections on ideological persistence and the politics of the countryside', *Landscape Research*, 13, 3, 1988, pp. 24–34

Cox, G., Lowe, P. and Winter, M., 'Private rights and public responsibilities: the prospects for agricultural and environmental controls', *Journal of Rural Studies*, 4, 4, 1988, pp. 323–37

Curry, N., 'Capital conspiracy in the countryside', *Town and Country Planning*, 57, 1, 1988, pp. 22–3

Gossop, C., 'Step forward for planning: environmental assessment begins next month', *Town and Country Planning*, 57, 6, 1988, pp. 166–8

Haigh, N., 'Environmental assessment', *Ecos*, 9, 4, 1988, pp. 7–10

Hall, D., McLaughlin, B., Cherry, A., Dower, M., Vinson, Lord and O'Riordan, T., 'The future for rural areas', *Town and Country Planning*, 57, 7/8, 1988, pp. 202–11

Hoggart, K., 'Not a definition of rural', *Area*, 20, 1, 1988, pp. 35–40

Holliday, J., 'Green planning in the battle for the countryside', *Town and Country Planning*, 58, 7/8, 1989, pp. 194–5

Labour Party Working Group; and Hall, P., Shepley, C. and Soley, C., 'Labour and the environment', *The Planner*, 74, 9, 1988, pp. 11–20

Lichfield, N., 'Environmental impact assessment in project appraisal in Britain', *Project Appraisal*, 3, 3, 1988, pp. 133–41

Lloyd, M., Rowan-Robinson, J. and Dawson, J., 'Policy adaption of Scotland: national planning guidelines and agricultural land resources', *Scottish Geographical Magazine*, 105, 1, 1989, pp. 19–24

McDonic, G., 'Planning in the countryside', *Planning Outlook*, 30, 1, 1987, pp. 23–6

Mowle, A., 'Changing countryside: land-use policies and the environment', *Geography*, 73, 4, 1988, pp. 318–26

O'Riordan, T., 'The politics of environmental regulation in Great Britain', *Environment*, 3, 8, 1988, pp. 5–9 and 39–44

Selman, P., 'Rural land-use planning—resolving the British paradox?', *Journal of Rural Studies*, 4, 3, 1988, pp. 277–94

Sinclair, G., 'Over the top and down to the root (radical rethink of rural planning)', *Ecos*, 9, 2, 1988, pp. 7–10

Walford, N., Lane, M. and Shearman, J., 'The Rural Areas Database', *Institute of British Geographers, New Transactions*, 14, 2, 1989, pp. 221–30

Watson, J., 'The UK implementation of environmental assessment', *Local Government Policy Making*, 15, 4, 1989, pp. 55–63

Wood, C., 'ETA and BPEO: Acronyms for good environmental planning', *Journal of Planning and Environmental Law*, May 1988, pp. 310–21

Wood, C. and Lee, N., 'The European directive on environmental impact assessment: implementation at last?', *Environmentalist*, 8, 3, 1988, pp. 177–86

Wood, C. and McDonic, G., 'Environmental assessment: challenge and opportunity', *The Planner*, 75, 11, 1989, pp. 12–18

Agriculture

Brotherton, I., 'Grant-aided agricultural activity in National Parks', *Journal of Agricultural Economics*, 39, 3, 1988, pp. 376–81

Buckwell, A., 'Economic signals, farmers' response and environmental change', *Journal of Rural Studies*, 5, 2, 1989, pp. 149–60

Eldon, J., 'Agricultural change, conservation and the role of advisers', *Ecos*, 9, 4, 1988, pp. 14–20

Ervin, D., 'Cropland diversion in the US and UK', *Journal of Agricultural Economics*, 39, 2, 1988, pp. 183–95

Ervin, D., 'Set-aside programmes: using US experience to evaluate UK proposals', *Journal of Rural Studies*, 4, 3, 1988, pp. 181–91

Gasson, R., 'Farm diversification and rural development', *Journal of Agricultural Economics*, 39, 2, 1988, pp. 175–82

Gasson, R. and Potter, C., 'Conservation through land diversion: a survey of farmers' attitudes', *Journal of Agricultural Economics*, 39, 3, 1988, pp. 340–51

Gibson, D., 'Set-aside and the environmental use of agricultural resources', *Environmental Education and Information*, 6, 4, 1987, pp. 279–89

Halliday, J., 'Dairy farmers take stock: a study of milk producers' reactions to quota in Devon', *Journal of Rural Studies*, 4, 3, 1988, pp. 193–202

Halliday, J., 'Attitudes towards farm diversification: results from a survey of Devon farmers', *Journal of Agricultural Economics*, 40, 1, 1989, pp. 93–100

Hodge, I., 'A reassessment of the role of County Council smallholdings', *Journal of Agricultural Economics*, 39, 2, 1988, pp. 243–53

Lobley, M., 'A role for ESAs', *Ecos*, 10, 2, 1989, pp. 27–9

Marshall, R., 'Agricultural policy development in Britain: rural land-use planning issues', *Town Planning Review*, 59, 4, 1988, pp. 419–35

North, J., 'Agricultural land use', *Ecos*, 9, 4, 1988, pp. 10–13

North, J., 'How much land will be available for development in 2015?', *Development and Planning*, 1, 1989, pp. 29–34

Owens, S., 'Agricultural land surplus and concern for the countryside', *Development and Planning*, 1, 1989, pp. 35–8

Potter, C., 'Environmentally Sensitive Areas in England and Wales: an experiment in countryside management', *Land Use Policy*, 5, 3, 1988, pp. 301–13

Potter, C., 'Making waves: farm extensification and conservation', *Ecos*, 9, 3, 1988, pp. 32–7

Potter, C. and Gasson, R., 'Farmer participation in voluntary land diversion schemes: some predictions', *Journal of Rural Studies*, 4, 4, 1988, pp. 365–75

Russell, N. and Power, A., 'UK government expenditure—implications of changes in agricultural output under the CAP', *Journal of Agricultural Economics*, 40, 1, 1989, pp. 32–9

Tapper, R. and Mounsey, H., 'Planning for Britain's changing farms', *Town and Country Planning*, 57, 19, 1988, pp. 279–81

Thirtle, C. and Bottomley, P., 'Is publicly funded agricultural research excessive?', *Journal of Agricultural Economics*, 39, 1, 1988, pp. 99–111

Conservation

Aitchison, J. and Hughes, E., 'The common lands of Wales', *Institute of British Geographers, New Transactions*, 13, 1, 1988, pp. 96–108

Anfield, J., 'The role of the planner in National Parks', *The Planner*, 74, 1, 1988, pp. 29–32

Barkham, J., 'Developing the spiritual (case for conservation)', *Ecos*, 9, 3, 1988, pp. 13–20

Barkham, J., 'Trusting the Counties (County Conservation Trusts)', *Ecos*, 10, 2, 1989, pp. 11–20

Benson, J. and Willis, K., 'Conservation costs, agricultural intensification and the Wildlife and Countryside Act 1981', *Biological Conservation*, 44, 3, 1988, pp. 157–78

Burnham, P., 'Returning set-aside land to nature', *Ecos*, 10, 1, 1989, pp. 13–17

Cahn, M., 'Losing inertia (a follow-up survey to D. Tyldesley's report on ecological work in local councils)', *Ecos*, 8, 4, 1987, pp. 34–6

Clark, A. and O'Riordan, T., 'A case for a farm conservation grant support unit', *Ecos*, 10, 2, 1989, pp. 30–5

Everett, S., 'European habitat protection: the draft directive', *Ecos*, 9, 3, 1988, pp. 37–40

Fenton, J., 'The ecology of environmentalism', *Ecos*, 8, 4, 1987, pp. 28–33

Ferguson, M., 'National Parks for Scotland', *Scottish Geographical Magazine*, 104, 1, 1988, pp. 36–40

Glasson, N., 'The use and effectiveness of the SSSI designation in the East Midlands region of the NCC', *Planning Outlook*, 30, 2, 1988, pp. 84–90

Goldsmith, E. *et al.*, 'Deep ecology: 67 principles of the ecological world view', *The Ecologist*, 18, 4 and 5, 1988, pp. 118–85

Goodier, R. and Maynes, S., 'UK biosphere reserves', *Ecos*, 9, 4, 1988, pp. 33–9

Halliday, J., 'Coastal planning and management: the contribution of District Councils', *Town Planning Review*, 58, 3, 1987, pp. 317–29

Hearn, K., 'The National Trust and nature conservation: problems for the next decade', *Ecos*, 9, 1, 1988, pp. 11–16

Jones, P., 'Urban fringe management projects in Scotland', *Scottish Geographical Magazine*, 103, 3, 1987, pp. 166–70

Jones, P., 'The development of groundwork', *Town and Country Planning*, 57, 12, 1988, pp. 346–7

Junghanns, D., 'Conservation designation in the Somerset levels: a study of local attitudes', *Landscape and Urban Planning*, 14, 6, 1987, pp. 451–61

Parker, K., 'Private national nature reserves?', *Land Use Policy*, 5, 4, 1988, pp. 365-9

Perring, H. *et al.*, 'Changing attitudes to nature conservation in the UK', *Biological Journal of the Linnean Society*, 32, 2, 1987, pp. 147-236

Roberts, G., 'Landscape and nature: integrated policies for National Parks', *Landscape Research*, 13, 1, 1988, pp. 6-9

Selman, P., 'Nature conservation and local plans', *Planning Outlook*, 30, 2, 1988, pp. 78-83

Shaw, M., 'The Broads Act', *Journal of Planning and Environmental Law*, April 1989, pp. 241-6

Sheail, J., 'The great divide (the NCC and the Countryside Commission)', *Landscape Research*, 13, 1, 1988, pp. 2-5

Tarn, J., 'The landscape and buildings of National Parks in a changing economic and social world', *Town Planning Review*, 58, 3, 1987, pp. 243-53

Taylor, G., 'National Parks at a time of change', *The Planner*, 74, 1, 1988, pp. 25-8

Tyldesley, D., 'Nature conservation: an assessment of Circular 27/87', *The Planner*, 75, 11, 1989, pp. 22-4

Wathern, P., Young, S., Brown, I. and Roberts, D., 'Recent upland land-use change and agricultural policy in N. Wales', *Applied Geography*, 8, 2, 1988, pp. 147-63

Willis, E., 'The Adult Training Programme and its implications for conservation organisations', *Ecos*, 9, 2, 1988, pp. 10-13

Willis, E., 'Working together for nature conservation? (The use of labour under MSC schemes)', *Ecos*, 9, 1, 1988, pp. 28-31

Willis, K. and Benson, J., 'A comparison of user benefits and costs of nature conservation at three nature reserves', *Regional Studies*, 22, 5, 1988, pp. 417-28

Willis, K. and Benson, J., 'Financial and social costs of management agreements for wildlife conservation', *Journal of Environmental Management*, 26, 1, 1988, pp. 43-63

Willis, K., Benson, J. and Saunders, C., 'The impact of agricultural policy on the costs of nature conservation', *Land Economics*, 64, 2, 1988, pp. 147-57

Extractive Industries

Gilder, P., 'Private water', *Countryside Commission News*, 33, 1988, pp. 4-5

Hellawell, J., 'River regulation and nature conservation', *Regulated Rivers—Research and Management*, 2, 3, 1988, pp. 425-43

Parker, D. and Sewell, W., 'Evolving water institutions: an assessment of two decades of experience', *Natural Resources Journal*, 28, 4, 1988, pp. 751-85

Purseglove, J., 'Crossroads for rivers and wetlands? (Water privatisation)', *Ecos*, 9, 4, 1988, pp. 21-5

Smith, T., 'Minerals planning in the post-Stevens era', *Land and Minerals Surveying*, 5, 1987, pp. 414-23

Synott, M., 'The consequences for development of water privatisation', *Development and Planning*, 1, 1989, pp. 62-4

Forestry

Boyd, J., 'Commercial forests and woods: the nature conservation baseline', *Forestry*, 60, 1, 1987, pp. 113-34

THE LIBRARY
BISHOP BURTON COLLEGE
BEVERLEY HU17 8QG
TEL: 0964 550481 Ex: 227

Brotherton, I., 'The case for (forestry) consultation', *Ecos*, 8, 4, 1987, pp. 18–23

Brotherton, I. and Devall, N., 'Does afforestation consultation work?', *Arboricultural Journal*, 11, 4, 1987, pp. 363–70

Brotherton, I. and Devall, N., 'Forestry conflicts in National Parks', *Journal of Environmental Management*, 26, 3, 1988, pp. 229–38

Brotherton, I. and Devall, N., 'On the acceptability of afforestation schemes', *Land Use Policy*, 5, 2, 1988, pp. 245–51

Brotherton, I. and Hetherington, M., 'Conservation as a restraint on afforestation in pressured and protected areas of upland Britain', *Biological Conservation*, 48, 2, 1989, pp. 129–49

Campbell, J., 'British forestry—an international perspective', *Commonwealth Forestry Review*, 67, 2, 1988, pp. 115–28

Griffin, N. and Watkins, C., 'The control of tree felling: recent developments in Statute and Case Law', *Quarterly Journal of Forestry*, LXXXII, 1988, pp. 26–32

House, A. and Souter, R., 'Afforestation and nature conservation: assessing the impact on plant species and communities', *Ecos*, 9, 2, 1988, pp. 25–9

Johnston, J. and Price, C., 'Afforestation, employment and depopulation in the Snowdonia National Park', *Journal of Rural Studies*, 3, 3, 1987, pp. 195–205

Mather, A., 'New private forests in Scotland', *Area*, 20, 2, 1988, pp. 135–43

Mather, A., 'Afforestation and planning', *Scottish Planning Law and Practice*, 26, February 1989, pp. 4–8

Mather, A. and Murray, N., 'Employment and private sector afforestation in Scotland', *Journal of Rural Studies*, 3, 3, 1987, pp. 207–18

Mather, A. and Murray, N., 'The dynamics of rural land-use change: the case of private sector afforestation', *Land Use Policy*, 5, 1, 1988, pp. 103–20

Reid, C., 'Afforestation: controls and controversies', *Journal of Planning and Environmental Law*, September 1988, pp. 610–14

Scrambler, A., 'Farmers' attitudes towards forestry', *Scottish Geographical Magazine*, 105, 1, 1989, pp. 47–9

Spilsbury, M. and Crockford, K., 'Woodland economics and the 1988 budget', *Quarterly Journal of Forestry*, 83, 1, 1989, pp. 25–32

Wilson, R., 'The political power of the forestry lobby', *Ecos*, 8, 4, 1987, pp. 11–17

Land use

Ash, M., 'Plus ça change (Is the green belt relevant anymore?)', *Town and Country Planning*, 57, 6, 1988, pp. 162–3

Bate, R. and Burton, T., 'Department (of the Environment) making little progress over land supply figures', *Planning*, 814, 14 April 1989, pp. 12–13

Bennett, A., 'Progress on new (rural) settlements (by Consortium Developments)', *The Planner*, 73, 11, 1987, p. 35

Falk, N., 'New approaches for green belt planning', *Town and Country Planning*, 57, 6, 1988, pp. 182–3

Hall, D., 'The case for new settlements', *Town and Country Planning*, 58, 4, 1989, pp. 111–14

Hooper, A., Pinch, P. and Rogers, S., 'Housing land availability: circular advice, circular arguments and circular methods', *Journal of Planning and Environmental Law*, April 1988, pp. 225–39

King, D., 'Grasping the nettle in the numbers game (shortfall in structure plan land allocations for the 1990s)', *Planning*, 4 December 1987, pp. 10–11

Kleinman, M. and Whitehead, C., 'Demand for new housebuilding 1986–2001', *Development and Planning*, 1, 1989, pp. 71–7

McConnell, R., 'The implementation and the future of development plans', *Land Development Studies*, 4, 1987, pp. 79–107

Munton, R., 'Green Belts: end of an era?', *Geography*, 71, 3, 1987, pp. 206–14

Rydin, Y., 'Joint housing studies: housebuilders, planners and the availability of land', *Local Government Studies*, 14, 2, 1988, pp. 69–80

Scrase, A., 'Agriculture—1980's industry and 1947 definition', *Journal of Planning and Environmental Law*, July 1988, pp. 447–60

Recreation

Elliott, R., Lloyd, M. and Rowan-Robinson, J., 'Land-use policy for skiing in Scotland', *Land Use Policy*, 5, 2, 1988, pp. 232–44

Elson, M., 'The urban fringe—will less farming mean more leisure?', *The Planner*, 73, 10, 1987, pp. 19–22

Hughes, C., 'Touring caravans and camping: a legislative review', *Scottish Planning Law and Practice*, 25 October 1987, pp. 68–71

Jones, P. *et al.*, 'Leisure provision in the countryside', *Local Council Review*, 38, 4, 1988, pp. 106–15

Kay, G., 'Routes for recreational walking', *Town and Country Planning*, 58, 3, 1989, pp. 78–81

Phillips, A. and Ashcroft, P., 'The impact of research in countryside policy development', *Leisure Studies*, 6, 1987, pp. 315–28

Sidaway, R., 'Access to the countryside for outdoor recreation: an Anglo-Dutch comparison', *Town Planning Review*, 58, 4, 1987, pp. 401–9

Wilman, E., 'Pricing policies for outdoor recreation', *Land Economics*, 84, 3, 1988, pp. 234–41

Socio-economic

Armstrong, H. and Fildes, J., 'Industrial development initiatives in England and Wales', *Progress in Planning*, 30, 2, 1988, entire issue

Banister, D. and Norton, F., 'The role of the voluntary sector in the provision of rural services—transport', *Journal of Rural Studies*, 4, 1, 1988, pp. 57–71

Champion, A., 'Recent changes in the pace of population deconcentration in Britain', *Geoforum*, 18, 4, 1987, pp. 379–401

Cloke, P. and Edwards, G., 'Housing association and local authority provision in rural housing markets', *Planning Outlook*, 30, 2, 1988, pp. 55–62

Cloke, P. and Little, J., 'Class distribution and locality in rural areas', *Geoforum*, 18, 4, 1987, pp. 403–13

Cowan, R., 'The Scottish rural economy—the north-west/south-east divide', *The Planner*, 75, 2, 1989, pp. 12–14

Dean, N., 'Transport in rural areas', *The Planner*, 74, 2, 1988, pp. 14–17

Derounian, J., 'Countrywork—how companies can help rural enterprises', *Town and Country Planning*, 58, 3, 1989, pp. 82–4

Green, R., 'Ten steps towards closing the poverty gap (and repopulating the countryside)', *The Planner*, 74, 6, 1988, pp. 14–16

Houston, G., 'Assessing the IDP for the Western Isles', *Scottish Geographical Magazine*, 103, 3, 1987, pp. 163–5

McCleary, A., 'The Highland Board reviewed: a note on the analysis of economic and social change', *Scottish Geographical Magazine*, 104, 3, 1988, pp. 171-5

Mitchell, D. *et al.*, 'Rural public transport today', *Local Council Review*, 38, 3, 1987, pp. 81-8

Nutley, S., 'Unconventional modes of transport in rural Britain: progress to 1985', *Journal of Rural Studies*, 4, 1, 1988, pp. 73-86

Robertson, G., 'Over the bridge to Skye (Integrated Development Programme in the Scottish Islands)', *Ecos*, 9, 1, 1988, pp. 2-10

Annual reports and accounts

List of annual reports and accounts produced by rural planning organisations 1987-9 Published by HMSO

Format: Author, *Title*, HC or Cmnd number, (Year of Publication)

Agriculture, Fisheries and Food, Ministry of
  Annual Review of Agriculture 1988, Cm. 299, (1988)
  Agriculture in the UK 1988 (Successor to the Annual Review), (1988)
  Environmentally Sensitive Areas. First Report, (1989)
Agriculture in Scotland, Department of
  Agriculture in Scotland 1986, Cm. 144, (1987)
  Agriculture in Scotland 1987, Cm. 435, (1988)
Ancient Monuments Board for Scotland
  34th Report, 1987, HC 2 (88-89), (1988)
British Tourist Authority
  Accounts 1986-87, HC 84 (87-88), (1987)
  Accounts 1987-88, HC 641 (87-88), (1988)
  Accounts 1988-89, HC 549 (88-89), (1989)
Chief Planning Inspector
  Annual Report 1986-87, (1988). See *Planning*, 751, pp. 6-7
  Annual Report 1987-88, (1988). See DOE press notice 674/88
Crofters Commission
  Annual Report 1987, (1988)
  Annual Report 1988, (1989)
Countryside Commission
  Accounts 1987-88, HC 636 (87-88), (1988)
  Accounts 1988-89, HC 526 (88-89), (1989)
Countryside Commission for Scotland
  Accounts 1986-87, HC 210 (87-88), (1988)
  Accounts 1987-88, HC 210 (87-88), (1988)
  Accounts 1987-88, HC (87-88), (1988)
Development Board for Rural Wales
  Accounts 1986-87, HC 77 (87-88), (1987)
  Accounts 1987-88, HC 657 (87-88), (1988)
  Accounts 1988-89, HC 557 (88-89), (1989)

Development Commission
  Accounts 1987–88, HC 652 (87–88), (1988)
  Accounts 1988–89, HC 551 (88–89), (1989)
English Tourist Board
  Accounts 1987–88, HC 589 (87–88), (1988)
  Accounts 1988–89, HC 498 (88–89), (1989)
Environment, Department of
  Report on Research and Development 1988 (1989)
Forestry Commission
  67th Annual Report and Accounts 1986–87, HC 171 (87–88), (1988)
  68th Annual Report and Accounts 1987–88, HC 69 (88–89), (1989)
  Forest Research 1987, (1987)
  Forest Research 1988, (1988)
General Register Office, Scotland
  Annual Report 1987, (1988)
  Annual Report 1988, (1989)
Highlands and Islands Development Board
  Accounts 1986–87, HC 237 (87–88), (1987)
  Accounts 1987–88, HC 237 (87–88), (1988)
Historic Buildings Council for Scotland
  Accounts for 1985–86, 1986–87, HC 99 (87–88), (1987)
Intervention Board for Agricultural Produce
  Annual Report 1987, Cm. 404, (1988)
  Annual Report 1988, Cm. 678, (1988)
  Accounts 1985, HC 68 (87–88), (1987)
  Accounts 1986, HC 564 (87–88), (1988)
  Accounts 1987, HC 564 (87–88), (1989)
Land Authority for Wales
  Accounts 1986–87, HC 86 (87–88), (1987)
  Accounts 1987–88, HC 645 (87–88), (1988)
  Accounts 1988–89, HC 518 (88–89), (1989)
National Heritage Memorial Fund
  Accounts 1987–88, HC 644 (87–88), (1988)
  Accounts 1988–89, HC 555 (88–89), (1989)
Nature Conservancy Council
  Accounts 1987–88, HC 637 (87–88), (1988)
  Accounts 1988–89, HC 554 (88–89), (1989)
Red Deer Commission
  Annual Report 1986, (1988)
  Annual Report 1987, (1989)
Scottish Development Agency
  Accounts 1987–88, HC 597 (87–88), (1988)
  Accounts 1988–89, HC 515 (88–89), (1989)
Scottish Tourist Board
  Accounts 1987–88, HC 550 (87–88), (1988)
  Accounts 1988–89, HC 471 (88–89), (1989)
Welsh Development Agency
  Accounts 1987–88, HC 593 (87–88), (1988)
  Accounts 1988–89, HC 516 (88–89), (1989)

THE LIBRARY
BISHOP BURTON COLLEGE
BEVERLEY HU17 8QG
TEL: 0964 550481 Ex: 227

Welsh (Wales) Tourist Board
 Accounts 1987–88, HC 562 (87–88), (1988)
 Accounts 1988–89, HC 525 (88–89), (1989)

List of annual reports produced by rural planning organisations 1987–9
Published by the Organisation

Format: Author, *Title* (Year of Publication)

Advisory Committee on the Landscape Treatment of Trunk Roads
 Report 1987 (1988)
Action for Communities in Rural England
 First Annual Report 1987–88 (1988)
Council for National Parks
 Annual Report 1986–87 (1987)
Council for the Protection of Rural England
 Annual Report 1987 (1988)
 Annual Report 1988 (1989)
Countryside Commission
 Annual Report 1987–88 (1988). See *Planning*, 788, p. 4
 Rights of Way legislation: 2nd Monitoring Report, CCP242 (1987)
Countryside Committee of Wales
 The Countryside in Wales 1988 (1988)
(Rural) Development Commission
 Annual Report 1986–87 (1987). See *The Planner*, November 1987, p. 6
 Annual Report 1987–88 (1988). See *Planning*, 793, p. 5
 Annual Report 1988–89 (1989). See *Planning*, 843, p. 6
Highlands and Islands Development Board
 Annual Report 1987 (1988)
 Annual Report 1988 (1989)
Nature Conservancy Council
 13th Report 1986–87 (1987). See *Planning*, 743, p. 10
 14th Report 1987–88 (1988). See *Planning*, 798, p. 9
 Corporate Plan 1988/89 (1988)
Scottish Consumer Council
 Bus deregulation monitoring study, Second Annual Report (1988). See *Planning*,
 784, p. 36
Scottish Tourist Board
 Annual Report 1987–88 (1988)
 Annual Report 1988–89 (1989)
Town and Country Planning Association
 Annual Report 1987/88 (1988)
 Annual Report 1988/89 (1989)
Transport and Road Research Laboratory
 Bus deregulation in Great Britain. A review of the first year (1987). See *Planning*,
 788, p. 15

Wales Tourist Board
  Annual Report 1987–88 (1988)
  Annual Report 1988–89 (1989)

Statistics

List of periodicals and statistical series containing information useful for rural planning
Published or sold by HMSO

Format: Author, *Series Volume, Year or Period Data refer to* and (Year of Publication)

Agriculture and Food, Ministry of
  Agricultural Statistics UK, 1986 (1988); and *1987* (1989)
  Farm Incomes in the UK, 1988 (1988); and *1989* (1989)
  Household Food Consumption and Expenditure, 1986 (1987); and *1987* (1989)
Central Statistical Office
  Annual Abstract of Statistics, 124, 1988 (1988); and *125, 1989* (1989)
  Regional Trends, 23, 1988 (1988); and *24, 1989* (1989)
  Social Trends, 18, 1988 (1988); and *19, 1989* (1989)
Environment, Department of
  Digest of Environmental Protection and Water Statistics 10, 1987 (1988); and *11, 1988* (1989)
  Housing and Construction Statistics 1976–86 Great Britain (1987)
  Housing and Construction Statistics 1977–87 Great Britain (1988)
  Housing and Construction Statistics, 30, June 1987, Parts 1 and 2 (1987); *31, Sept 1987*, Part 1 (1987) and Part 2 (1988); *32, December 1987*, Parts 1 and 2 (1988); *33, March 1988*, Parts 1 and 2 (1988); *34, June 1988*, Parts 1 and 2 (1988); *35, Sept 1988*, Parts 1 and 2 (1989); *36, December 1988*, Parts 1 and 2 (1989); and *37, March 1989* (1989)
  Local Housing Statistics, 82, July 1987 (1987); *83, October 1987* (1987); *84, January 1988* (1988); *85, April 1988* (1988); *86, July 1988* (1988); *87, October 1988* (1989); *88, January 1989* (1989); and *89, April 1989* (1989)
General Register Office, Scotland
  Population Estimates, Scotland, 1987 (1988); and *1988* (1989)
Office of Population Censuses and Surveys
  General Household Survey, No. 15, 1985 (1987)
  Key Population and Vital Statistics, Series VS, 13, 1986 (1988); and *VS 14, 1987* (1989)
  Key Population and Vital Statistics, Series PP1, 9, 1986 (1988)
  Population density and concentration in England and Wales 1971 and *1981* (1988)
  Population Projections, PP2, No. 15, from mid 1985 (1987)
  Population Projections, PP3, 7, 1985–2001 (1988)
  Population Trends, 49, Autumn 1987 (1987); *50, Winter 1987* (1987); *51, Spring 1988* (1988); *52, Summer 1988* (1988); *53, Autumn 1988* (1988); *54, Winter 1988* (1988); *55, Spring 1989* (1989); and *56, Summer 1989* (1989)

Scottish Development Department
Scottish Housing Statistics 1986 (1987)
Transport, Department of
National Travel Survey. 1985/86 Report. Part 1, *An analysis of personal travel.*
Part 2, *A technical guide* (1988)
Transport Statistics Great Britain 1976–86 (1987)
Transport Statistics Great Britain 1977–87 (1988)

List of periodicals and statistical series containing information useful for rural planning
Published by the Organisations involved.

Format: Organisation, *Series or one-off title*, (date of publication), Address if out of the ordinary, Authors if useful.

Agriculture and Food, Ministry of
  Output and Utilization of farm produce in the UK 1980–86 (1987), Lion House, Willowburn Trading Estate, Northumberland, NE66 2PF
Countryside Commission
  CCD16, *A compendium of recreation statistics 1984–86* (1987)
County Planning Officers Society
  Open-cast Coal-mining statistics 1986–87 (1988), County Planning Department, County Hall, Durham, DH1 5UF. See *Planning*, 758, p. 11
Development and Planning
  New annual journal produced by the Department of Land Economy at the University of Cambridge. Edited by D. Cross and C. Whitehead. The first issue (1989) was published by Policy Journals of the Old Vicarage, Hermitage, Newbury, Berks, RG16 9SU, and was 102 pages long. See *Town Planning Review*, 60, 4, 1989, pp. 476–8 for a review
Environment, Department of
  House projections 1986–2001 (1987). Available from Room P3/021, 2 Marsham Street, London, SW1P 3EB. See *Planning*, 756, p. 1
  Land for housing. Progress Report 1987 (1987). See *Planning*, 745, p. 6. *Progress Report 1988*, (1989). See *Planning*, 805, p. 3. Both available from Publication Sales Unit, Victoria Road, South Ruislip, Middlesex, HA4 0NZ
  Land-Use Change in England—Statistical Bulletin (88) 5 (1988). See *Planning*, 777, p. 1. Available from South Ruislip as above
Forestry Commission
  Forest Health Survey 1987. Part 1: *Results* (1987). Part 2: *Analysis and Interpretation* (1988). Both by J. Innes and R. Boswell
Landscape Institute
  Landscape Institute Yearbook, 1988 (1988)
  Landscape 89: The Environmental Review. Landscape Design Trust Yearbook (1989). Available from 5A West Street, Reigate, Surrey, RH2 9BL
Laurence Gould Consultants
  Land-Use Change Statistics Research Project (1989), Birmingham Road, Saltisford, Warwick, CV34 4TT

London and South East Regional Planning Conference (SERPLAN)
  Housing land supply and structure plan provisions in the South East (1988)
  Regional trends in the South-East, the South-East Regional Monitor 1987–8 (1988)
Office of Population Censuses and Surveys
  Mid-1987 population estimates for England and Wales (1988). See *The Planner*,
    September 1988, p. 6
Savills
  Savills IPD—Agricultural Performance Analysis 1987 (1987)
Scottish Development Department
  Land-Use Change in Scotland 1988 (1989)

7 The social and economic restructuring of rural Britain

Richard Munton

This brief report introduces some aspects of the London programme being conducted under the ESRC's Countryside Change Initiative. The programme seeks to elucidate the complex processes which underlie the uneven development of rural Britain. These processes result from the interaction between local and non-local forces, especially the relations between international capital, the regulatory functions of the state and local class interests (Marsden and Murdoch, 1990), but unlike other locality studies which have focused upon adjustments to local labour markets (e.g. Cooke, 1989), this programme pays particular attention to the land development process (LDP). The primary purpose is not to explain the changing use and management of land but to use the LDP as a means of understanding the social and political recomposition of rural areas and to assess its consequences for different interests in an era of deregulation and privatisation (see Flynn *et al.*, 1990).

The programme's methodology requires an analysis of non-local forces for change and how their requirements are mediated by local circumstances. The non-local forces include the major corporate interests engaged in rural development, such as those in the food system and construction industry, those responsible for the formulation and implementation of public policy (e.g. MAFF, RDC) and the endeavours of national amenity and environmental bodies. Background reports have been prepared on recent changes to the economic structure of the food chain (see Ward, 1990) and private sector housebuilding. Three characteristics are common to both reports. First, production continues to be concentrated in the hands of an ever smaller number of large companies; second, the tendency among these big corporations is to have a declining proportion of their activities directed towards rural Britain, increasing the risk of severe disruption to the local economy; and third, there is the greater direct involvement of banking capital in the food chain (Marsden *et al.*, 1990) and financial institutions in the housing sector. The latter is reflected in the recent purchase and restructuring of estate agency chains by Lloyds Bank and Abbey Life (Black Horse Agencies Ltd.), General Accident (GA Property Services), Prudential Corporation (Prudential Property Services) and the Halifax Building Society (Halifax Property Services).

At the local level of inquiry, the concern is to establish the changing divisions and distribution of property rights between different interests in the rural community as a consequence of land development. The LDP is often fiercely contested with the outcome (or non-outcome) of each development contributing to a constantly evolving local political and social context within which the next case occurs. A holistic analysis is therefore called for but this is complicated by the enormous number and range of LDPs, some lying beyond the remit of the planning system. They vary from speculative housing development to barn conversions, from mineral extraction to leisure development, and from affordable housing to farm diversification (see Grove-Hills *et al.*, 1990). The local investigations are being conducted in three contrasting localities with different economic histories, current development pressures, class fractions and political compositions. The districts are Allerdale (Cumbria), East Devon and Aylesbury Vale (Bucks.). The primary field method is the case study developed from detailed, unstructured interviews with representatives of the interests involved. Two approaches are being used.

First, subject only to the broad objectives of the programme, each locality is being 'allowed to speak for itself', with the case studies being selected to reflect the local nature of contestation. These include examples of all the more important LDPs, complemented by clusters based on three contrasting villages in each district for which detailed histories of all developments to have occurred during the 1980s are being compiled. Field enquiry is in progress and given the methodology the results are difficult to interpret out of context. But the case of the Lostrigg open-cast coal site in Allerdale is a straightforward and effective illustration. In a political and cultural context where coal-mining has long been regarded as vital to the local economy, the NCB (now British Coal) had never failed, until last year, to obtain planning permission for its open-cast operations. Even allowing for one or two special features of this particular planning applica-tion, its rejection can be largely attributed to a change in local political representation. This in turn reflects a change in the social composition of the rural Cumbrian population which is increasingly privileging consump-tion rather than production objectives for the countryside.

Second, to ensure a more direct form of comparison between the three localities and a more direct link between the local and the non-local, three further analyses are being conducted. These concern the housing and agricultural LDPs, and the provision of environmental goods. The investigations will proceed in an iterative manner between the 'strategic' and the local. Interviews with the non-local interests are defining an agenda (e.g. how best to contain speculative housing pressures and to provide affordable housing), to be pursued within each locality, the local experience then to be debated with representatives of the strategic bodies.

Note

The London programme is directed by Philip Lowe, Terry Marsden and Richard Munton. It runs from 1989 to 1992. A fuller account of its methodological and theoretical perspectives is contained in a series of Countryside Change Working Papers prepared jointly with the Countryside Change Unit, Department of Agricultural Economics, University of Newcastle, Newcastle-upon-Tyne NE1 7RU. These may be obtained from the Unit's Secretary.

References

Cooke, P. (ed.), 1989, *Localities: a comparative analysis of urban change*, Unwin Hyman, London

Flynn, A., Lowe, P. and Cox, G., 1990, *The rural land development process*, Working Paper 6, Countryside Change Series

Grove-Hills, J., Munton, R. and Murdoch, J., 1990, *The rural land development process: evolving a methodology*, Working Paper 8, Countryside Change Series

Marsden, T. and Murdoch, J., 1990, *Restructuring rurality: key areas for development in assessing rural change*, Working Paper 4, Countryside Change Series

Marsden, T., Whatmore, S. and Munton, R., 1990, 'The role of banking capital in British agriculture', T. Marsden and J. Little (eds), *Perspectives on the food system*, Gower, London

Ward, N., 1990, 'A preliminary analysis of the UK food chain', 15: Food Policy 439–41

8 Countryside change: some Newcastle research programme findings at Year One
Ken Willis

The countryside is changing in a number of ways and in respect to a variety of forces. How these are assessed and their impact determined partly depends upon the methods of analysis adopted. Research at the Newcastle Countryside Change Unit (CCU) essentially views changes (intervention) as a response to market (non-market) price (preference) signals (Harvey *et al.*, 1989). This contrasts with, but also complements, research at the Rural Studies Research Centre, UCL, which essentially focuses on another aspect of countryside change, the actors and agencies involved in the process of change, explored through qualitative and ethnographic research methods. Research methods employed at Newcastle are more quantitative and rooted in standard micro-economic theory.

Environment

Research into aspects of the environment at Newcastle has investigated such issues as the value of forest recreation and informal recreation along inland waterways, through travel cost and contingent valuation methods. The individual travel cost model (ITCM) was adopted for the first time in Britain to deal with the particular problems of assessing linear forms of recreation provision and to value different aspects of the facilities provided, rather than adopting the traditional Clawson-Knetsch zonal travel cost model (ZTCM). The ITCM can estimate the value of particular recreational activities with a fewer number of observations than that required for a ZTCM; this provides consumer surplus estimates of benefits, to waterways and forests, to set alongside the subsidies from government to maintain these rural land uses and facilities.

Results indicate that while the consumer surplus from recreation along certain canals fails to offset the cost of maintaining them (Willis, Garrod and Dobbs, 1990), for inland waterways in general consumer surplus exceeds government subsidies, and for particular canals the benefit/cost ratio is extremely high (Willis and Garrod, 1991a). Considerable contrasts in the value of forest recreation can be seen between ZTCM, ITCM and contingent valuation (CV) estimates (Willis and Garrod, 1991b). While CV is subject to biases, they are controllable, and CV should be viewed optimistically (Garrod and Willis, 1990a) as a means of valuing countryside change. The ITCM suggests forest recreational values vary spatially by forest district, and what while recreation benefits match the forest recreation and amenity subsidy, they may not exceed total subsidies to forestry. All of these results have considerable policy implications for future funding of such activities in rural areas, and the spatial distribution of future recreational provision in the countryside.

Research has also been able to demonstrate through ANOVA (analysis of variance) that house prices vary significantly by ITE (Institute of Terrestrial Ecology) landscape type, suggesting that different landscapes provide significantly different benefits (Garrod and Willis, 1990b).

The research has typically provided a total valuation of the recreational site, rather than indicating the value of marginal changes to the site if some facilities are provided or withdrawn. Clearly impact should be measured as the value of marginal changes in the countryside. The next stage of the research in the environment field will be to explore the value of changes in countryside attributes in the Yorkshire Dales and the Forest of Dean.

Countryside management

The need to incorporate environmental stocks and flows into national accounts has been stressed by Pearce et al. (1989), in order to ensure that welfare losses due to natural and environmental resource depletion, as well as environmental benefits, are taken into account in decision making. Adger and Whitby (1991) have compiled such a set of environmental accounts for the agricultural and forest sector. Difficulties were encountered due to the paucity of data on the environmental costs and benefits of particular rural land uses and the difficulty of aggregating the data to the national situation. But results suggest that agriculture and forestry land uses provide major environmental benefits which might add 20 per cent to the net product of these industries. Most benefits accrue from green belt designation. There are some offsetting negative effects, but these costs appear to be small, although the evidence is incomplete. Results should be judged against fully specified satellite accounts which indicate the physical magnitudes to be evaluated.

Research on the countryside begs the question as to how decisions will be made on particular projects and policies. Environmental impact assessment (EIA) and cost benefit analysis (CBA) are two commonly employed decision aids. But in a review of these, Adger and Whitby (1990) reached the conclusion that both had important imperfections which laid them open to abuse and capture by individual agencies pursuing their narrower objectives. The only safeguard against such capture is greater transparency in the public sector: only full disclosure of calculations and assessment guarantee better rural land-use policy and planning decisions.

References

Adger, N. and Whitby, M. (1990), *Appraisal and the public good: environmental assessment and cost benefit analysis*, Countryside Change Working Paper Series WP7, Department of Agricultural Economics and Food Marketing, University of Newcastle-upon-Tyne

Adger, N. and Whitby, M. (1991) 'Accounting for the impact of agriculture and forestry on environmental quality', Paper presented to the September Conference of the European Association of Environmental and Resource Economists, Lisbon

Garrod, G.D. and Willis, K.G. (1990a), *Contingent valuation techniques: a review of their unbiasedness, efficiency and consistency*, Countryside Change Working Paper Series WP10, Countryside Change Unit, Department of Agricultural Economics and Food Marking, University of Newcastle-upon-Tyne

Garrod, G.D. and Willis, K.G. (1990b), 'Assessing the impacts and values of agricultural and rural landscapes: an application of non-parametric statistical methods', Paper presented to the April conference of the European Association of Environmental and Resource Economists, Department of Economics, University of Venice, Italy

Harvey, D., Whitby, M., Willis, K., Allanson, P., Adger, N. and Garrod, G. (1990), *Markets policies and countryside change*, Countryside Working Paper Series WP3, Department of Agricultural Economics and Food Marketing, University of Newcastle-upon-Tyne

Pearce, D., Markandya, A. and Barbier, E. (1989), *Blue print for a green economy*. Earthscan, London

Willis, K.G. and Garrod, G.D. (1991a), *On-site recreation surveys and selection effects: valuing open access recreation of inland waterways*, Working Paper (forthcoming)

Willis, K.G. and Garrod, G.D. (1991b), 'An individual travel-cost method of evaluating forest recreation', *Journal of Agricultural Economics* (forthcoming)

Willis, K.G. Garrod, G.D. and Dobbs, I.M. (1990), *The value of canals as a public good: the case of the Montgomery and Lancaster canals*, Countryside Change Working Paper Series WP5, Countryside Change Unit, Department of Agricultural Economics and Food Marketing, University of Newcastle-upon-Tyne

9 Splitting nature
Ian Brotherton, University of Sheffield

In the late 1940s the British Government was persuaded by pressure from voluntary concerns to give official recognition and support to countryside conservation and recreation. Initially two agencies were established. The *Nature Conservancy* was charged with providing scientific advice on the conservation of native flora and fauna, with establishing and managing nature reserves and with developing supportive research. The *National Parks Commission* was charged with designating, for ministerial confirmation, national parks and areas of outstanding natural beauty and with advising on their planning and management for landscape conservation and recreation purposes. Thus, the Nature Conservancy dealt with nature conservation and did so throughout Britain; and it had an executive role as a landowner and manager. In contrast, the National Parks Commission was concerned with landscape conservation and outdoor recreation but only within designated areas in England and Wales; and its role was essentially advisory and supervisory. Thus began what many conservationists have regarded as the great divide in conservation policy and practice, with the purposes of nature conservation and landscape conservation pursued by separate central government agencies.

While the two bodies have established substantial links and generally not unharmonious working relationships through the intervening years, they have developed on substantially separate courses. The Nature Conservancy, established in 1949 under Royal Charter with a high degree of independence, was brought under the wing of a newly established research council in 1968. Then, in 1973, following a general government move to fund research on a customer-contractor basis, most, though not all, of the Nature Conservancy's research function was removed to a new body the Institute of Terrestrial Ecology which remained under the Natural Environment Research Council. The remaining functions involving the establishment and management of nature reserves and the giving of advice and grants in furtherance of nature conservation, went to a renamed *Nature Conservancy Council* under the Department of the Environment. Through the 1970s and 1980s, the Nature Conservancy Council substantially developed its interest in the wider countryside as well as giving much time and attention to designated sites in the 1980s, following the substantially improved arrangements for the protection of Sites of Special Scientific Interest contained in the 1981 Wildlife and Countryside Act.

Meanwhile, the National Parks Commission having designated 10 national parks in England and Wales in the 1950s and a number of areas of outstanding natural beauty continued to advise on their planning and management until the 1986 Countryside Act introduced its successor organisation, the *Countryside Commission*. The new Commission continued the work of the old but was additionally required to advise upon and grant aid the maintenance and enhancement of rural landscape and provision for its enjoyment throughout the whole of England and Wales. A year earlier, landscape conservation and recreation in the countryside were also legislated for in Scotland and, since 1967, these purposes have been pursued by the Countryside Commission for Scotland.

These organisations (certainly in England and Wales and recently also in Scotland) have enjoyed substantial support from the many voluntary bodies that concern themselves with countryside conservation and recreation in Britain. As a result, not only have they survived some dangerous moments, but their powers, resources and influence have grown steadily over the years. Certainly some influential conservationists have argued that the Nature Conservancy Council and the Countryside Commissions should be merged, to avoid what is seen as an artificial and unhelpful separation of nature and landscape and to provide a single more substantial body, better able to stand up to the major departments of government. But in general, the Council and the Commissions have received substantial support within the conservation world.

What happened next, on 11 July 1989, came as a bombshell, particularly to the Nature Conservancy Council and to its supporters in the voluntary conservation sector. With minimal conservation, the government announced its intention to fragment the Nature Conservancy Council into three country agencies; to separate the Countryside Commission (for England and Wales), into two country organisations (the Countryside Commission for Scotland already having a separate existence); and to combine the resulting nature and landscape agencies in Scotland (to form the Scottish National Heritage Agency) and in Wales (to form the Countryside Council for Wales) but not in England where the Countryside Commission and the Nature Conservancy Council for England will operate as separate agencies. Many reasons have been given for the proposed change. Thus, government has presented it as a rationalisation of countryside functions, the devolution of responsibilities in particular being claimed as a major improvement. In contrast, some conservationists at least have seen the proposals as emanating from the Scottish Office which, it is argued, has resented the anti-development stance taken by the Nature Conservancy Council, notably in relation to afforestation proposals in Scotland.

The reactions from the conservation world were as predictable as they were hostile; and they were, arguably, over-done. Thus, the dismemberment of the Nature Conservancy Council is not a cost-cutting exercise.

Funding the new structure will almost certainly cost the government more. And in Scotland and Wales at least, conservation will be developed and delivered as a unified and devolved service.

But if a unified service is good for Scotland and Wales, why not for England? And will the country organisations go their separate ways? Given a devolved structure, who will attend to conservation issues with UK or international dimensions, clearly crucial given the increased importance now afforded to trans-national and global environmental problems? These and similar questions have been pressed hard by conservationists and have been hotly debated in both Houses of Parliament. The voluntary conservation organisations have been largely united in their opposition to the splitting of the Nature Conservancy Council and have pressed for the removal of the offending Part VII from the Environment Protection Bill. But the government appears determined to press ahead with its proposals and it has not been seriously opposed in this by the opposition parties which have at least seen merits in the devolutionary aspects.

The government's only significant concession to date is a proposal to place upon the three country bodies a duty to establish a Joint Nature Conservation Committee. This JNCC would tackle conservation issues with a UK or international dimension (but will not concern itself with co-ordinating overviews on countryside and landscape conservation issues) and would establish common standards for the work of the three country agencies (formal arrangements involving Northern Ireland are also proposed). Half of the members of the JNCC would be drawn from the three country agencies, the remaining half including the Chairman being independent members appointed directly by the Environment Secretary. The JNCC would have its own budget and a staff complement of up to 50.

Assuming that the proposals are enacted more or less in their current form, as seems likely, what will they achieve? Will they improve, or worsen things, from the conservation point of view? It is at present impossible to say. The answer will depend in part on the resources allocated to the new bodies and on that the government has yet to pronounce, apart from saying that the funding will be 'adequate'. It will also depend on the members appointed to run the new bodies, and on their resolve. And it will depend perhaps crucially on the effectiveness of the JNCC, and on the role that both the country agencies and ministers allow it to play. But amidst the current conservationist gloom, there is perhaps some reason to be optimistic. Thus, it seems likely that the Scottish and Welsh Offices will be keen to make their new-found responsibilities work to the reasonable satisfaction of conservation interests; and if, and when, the JNCC and the three country agencies speak with a united voice, as they may well on crucial issues, government is likely to take note.

But when the dust has settled, the episode is likely to be seen as little more than a piece of opportunistic politicking. Arguably, more fundamental change in the organisational structure of conservation is needed. Government, it would be seem, still sees conservation as an add-on, a special but discrete interest to be dealt with by semi-autonomous agencies. Such agencies certainly have value and the independence afforded to the Nature Conservancy Council and the Countryside Commissions in the past has enabled them to lobby government and to secure greater acceptance of the conservation case. But if conservation is to imbue all government work, as the forthcoming Environment White Paper may propose, conservation thinking will need to be brought squarely within the mainstream of government policy-making. This, and the current realignment of agricultural and other rural policy, suggests that the soon-to-be enacted changes in the organisation of conservation in Britain could be short-lived.

Section III:
Europe

edited by
David J. Briggs

Introduction

David J. Briggs

Europe is a diverse and complex region, not only politically but environmentally and socially. It is a region which is also undergoing radical change, with far-reaching consequences for the rural environment and rural communities. This section of the Yearbook is therefore aimed at assessing and analysing the changes which are taking place, and their potential implications for rural areas, e.g.:

1. by reviewing international legislation and policy initiatives likely to impinge on rural areas;
2. by examining in some detail the motives and processes behind specific policy developments;
3. by considering the impacts of policy and other broad-scale developments on more local rural areas in Europe.

In this issue, therefore, I review the proposals for the European Environment Agency—undoubtedly one of the major environmental initiatives in the EC in recent years. Helen Groome and Franca Batigelli look at the effects of national and EC policies (the former on forestry, the latter on agricultural intensification) on two specific regions. Krzysztof Mazurski considers the impacts of the liberalisation of Poland on the country's agriculture and rural environment. All four papers are an attempt to look beyond the immediate objectives and terms of the policies involved to their wider implications.

During the years ahead, the aim will be to continue this philosophy to the European section: in particular, to try to bridge the gap between policies which are generally adopted in pursuit of some broad and common (often national) good, and the problems, needs and effects in individual regions. In 1991–2, issues of obvious concern will thus be the changes in agricultural policy—arising from GATT and the Community's attempts to reduce surpluses and costs—and their effects on rural areas.

The reunification of Germany and other changes in eastern Europe are also likely to be of continuing importance. Policy on rural areas is also being driven in many cases by longer-term social and environmental processes, for example, the demographic shift which is currently occurring in Europe, and by global warming. Contributions and comments on these and other topical issues are therefore welcome.

10 Land consolidation and agrarian policy in the Friuli-Venezia Giulia region, Italy

Franca Battigelli

Introduction

Friuli-Venezia Giulia is one of five Italian regions which were granted special status in 1947, the others being Val d'Aosta, Trentino-Alto Adige, Sicily and Sardinia. It was not until 1963, however, that the region was officially established, largely due to the delay caused by the controversy over the country's eastern border following World War II[1]. Under its new status, the region gained wide-ranging powers, though with varying levels of autonomy. These included major responsibility (i.e. total autonomy within the terms of the Italian Constitution and subject only to national and international laws) over agriculture and forestry, land reclamation, land consolidation, irrigation, agrarian reform, land improvement, fishing and animal breeding. Since 1978, when various government powers were decentralised, all Italian regions have acquired a degree of self-government in certain social and economic fields. Yet, even now, the five autonomous regions are notable for their degree of independence, especially in the area of agricultural policy, in which they have the responsibility not only to apply the directives issues by the Italian government and European Community, but also to take and apply decisions of their own.

In principle, this position of autonomy should enhance the ability of the Friuli-Venezia Giulia region to tackle its agrarian problems and improve its agricultural sector for, unlike remote and central governments, it should be able to respond to problems at close quarters. Nevertheless, many problems remain unsolved, and the benefits of land consolidation especially are now being reassessed. This paper outlines the policy context and nature of land consolidation in Friuli-Venezia Giulia, and discusses some of its impacts on the rural environment.

Regional agricultural policy

During the early years of regional autonomy, until the late 1970s, agriculture policy development concentrated mainly on functional reorganisation of the sector. This involved setting up various agencies with responsibility for agriculture, and defining how they should operate. In addition, programmes of direct aid were introduced, under which financial compensation was available for damage caused by natural disasters, and support was given for the improvement of rural housing, for land reform and consolidation. Lastly, a system of selective grants was proposed in order to encourage the development and consolidation of specific sectors of agriculture (e.g. livestock farming and cash crop production). Livestock farming, in particular, was a focus for support: this covered both the important area of cattle breeding and the more minor sectors of rabbit, poultry and silkworm farming. Support is provided by regular—normally financial—aid giving help with running costs, modernisation of equipment and production methods, preventive medicine and genetic improvement of livestock.

Underlying these actions was a common theme: the protection of agricultural incomes and support for farming families. This, in turn, was part of a wider socio-economic policy, aimed at reducing both regional inequalities (e.g. between the lowlands and uplands, and the sub-regions of Friuli and Venezia Giulia) and structural imbalances (i.e. between different sectors of production). Although these problems had existed since the region's establishment, during the 1970s they were exacerbated by the rapid industrial growth which occurred in the Friulian plain. In compensation, large quantities of financial aid were therefore directed at agricultural support. Lack of selectivity in the allocation of this aid, however, reduced it essentially to a form of welfare support, which did little to tackle the basic problems of the region.

Since the mid 1970s, attempts have been made to introduce more comprehensive and effective development programmes. These were intended to involve the entire agricultural sector, rather than individual parts, and were aimed at raising production by increasing the technical and economic efficiency of agriculture. To this end, a range of legislation was passed, covering incentives for agricultural co-operation, professional training and technical assistance, new financing of public land reclamation projects, land improvement and the construction of forest roads.

At the same time, this trend towards structural improvement and cross-sectoral development was reinforced by various national and EC policies. Regional Law 62, for example, passed in 1978, dealt with the application of EC directives on agricultural reform,. In 1981, the so-called 'Four Leaf Clover' law—adopted at the national level four years earlier—was applied at the regional level by the adoption of six development programmes. These covered irrigation, utilisation of hill and mountain land, fish and

THE LIBRARY
BISHOP BURTON COLLEGE
BEVERLEY HU17 8QG

livestock farming, fruit and vegetable production, wine, Mediterranean crops and the establishment of co-operatives.

More recently, however, the wider context of agricultural policy has undergone a radical change. Continued and accumulating food surpluses, together with renewed concern about the effects of modern farming on the environment, provoked a fundamental reassessment of the European Community's agricultural policy. During the late 1980s, new measures were thus introduced under the CAP, aimed at encouraging diversification and set-aside, at reducing production levels and at protecting environmentally sensitive areas. In line with these policies, legislation on set-aside was adopted by the Friuli-Venezia Giulia region, in 1989. To date, however, these new trends in agricultural policy have had little effect. Farmers in the region tend to regard them as premature, given the need which still exists for modernisation and intensification, in the face of the imminent increase in competition likely to arise from the creation of the Single European Market in 1992.

The need for land consolidation

The agriculture of Friuli-Venezia Giulia, therefore, could still benefit from further land consolidation and rationalisation. In several areas of the region land has been undergoing a prolonged and far-reaching process of subdivision and fragmentation, which has led to an agrarian landscape characterised by a patchwork of small and scattered plots. Several historical factors have contributed to this: the gradual break-up of the large estates of the manorial system; the expropriation and redistribution—that took place under the Napoleonic regime—of land belonging to religious institutions; the privatisation of common lands, initially on a *de-facto* basis and, after 1853, legally; the increase in taxation after Friuli's incorporation into the Italian kingdom in 1866; and, above all, the practice of partible inheritance. This pattern has tended to be fossilised by the stagnation of the land market, as a consequence of the innate unwillingness of Friulian farmers to sell their own land, and, nowadays, by the expectation in urban fringe areas of future substantial increases in land prices in response to urban growth. The consequence has been a continued reduction in farm size, such that many holdings are today too small to support the families which run them, and unable to compete either nationally or internationally. By 1970, for example, 56 per cent of farms in the region were smaller than 3 ha in size, and over half were divided into four or more separate parcels.

For these reasons alone, there is clearly an urgent need for land consolidation in the area as shown in Figure 10.1. The Friulian plain—the main focus of agriculture in the region—can, however, be divided into two regions: an upper zone composed of coarse and loose alluvial deposits,

FRAGMENTED PROPERTIES

ROADS

0   100m   200m   300m

Figure 10.1 *The traditional pattern of fragmented and scattered holdings in the Commune of Pradamano, Udine, before consolidation*

Source: Consorzio di Bonifica Stradalta, Udine

such as sand and gravel, and a lower alluvial plain consisting of argillaceous sediments. In the former, soils are light and highly permeable, and suffer from droughtiness despite the high rainfall: irrigation is consequently required. In the latter, the soils are heavy, clayey and impermeable, and there is a need for improved land drainage. In both areas, however, the small size and fragmentation of holdings mean that technologies such as irrigation or land drainage cannot easily be applied.

In the case of irrigation, for example, fragmentation greatly increases both the cost and complexity of installing the network. Typically, small, unconsolidated plots require around 100 m of piping per hectare, compared to around 70 m/ha in consolidated holdings. At the same time, small land parcels inhibit the efficient use of sprinklers. Consolidation thus needs to be seen as part of a more general plan for land reform and improvement, including provisions to extend irrigation in the upper plain, and land drainage in the lower.

The legal framework

The main legal instrument controlling land consolidation in Italy remains the old national law on land reclamation, introduced in 1933. This law states that, in districts which are suitable for economic and social development, programmes of land reform and improvement should be established, including, if appropriate, land consolidation. Under the law, responsibility for drawing up and implementing these programmes lies with the Ministry for Agriculture and Forests, although the Ministry may delegate these responsibilities to a purposely established Land Reclamation Agency, in which all the landowners involved in the project take part. It should also be noted that land consolidation in this context can only be applied on a property basis and not—as would often be more efficient and effective—on a farm basis. (A property is defined by ownership; a farm, on the other hand, may include rented land which is thus excluded from the consolidation process.)[2]

With the creation of the autonomous region of Friuli-Venezia Giulia, responsibility for consolidation was handed over to the regional administration, which grants concessions for the planning, implementation and management of drainage and consolidation operations to Land Reclamation Agencies. To enable this process, a specific regional law was passed in 1965, which provides financial aid for up to 98 per cent of the total cost, so that the landowners are required to pay relatively small sums for the whole operation. More recently, in 1983, Law Number 44 was adopted, defining the whole region as a 'land reclamation district'. This allows support for land consolidation to be granted throughout the region.

Advantages and disadvantages of land consolidation

During the 1930s, and again during the post-war period, extensive land drainage and consolidation operations were carried out on the damp and marshy land of the lower Friulian plain, as far as the coast. From the late 1960s, consolidation and irrigation work was started on the upper plain. In this way, between 1934 and the present day, over 25,000 ha of land has been consolidated in the region to produce the type of pattern shown in Figure 10.2. This constitutes almost half of the land consolidation in the whole of Italy over this period.

All the consolidation projects which have been carried out in the region have produced undoubted positive economic results. Rationalisation of properties and reorganisation of land distribution have reduced the proportion of unexploited land and decreased the working hours required for farm operations. In addition, they have made the use of farm machinery more efficient, and thereby allowed equipment costs to be paid off more quickly. This, in turn, has reduced production costs. Furthermore, irrigation—using sprinkler systems—has raised crop yields and led to a sharp increase in farm productivity. As a result of these improvements, land values in the consolidated areas have also risen significantly.

In the same way, land consolidation has generated a range of social benefits. Legal conflicts over land ownership and over access to single plots have declined. Working conditions have improved; the status of farmers, their quality of life and their public image have therefore risen and as a consequence young people are being attracted back into agriculture, which at present is dominated by elderly workers.

The socio-economic aims of the 1933 law have therefore been largely achieved in these areas. Nevertheless, during the last ten years, criticism of the land consolidation scheme has begun to grow, and today the whole issue of consolidation is being reconsidered. Some of this criticism comes from the farmers themselves, who accept the need for land consolidation as well as for irrigation, but have begun to challenge the ways and methods by which traditional consolidation has been carried out. Small landowners especially—many of whom work part time—have gained only marginally from the improvements in management and economic benefits, while they have often been hard hit by the costs both of consolidation itself and of the purchase of land necessary to reach the minimum farm size required.

A number of legal uncertainties are also beginning to emerge. In particular, for projects planed in the 1970s, there are doubts about the legality of the ruling which forces landowners—by means of cash payments—to achieve the minimum size defined for consolidated farm units. Equally, there is some dispute about the attenuated procedures which some of the Land Reclamation Agencies have adopted in recent years to avoid bureaucratic delays. These have involved carrying out consolidation

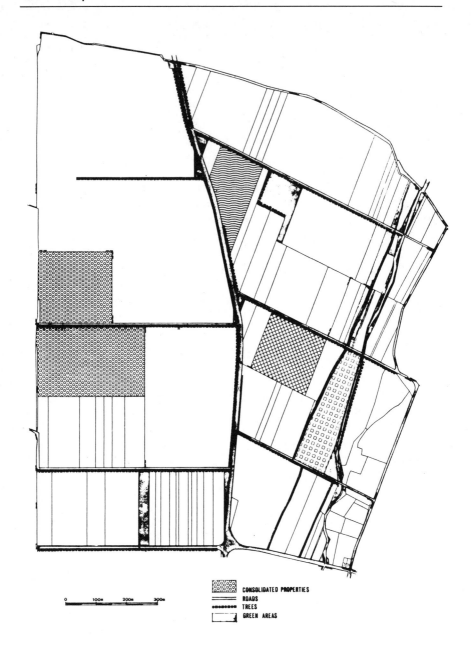

CONSOLIDATED PROPERTIES
ROADS
TREES
GREEN AREAS

0   100m   200m   300m

Figure 10.2 *The rationalised pattern of holdings resulting from a second-generation consolidation scheme in Pradamano, Udine. Intermixed trees, hedgerows and plots of woodland interrupt the geometric landscape, and also the original layout of roads has basically been preserved.*

Source: Consorzio di Bonifica Stradalta, Udine

works (e.g. construction of the rural road network and reorganisation of land parcels) and installing irrigation systems before the project is fully approved by the regional administration. It is argued that this contravenes the 1933 land reform law by not providing sufficient opportunity for any complaints or appeals to be lodged by the landowners.

More generally, questions are being posed about the cost effectiveness of land consolidation schemes. The costs of consolidation are presently estimated at 8–9 million lire per hectare, the vast majority of which comes from the public purse. It is therefore being asked whether other, less costly means might exist of achieving the economic benefits; or whether the schemes are appropriate at all. In particular, it has been argued that such consolidation is part of an agrarian policy which is aimed at intensification and increasing output—a policy which has now been rendered obsolete by the existence of agricultural surpluses, the shift in demand to high quality food, and the recent 'greening' of the CAP.

Yet above all, the challenge to land consolidation is coming from outside the agricultural world: from both environmentalists and from those concerned with protecting regional identity who fear adverse impacts on the ecological, historical and cultural value of the land and landscape. Objections from environmentalists are targeted mainly at projects dating from the 1970s, which were based on the so-called MUP (minimum plot size). According to this, each parcel within the new layout must be between 5,000 and 10,000 m^2 in area, and strictly rectangular. Moreover, as part of the consolidation process, various preparatory works have to be carried out: obstacles (such as trees, hedges, thickets or ditches) are removed, disused roads and tracks are covered over, the land is levelled, and a new road network between the fields is built.

Since 1970, over 6,000 ha of land have been consolidated using the MUP approach. Technically, of course, it is sound. It maximises rationalisation of land use, minimises the requirements for and costs of irrigation pipes and avoids 'wastage' of land. Nevertheless, the approach clearly leads to a fundamental change in the traditional rural landscape. The ancient and irregular bocage-type landscape is replaced by the regular and artificial geometry of a chess-board, and by a monocultural open field.

Environmental impacts: two generations in conflict

Land consolidation, which in the upper Friulian plain is invariably associated with irrigation, is having a variety of both direct and indirect effects on the ecology and landscape of the region. The removal of hedgerows and trees, for example causes:

1. the loss of natural compartmentalisation of the area, and the removal of vegetational barriers to the spread of disease and parasites;

2. the loss of natural and semi-natural habitats which support a wide
   range of plant and animal species, with a consequent reduction in
   species diversity and a general ecological impoverishment of the area;
3. the loss of protection against wind afforded by hedgerows, resulting in
   a probable increase in soil erosion during fallow periods, and damage
   to crops by wind during the vegetative period; and
4. modification and microclimate, with an increase in temperature and
   evapotranspiration, and a reduction in atmospheric humidity.

Irrigation, similarly, has a wide array of both direct and indirect effects.
The increased availability of water for agricultural use encourages cultivation of those cash crops which respond most effectively to irrigation
(originally only maize, but nowadays soya as well). This, in turn,
encourages the trend towards monocultures without rotation. The uninter-
rupted cultivation of a single crop—both spatially and temporally—is
probably economically questionable; it certainly has severe environmental
effects; it gives rise to a simple and repetitive landscape; and it leads to
increased use of fertilisers and pesticides, and thereby results in increased
water pollution. In the case of soya, levelling of the soil—carried out to
make harvesting easier—also reduces infiltration capacity and increases the
risk of runoff and erosion.

In addition, abstraction of water for irrigation is beginning to deplete
both ground and surface waters, not only in the lowlands but also in the
mountains, where several irrigation plants already exist and others are
planned.

As already mentioned, the last ten years have seen growing concern
about both agricultural surpluses and the environment in the European
Community. As a result, increasing attention is now being given to the
'greening' of agricultural policy, at the Community level. Similar principles are also beginning to drive agricultural policy in the Friuli-Venezia
Giulia region. Regional Law 44/1983, for example, obliges all land
consolidation projects to be accompanied by a Plan for the Conservation
and Restoration of Vegetation. Article 8 states the intention to protect and
improve woodlands (and in some cases to provide for their establishment)
and to safeguard features of the natural environment, for example, tree-
lined riverbanks, since such features are ecologically positive both for the
local fauna and flora, and for agricultural productivity. Subsequent
supplementary regulations state specifically that districts undergoing land
consolidation must retain a green area equal to that which previously
existed, or, if no green area did exist, to ensure that vegetation is planted
over at least 1.5 per cent of the consolidated land.

Greater ecological awareness, expressed through such legislation, is
therefore helping to produce a new generation of land consolidation
projects which are more sympathetic to the environment, whilst still
faithful to the fundamental objective of farm rationalisation. These aim to

achieve legal consolidation of properties and to install irrigation without
the necessity for major physical modifications to the land. One example is
the consolidation of 620 hectares of land in the commune of Pradamano,
to the east of Udine, in 1986. Before work began, a habitat census was
conducted, listing all woodlands, hedgerows, tree lines and natural
meadows, which were then classified according to their botanical and
environmental value. Thus here—as elsewhere—attempts have been made
to design a new layout which met technical and legal requirements and
was compatible with the pre-existing rural landscape.

Another innovative feature of this scheme was the action taken to
conserve individual mature trees (e.g. of mulberry). These form an
integral part of the traditional landscape, yet in many cases needed to be
removed. Rather than simply destroy them, a technique developed in
Germany was adopted, by which the trees were lifted and replanted on
nearby sites. This has allowed about 600 mature trees and 2,000 hectares
of woodland to be saved, albeit in a site different from the original one.
In some cases, poor and gravelly soils have also been improved in quality
by the artificial addition of topsoil and humus. Other devices to protect
the environment have included the conservation of permanent
(unploughed) grassland, and the creation of cover and 'green routes' for
wildlife. This 'green plan' has added only 7–8 per cent to the total cost
of the consolidation scheme.

In terms of their environmental implications, these new consolidation
projects are clearly a significant improvement on earlier schemes. Nevertheless, they are still far from ideal. Environmental conservation is, in
fact, restricted to only a few sites or features in the area concerned; these
are reduced to the status of a 'reserve', divorced from the rest of the landscape, little more than green islands within a sea of intensive land use.
The existence of legal requirements for conservation has also, in some
cases, had a detrimental effect: some landowners have ploughed up natural
habitats and grubbed out trees prior to consolidation in order to avoid the
regulations.

Considerable scope yet exists, therefore, to improve the land consolidation schemes in this region (and elsewhere in Italy), and to make the
ecologically more sensitive. This, however, will require a fundamental
change in the way these schemes are perceived and planned. It will require
that the natural and cultural environment is no longer seen as the enemy
of development, as an anachronism needing to be swept away or confined
to tiny oases. Instead, the policy-makers, planners, engineers and farmers
concerned need to recognise the environment as both an economic and
cultural resource—a source of raw materials and energy, and at the same
time a major contributor to a better quality of life. For the future it may
thus be hoped that a third generation of land consolidation projects will
evolve, which will take a more holistic view of the relationships between
agriculture, environment and quality of life in the region, and which will

involve a commitment to qualitative as well as quantitative development.

Notes

1. It should be noted that the new administrative Friuli-Venezia Giulia region was established by the union of two different subregions, each having its own historical, cultural and economic identity. Friuli, which comprises the two provinces of Udine and Pordenone, dominates both in terms of area (91 per cent out of the 7800 km² regional area) and population (about two-thirds of the present 1,200,000 people of the region). The small Venezia Giulia subregion is what remains of what was a larger area prior to World War II, and is now composed of the provinces of Trieste (the town of Trieste—240,000 people in size—being the regional capital) and Gorizia.
2. This distinction between properties and farms also complicates analysis. Because official statistics are always based on properties, quantitative information on farms is rarely available. Nevertheless, in Friuli-Venezia Giulia—and especially in the upper plain, where owner-occupied farms predominate—less than one-third of the farms use leasehold land, and the discrepancy tends to be small.

Acknowledgements

The author wishes to thank Fiona Drew (then of Huddersfield Polytechnic) for translating this paper from the original Italian. Thanks are also due to Thelma Miller for word-processing the various manuscripts.

11 Problems of Polish agriculture

K.R. Mazurski

Historical context

The condition of Polish agriculture is today both serious and complex. The reasons for this are largely historical. Since 1945 the country has been subjected to an intensive process of nationalisation and industrialisation as part of the creation of a socialist economy. For many years, therefore, agriculture has been neglected, as attention has focused almost exclusively on the needs of industry and urbanisation. In the process, much land has been lost from agriculture, although farmland still covers 61 per cent of the national area (Buchhofer, 1982). As a result of this neglect, Polish agriculture has become increasingly backward both technologically and structurally.

The character of farming in Poland is nevertheless unusual for a socialist country, in that it is dominated by privately owned farms. This is to a great extent a consequence of the failure of collectivisation. Between 1948 and 1953, collectivism was pursued vigorously, farms being brought into the collective system often under duress and under threat of reprisals (together, in many cases, with unlawful imprisonment). In 1956, however, in the so-called 'October reversal', this period of extreme Stalinism waned, and a minor liberalisation occurred. As a result, many of the agricultural co-operatives broke up. Meeting no major reprisals, they survived as private farms, and indeed in succeeding years attracted considerable favour from the state administrations. In contrast, in the areas taken over from Germany in 1945 (e.g. Silesia, Pomerania), and where there had originally existed mainly large farms, nationalisation resulted in the creation of state farms. Today, in north-eastern Poland, socialised farms (state agricultural farms and co-operatives) cover 50–60 per cent of farmland; in western Poland 40–50 per cent. Elsewhere, however, they are far less frequent, accounting for as little as 1 per cent of the area in voivodships (the main administrative units of Poland) in the so-called 'eastern wall'—the area along the border with the Soviet Union.

Polish agriculture is thus typically a peasant system with all the implications that this brings. Farms are, for example, generally small: some 4 million farms are less than 5 ha in size, and this number has remained almost unchanged for the last 30 years. Typically, too, farm units are often highly fragmented. Until recently, there were also restrictions on the expansion of farms beyond 50 ha, and an almost complete lack of land-flow between landowners of any kind. Whereas, until 1939, Poland was a major food exporter, since 1945 it has, thus, becoming increasingly a net importer.

Since 1980, however, change has begun to occur. As a result of the activities of the Trade Union *Solidarnośc* and conflicts within the Communist Party, PZPR, the Polish economy has been affected in almost all its aspects—agriculture included. Initially, the effects on agriculture were undoubtedly negative, food markets being destabilised and food distribution systems often failing. By late 1981 the food supply situation was critical (Buchhofer, 1981). Yet, since then, the reforms have started to have effect, and on 1 January 1990 a market-based system was introduced throughout the economy. It is as yet too early to determine how agriculture will adapt to these new circumstances. What remains clear is that, while there is an urgent need to return to normal productive operations, the problems facing agriculture are still daunting.

Environmental factors

Chief amongst these problems are environmental conditions. The natural environment in Poland is seriously degraded, albeit to different degrees and in different ways in different parts of the country. The situation is most severe in Upper Silesia—in the vicinity of Katowice (the Upper Silesian industrial district) and around the copper foundries of Lower Silesia (e.g. Legnica-Głogów). Here pollution is causing almost complete devastation of the rural environment. More generally, some 27 'ecologically threatened areas' as shown in Figure 11.1 can be defined, covering about 11 per cent of Poland's land area, in which about one-third of the population (around 11 million people) live.

These environmental problems derive from a number of sources, including:

1. industrial emissions and discharges, which have been excessive due to the lack of concern for environmental impacts, both in the past and more recently (especially in the foundries of Cracow, Warsaw and Katowice, and the refineries in Gdańsk);
2. inputs of pollutants from surrounding countries, especially East Germany and Czechoslovakia; over 51 per cent of SO_2, for example, comes from external sources (Mazurski, 1986a);
3. domestic emissions.

Due to the geographic intimacy of urban and rural areas in Poland (Mazurski, 1976b) a large proportion of the ecotoxins are deposited on

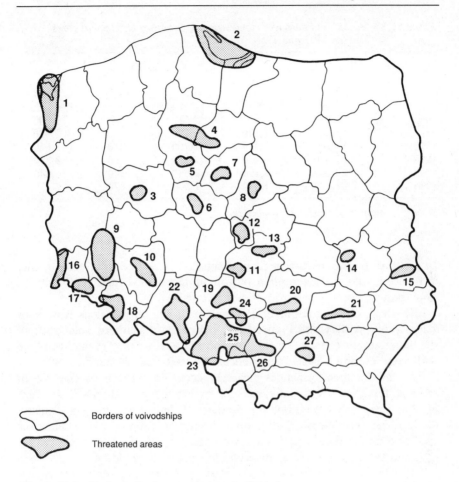

Figure 11.1 *Ecologically threatened areas in Poland*

farmland. Given that 51 per cent of Poland consists of sandy post-glacial soils with a low nutrient status and buffering capacity, the effects of these pollutants are often marked. Acid deposition represents a particular concern. The extensive use of brown coal, with a high sulphur content, results in the annual emission of around 5.2 million tonnes of SO_2—a figure which is growing rapidly. Together with high levels of input from transnational sources this is causing a rapid acidification of the soil. The most obvious consequences have been forest damage (Mazurski, 1990). Between 1967 and 1986, for example, the area of Polish forest showing detectable damage increased from 1,800 km^2 to 7,300 km^2—some 8 per cent of the total as shown in Table 11.1, mainly in the south of the country (see Figure 11.2). Agricultural production is also affected, in the Upper Silesian industrial district crop yields are typically reduced by 20 per cent; however: around other urban areas a loss of only 5–7 per cent occurs.

Table 11.1 *Health conditions of Poland's forests, according to damaged zones between 1967 and 1986*

Year	Total area	Zones km^2			
		I	II	III	Total
1967	78,000	—	—	—	1,800
1971	86,520	1,140	790	460	2,390
1976	87,260	2,350	1,100	210	3,660
1980	87,540	2,470	1,090	260	3,820
1983	88,200	4,190	1,990	300	6,540
1986	88,470	5,010	2,000	370	7,370

Note: I — lightly damaged; III — hardly

Source: Mazurski, 1986a

In addition to this reduction in productivity, it is clear that crop quality is reduced, whilst consumption of contaminated foodstuffs represents an important means of exposure of humans to toxins.

Elsewhere, other environmental problems exist. Most serious is perhaps soil erosion, as shown in Figure 11.3, especially in southern Poland where the mountainous terrain, loessic soils and seasonally heavy rainfall combine with poor cropping practices to encourage soil loss (Mazurski, 1989a).

Poor management practices similarly occur in relation to the use of artificial fertilisers. Nationally, rates of application are only 60–70 per cent of west European levels, but the presence of light soils, the poor quality of fertiliser production (with high levels of impurities), careless or excessive applications and inadequate conservation of soil organic matter combine to cause structural deterioration and soil pollution.

These problems are further aggravated by the poor sewerage infrastructure and inadequate water supply network in many rural areas. Today, over 70 per cent of farms still rely on their own wells for water, and 76 per cent of these are contaminated either by chemicals or, more commonly, by bacteriological pollutants. Recent declines in rainfall and increased water abstraction have also contributed to a fall in the regional water table of 40–100 cm in the last 10 years. As a consequence, many villages now depend on tankers for their water supply. Water resource problems therefore inhibit agricultural production and pose a significant health threat in rural areas.

Social factors

The years of decline in rural communities, and the overemphasis on industrialisation, have caused wider social changes in Poland. Chief amongst these has been rural depopulation, as farming families have

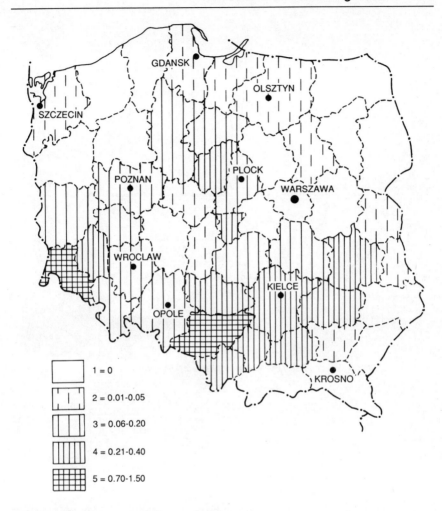

Figure 11.2 *Health conditions of Polish forests (% of areas damaged)*

migrated to the towns. Whereas only 30 per cent of the population was urbanised in 1945, today over 60 per cent live in towns. Wide salary and price differentials between town and country—giving rise to low levels of saving for farmers—the scarcity of domestic goods in rural areas and positive assistance for the families of farmers who move to towns have all encouraged the process.

Migration has, as elsewhere, been most rapid amongst the young. As a result, the average age of the rural population is rising, farmers are often forced to run their farms alone, without help from their sons, and as a consequence productivity has tended to fall. At the same time, low pensions and difficulties in selling farms—often resulting in the need to transfer the land to the state in return for a pension—have created low

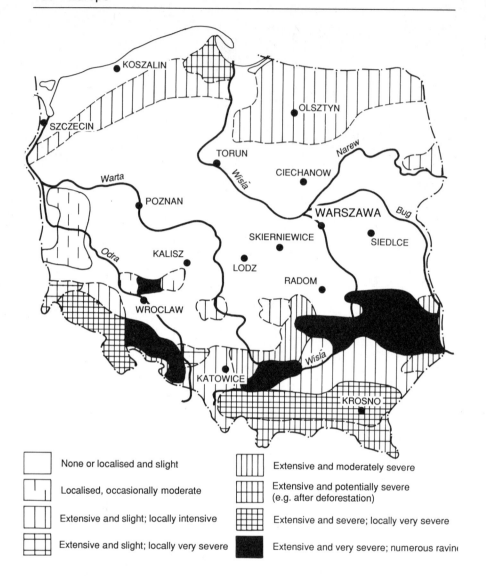

Figure 11.3 *Extent of soil erosion in Poland*

standards of living for many rural communities, especially the old. None the less, some exceptions do occur. In areas such as the Poznań region, for example, state farms have helped to improve productivity and raise standards of living. Inevitably, much depends upon the attitudes and aptitudes of the people concerned, independent of the political context.

Related to these changes has been a marked deterioration in the status of women in rural economy. Lacking support from their children, farmers have increasingly had to rely on their wives, not as partners in the running of the farm, but as basic labourers. Women have thus become responsible not only for housekeeping but for fundamental and menial farm work, such as tending livestock. The lot of many women in rural areas has thus become definably harder, with increased physical toil and reduced opportunities to work outside the farm.

Economic factors

One of the main obstacles facing any attempt to rationalise farming and increase productivity in Poland is the fragmentation of farms. This problem is most acute in central and south-eastern Poland (Olszewski, 1985). In these regions, farms of no more than 1–1.5 ha not untypically comprise as many as 100 separate fields; 20–30 per cent of these are often left uncultivated because of their distance or isolation. This situation has arisen as a result of overpopulation, and the strong tradition of partible inheritance. The small, fragmented farms which now exist clearly provide an inadequate resource base for many farmers. Not surprisingly, they have, thus, turned to alternative, rural industry for a source of secondary employment.

This situation—of small farm size, fragmented holdings and dual employment—has contributed to the lack of agricultural mechanisation. To support the large, state farms, plants have developed producing heavy agricultural machinery. This is totally unsuitable for the small, private farmstead. Even if lighter machinery were available, however, it is unlikely that many farms would be able to afford its purchase. Without considerable structural reorganisation, therefore, mechanisation of Polish agriculture will continue to be minimal (Morgan, 1989).

With the resurgence of democracy, since 1989, and the recognition of the disparity between urban and rural areas, attempts are now being made to redress the situation. Opportunities for any real progress remained limited, however, so long as the state monopoly of the agricultural market persisted, and while market prices for agricultural produce were kept artificially low. Faced with growing public pressure, the Communist government under Mieczyslaw F. Rakowski thus attempted to open up the agricultural market, in August 1989. The immediate result was a rapid rise in prices, without any significant improvement in delivery. Whilst small farmers had the capacity to sell directly to the public, they had no opportunity to increase production; on the other hand, because of the volume of goods involved, large producers still had to operate through established, state monopolies.

With the formation of the coalition government, under Tedeusz Mazowieki, in September 1989, a programme of more radical economic reform was initiated. This abandoned production targets for many goods and agricultural products. The result, however, has again been a sharp

THE LIBRARY
BISHOP BURTON COLLEGE
BEVERLEY HU17 8QG
TEL: 0964 550481 Ex: 227

increase in prices, with industrial prices rising by 200–300 per cent or more. The implications for agriculture are serious. Farmers have cut back on their already limited purchases of machinery, fertiliser and other inputs, and yields are consequently expected to fall.

In a true market economy, these changes might be expected to lead to a rise in price due to shortages of supply and thus some compensatory feedback to farm incomes. In the current state of the Polish economy this seems unlikely. Prices of other consumer goods are high. Incomes, on the other hand, are being restrained as a part of the government's anti-inflation policy. Unemployment is also beginning to develop, with around 400,000 out of work by May 1990. As a result, disposable income is falling, and the demand for meat and processed foodstuffs has declined. At the same time, the evolution of retail trading has meant that increased administrative and middlemen charges are being added to market prices, further squeezing farm revenues.

In the light of the surplus supply, processing companies are reducing their purchase of farm goods. Paradoxically, therefore, the shops are now full of food, yet deliveries have declined, and farmers are unable to sell their output. In an attempt to combat the situation, the government is now intervening to purchase livestock. In the three months to April 1990, 45,000 tonnes of meat were stockpiled in this way.

Detectable changes in the food market are nevertheless occurring. In particular, the development of street and mobile trading, although primitive, is helping to break down the trade monopolies by eliminating middlemen. Prices are as much as 50 per cent lower than those in the formal market place, thereby encouraging demand. The competition provided is also forcing state shops to reduce prices. Gradually, a more stable and balanced price structure is thus evolving, which, in time, may help to stimulate supply and reinvigorate Polish agriculture.

Even so, investment in agriculture remains low. Prices of machinery and other agricultural inputs are high and interest rates increasing. Inflation is falling—from 37 per cent per month in January 1990 to 25 per cent in February, 7 per cent in April and less than 1 per cent in May—but it is still a major cause for concern. Uncertainty about sales similarly deters farmers from the commitment to invest. Long-term improvements in production are thus being jeopardised. In response, in late February 1990, the government introduced a system of special agricultural credits covering, *inter alia*, arable land and machines.

At the time of writing, the situation of the state farms and co-operatives is less clear, for annual accounts are only produced in mid-year. The abandonment of production targets, and the need for major social provisions for the workers involved, will almost certainly highlight their general inefficiency. Widespread bankruptcy and closure are anticipated. As yet, policies for coping with these developments are lacking.

Conclusions

From what has been said, it is clear that agriculture—the foundation of rural life in Poland and a major component of the country's economy—is entering a critical period as the country adjusts to a market economy. Amongst many other needs, two general and fundamental changes are essential. The first is the establishment of new structures for the purchase, distribution and marketing of food. The second—and perhaps even more fundamental—is the restructuring of agriculture itself. Farms must be rationalised, enlarged and made more specialised. Levels of intensification must rise. Only in this way will the living standards in rural areas be raised. Such changes will, however, carry with them a substantial cost. The character of rural society in Poland will change; already, the government has warned of the need to close small and inefficient farms. Impacts on the environment are also likely to increase. Development will not take place without problems. In the years ahead, however, agriculture in Poland must adopt west European methods if it is to survive, and if it is to compete with—or find a place within—the European Community.

References

Buchhofer, E., 1981, 'Polen in der Ernährungskrise', *Geographie Heute*, **8**, 2–10

Buchhofer, E., 1982, 'Flächennutzungsveränderungen in Polen', *Marburger Geographischen Schriften*, **88**, 145–74

Mazurski, K.R., 1986a, 'The destruction of forests in the Polish Sudetes Mountains by industrial emissions', *Forest Ecology and Management*, **17**, 303–15

Mazurski, K.R., 1986b, 'Stadt und landwirtschaftliche Gebiete—sanitärökologische Zusammenhänge', *Forum Städte-Hygiene*, **37**, 262–4

Mazurski, K.R., 1988, *Antropogeniczna destrukcja srodowiska rolniczego Dolnego Slaska*, Wrocław: Akademia Rolnicza, pp. 14 (Eng. sum)

Mazurski, K.R., 1989a, 'Counteracting soil erosion in Poland', *Applied Geography*, **9**, 115–21

Mazurski, K.R., 1989b, 'The destruction of the agricultural environment in Lower Silesia, Poland', *Biological Wastes*, **27**, 245–55

Mazurski, K.R., 1989c, 'Wasserprobleme der polnischen Landwirtschaft', *Z. f. Kulturtechnik and Landentwicklung*, **30**, 261–7

Mazurski, K.R., 1990, 'Industrial pollution: the threat to Polish forests', *Ambio*, **19**, 70–4

Morgan, W.B., 1989, 'Recent government policy and private agriculture in Poland', *Resource Management and Optimism*, **6**, 291–305

Olszewski, T., 1985, 'Die Agrarregionen Polens', *Osteuropa*, **12**, 908–15

12 Conflicts caused by imbalances in forest policy and practice in the Basque Country
Helen Groome

Introduction

Forest policy in the Basque Country (in the Basque language, Euskadi) has changed dramatically in recent decades. As in other countries, it has had to adapt to changing scientific knowledge, changing economic conditions and demands, changing technologies and changing public awareness and fashions regarding product quality and environmental issues. The effects have been far from equitable, for different interest groups (scientists, farmers, industrialists, naturalists, foresters, politicians etc.) have not always been able to exert the same pressure on policy-makers, nor gain equally from the results. The clear hegemony of concrete economic interests in Basque forest policy and practice has therefore led to numerous conflicts, both within the forest sector itself and between forest and other interests.

Numerous external processes have influenced Basque forest development. These include:

i.   the gradual penetration of market forces in rural Euskadi, with the need for ever shorter investment cycles, product specialisation and the shift from local-rural to external-urban demand satisfaction;
ii.   rapid industrialisation from the nineteenth century onwards, with an unprecedentedly high demand for wood;
iii.   common land privatisation (enclosures); and
iv.   changing degrees of home rule.

Simultaneously, a whole series of developments within the forest sector itself have influenced the evolution of woodland management in the Basque Country. These include:

i.   the rapid rise in demand for cellulose-based products (Hutchinson, 1953; FAO, 1964);

ii. the introduction of, and experimentation with, quick-growing species—basically eucalyptus and *Pinus insignis* (Adan de Yarza, 1913; Mesanza, 1987);
iii. the mechanisation of forest practices;
iv. the introduction of chemical pesticides and fertilisers.

Faced with the dilemma of how to guarantee sufficient forest resources for a growing population, two schools of thought developed amongst foresters during the twentieth century. On the one hand, there was a strong tendency—most clearly reflected in the 1966 World Forest Congress held in Madrid—which argued in favour of obtaining 'maximum profitability' as shown in Figure 12.1a, through what was termed 'orchard silviculture'. This required the employment of heavy machinery, chemicals, monocultures, quick-growing species, etc. (Susaeta, 1966). Crematistic values dominated, forests offering few positive externalities such as soil conservation, landscape harmony or cultural benefits, whilst society as a whole had to assume the costs of negative externalities such as soil erosion, altered hydrological cycles and insect infestation. It was an approach which thereby engendered conflict between the various users of the land resource.

The alternative approach, which received growing attention in later World Forest Congresses (Secretariado VII Congreso Forestal Mundial, 1972a and 1972b; Clawson, 1975; Synott and Kemp, 1976; Nair, 1983, Pardo, 1985; Sholto Douglas and Hart, 1985), opted for maximisation of the welfare benefits to be gained from forest policy (see Figure 12.1b). This underlined not only economic but also cultural, social and environmental needs. It thus attempted to minimise negative and maximise positive externalities. 'Natural silvicultural techniques' (Leibundgut, 1960) were promoted, harmonising technological advances with physical and social potential: natural vegetation regeneration; species diversification; multi-functional woodlands; and integrated methods to combat insects. Clearly, such a model of forest development maximises the number of interests that benefit from woodland policy, through horizontal integration, and thus avoids or reduces conflict (Figure 12.1c).

In general, during the twentieth century the objective guiding forestry in the Basque Country has been the search for maximum profitability. This has been conducted regardless of social, cultural or environmental costs, or, indeed, of given industrial needs. Landowners looked for maximum rents whilst certain industries gained cheap raw materials. As is outlined below, the resulting practices have provoked numerous conflicts within rural Euskadi.

Before, however, considering such conflicts, it is worth briefly mentioning the geographical and historical variations in Euskadi, for these have resulted in regional differences in the impacts of forest policy (Figure 12.2). A distinction should be made between the northern coastal and

a)

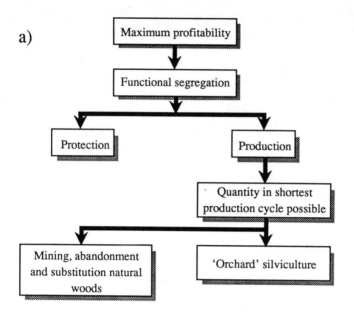

b)

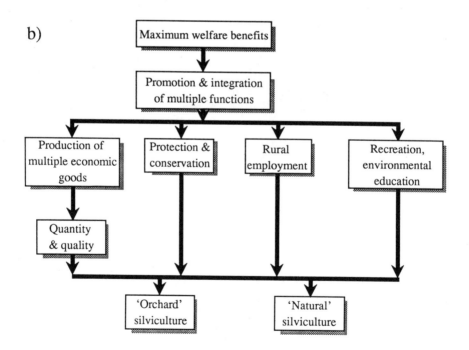

Figure 12.1   *a. Forest policy model promoting maximum profitability*
                  b. Forest policy model promoting maximum welfare benefits

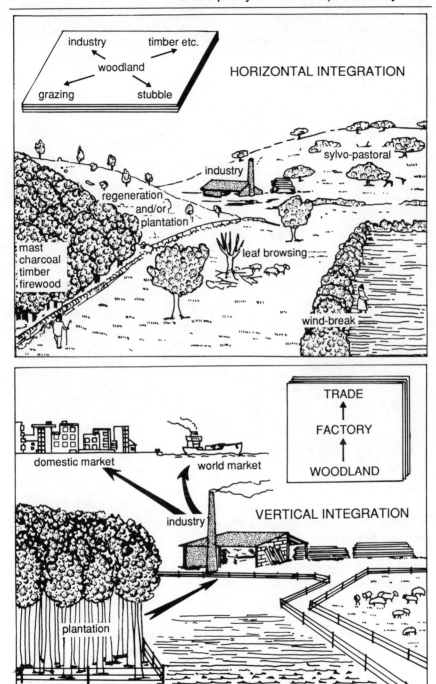

Figure 12.1 *c. Vertically and horizontally integrated woodland management*
Source: Author's design

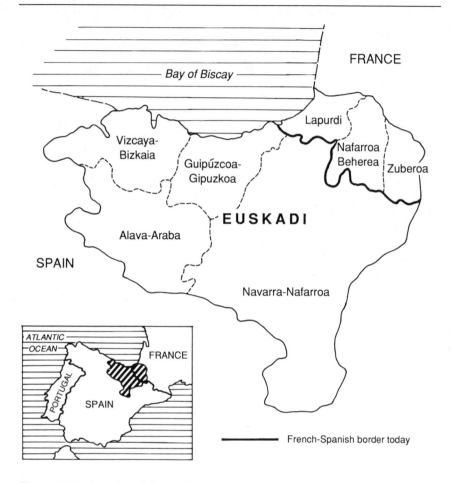

Figure 12.2 *Location of the southern Basque Country*

Pyrenean areas, which are typically Atlantic in climate, and the southern areas of Alava and Navarra which are characterised by Mediterranean conditions. Annual rainfall diminishes towards the south-east, whilst summer temperatures rise. The southern-most regions of Navarra and parts of Alava also possess less abrupt relief. Basque forestry has thus been characterised by its diversity (Llorca, 1984; Ruiz Urrestarazu, 1986). Differing degrees of self-government (Alava and Navarra retained their own forest administration whilst Vizcaya and Guipuzcoa were administered from Madrid) and differing intensities of urban-industrial development (strongest in Vizcaya and Guipuzcoa) have also contributed to variations in forest policy and practice.

A rough division can therefore be made between Vizcaya and Guipuzcoa, on the one hand, and Alava and Navarra on the other. The latter also retained a far higher percentage of common lands following the enclosure and privatisation processes of the nineteenth century and, simultaneously, a larger area of natural woodland vegetation, characterised by beech, oak, hornbeam, ash, etc. Vizcaya and Guipuzcoa, conversely, lost many common lands, witnessed a far greater degree of deforestation and became the major focus of forest monocultures employing quick-growing species (Echeverria Ballarin, 1933a and 1933b); Ministerio de Agricultura, 1986; Eusko Jaurlaritza, 1988). These circumstances explain why the conflicts mentioned in this article are most evident in Vizcaya and Guipuzcoa.

Environmental conflicts

The main environmental conflicts currently observed in the Basque forest sector are due to the low number of species and the type of silvicultural techniques promoted by forest policy. As Figure 12.3 reveals, Vizcaya and Guipuzcoa face the greatest problem. These provinces contain 85.7 per cent of the 183,084 ha of monocultures employing quick-growing species: one single species, the Monterrey pine, accounts for 65.6 per cent and 56.5 per cent of the total forests area of Vizcaya and Guipuzcoa respectively (40 and 34 per cent of their total surface area). Plantations with slow-growing species represent less than 1 per cent of the total afforestation undertaken in these provinces since the start of the century, despite the fact that many such species provide good quality wood. Species diversity is, however, greater in Navarra and Alava where natural, slow-growing broadleaf and coniferous woodland still predominates.

This reliance on artificial monocultures in much of the Basque Country has had a range of ecological and wider environmental impacts. One of the most important has been the depletion of the genetic resource. Current planting policy, the lack of research into native species in Euskadi, and a lack of management in general, have together led to a gradual degeneration of the natural woodlands which do survive. Today, good quality slow-growing conifer and deciduous seedlings are not available in Basque tree nurseries and have to be imported (for example, from Belgium for new beech plantations in Navarra and Guipuzcoa), with the added risk of importing new diseases with the plants.

In addition, lack of rural planning norms has led to the gradual spread of continuous pine plantations with no fire breaks to separate them. This is an all important factor in the rapid propagation of the forest fires that affected 25,000 ha in Vizcaya in December 1989.

Various environmentally-damaging silvicultural practices are also associated with these forests. The plantations, for example, are highly susceptible to insect damage and disease. In response, blanket applications of chemical insecticides are often made: previously DDT, but now Diflubenzuron with a petrol base. (An integrated biological approach to disease and insect control involving species diversification, insectivorous

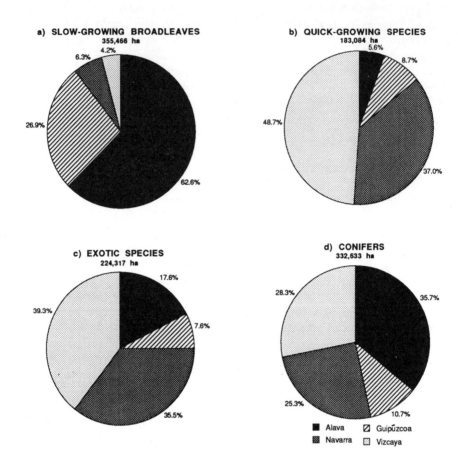

Figure 12.3 *Species composition of woodland areas, by province (percentage)*

Note: A — Alava
    G — Guipuzcoa
    N — Navarra
    V — Vizcaya

Source: Based on data from Ministerio de Agricultura, 1986; Eusko Jaurlaritza, 1988

birds etc. has yet to be seriously considered.) Similarly, short-rotation monocultures cause greater, specific nutrient depletion. To counteract this, synthetic fertilisers are now being applied at an ever greater scale in Basque plantations. Clear-cutting, terracing and downslope ploughing with heavy machinery are also increasingly carried out, as forest practices become more mechanised.

All these practices have far-reaching environmental effects. Runoff and erosion are encouraged, clogging ditches and channels, altering hydrological patterns and carrying pesticides and fertiliser residues into streams. Poor methods of application also allow drift of pesticides and fertilisers onto neighbouring lands. Extensive damage is thus occurring to what has been until now one of the least agriculturally polluted areas of Europe.

Economic conflicts

The economic conflicts caused by Basque forest policy are equally varied. Firstly, plantation encroachment in common lands is gradually leaving hill farmers without vital resources for livestock. This not only blocks access to water points and closes traditional tracks, but—given the lack of planning and public participation in forest decision-making processes—may lead to direct confrontation. Additionally, the high density of forest rides being introduced (currently with EC grants) is causing a high net loss of land resources.

Secondly, inadequate distances have been stipulated to regulate the land left between plantation and pasturelands. This is causing serious microclimatic effects due to shading in an already damp climate, and due to sapling emergence and leaf fall. Thirdly, insect invasions (such as *Thaumetopoea pitycampa*) also directly affect day-to-day farm work and cause serious health problems. The massive application of chemical products to combat such insects may have as yet unidentified secondary and long-term effects on livestock, crops, pasturelands and hydrological resources.

As far as industrial interests are concerned, the type of forestry practised in Vizcaya and Guipuzcoa has directly benefited those industries employing low-quality wood (such as paper and chipboard industries which reduce all wood to their basic fibres) and completely marginalised those industries employing large sized, good quality timber (basically the furniture and building trade). Quick-growing species felled after short rotations contain much juvenile wood of low structural quality (Senft *et al.*, 1985; Walford, 1985) and are therefore best suited for cellulose or packaging purposes. Furniture makers and builders need mechanically resistant wood, the plantation of which has been abandoned due to their long growth cycle. The low quality of most Monterrey pine wood—which accounts for 79 per cent of all wood produced in Euskadi—has eventually led to research into the species' genetic improvement, pruning and thinning techniques, and better logging methods, in order to improve market prices and diversify its use (Michel, 1984; INIA-CTM, 1988). There is in fact a determined effort to introduce the Monterrey pine into good quality wood markets. Whilst in itself a laudable change, this policy may nevertheless have adverse repercussions. In particular, it may deter the introduction of slow-growing species such as beech and oak, for which the climatic conditions in the Basque country are particularly suited. Calls by quality timber-using firms for changes in plantation policy have been made, but without effect (Piera, 1985). Meanwhile, mining of tropical forests, and the limits placed on the export of logs, mean that Basque and Spanish furniture makers can no longer rely on such sources for their future raw materials (Queen, 1949; Robins, 1981).

Afforestation in the Navarra and Alava region is not keeping pace with felling. As a result, the forests which supply good quality timber are gradually being depleted. In addition, the lack of research into species improvement means that wood quality is often inferior to that of other European sources.

Current economic conditions make grants increasingly necessary even for short rotation plantations (Elvira Martin and Pellon Arregui, 1976, Banco de Bilbao, 1986; Kreysa and Last, 1987). This is revealed by decrees such as 2/1988 Grants for the Promotion of Forest Production and Conservation in Bizkaia. Narrow economic margins mean woodland owners rarely undertake necessary silvicultural management tasks such as pruning, thinning and undergrowth clearance. Consequently, product quality is reduced (knotty wood), while the risk of fires (dry biomass accumulation) and insect infestation is increased. At the same time, the possibility of silvopastoral exploitation is limited since controlled woodland pasturage is not encouraged.

Various interest groups are thus now calling for plantations and forestry related grants to be linked to obligatory management plans, designed to give specific economic, environmental and social benefits. The argument is also being advanced that, without such plans, current forestry policies and practice will lead to intergenerational conflicts. In their absence the wider, longer-term interests of future generations are being sacrificed for the narrow, short-term economic interests of the present as the soil resource is depleted and lower productivity land is handed down.

Cultural conflicts

Because of the complex, often subjective nature of the problems involved, the cultural conflicts posed by forestry policy are harder to evaluate. Recent policies have undeniably led to important changes in traditional, historically important, vegetational associations: the oak is a clear example, representing as it does the very existence of the Basque nation. They have also resulted in the replacement of traditional multi-functional landscapes by monocultures.

At the same time forest policy and practice is enhancing those processes which encourage rural depopulation and unemployment. Indeed, at the very moment when the EC is calling for the maintenance of the rural population (Comision de las Comunidades Europeas, 1988), that in Euskadi is declining. As a consequence, not only people, but tradition and knowledge are being lost.

Towards a balanced forestry policy

Woodland management is clearly a social and environmental activity as much as an economic one, for woodlands are a fundamental part of both cultural and natural systems. Future forest policies should be guided by recognition of this fact. To achieve it, and to avoid the conflicts which otherwise occur, four basic steps are necessary in the Basque country:

1. Multi-disciplinary rural planning, with the participation of all interest groups, is indispensable in order to reduce intersectorial conflicts and lay the foundations for physically sound land management and exploitation.
2. Species diversification is necessary to reduce conflicts of raw material supply, increase market flexibility, reduce environment conflicts and enhance cultural and historical awareness and harmony. Such a policy clearly calls for a new approach to forest grant aid, guaranteeing an annual income for landowners (private and public) to compensate the long production cycle of natural woodland management or plantations, particularly in the case of slow-growing species.
3. Silvicultural techniques should be adjusted to the particular physical conditions of Atlantic and Mediterranean Euskadi in order to reduce both intergenerational and environmental conflicts.
4. Research into species characteristics, genetic improvement and wood quality is urgent, above all for native, slow-growing species, given their complete marginalisation in the past.

The forest resources of areas such as this are vital, not only for the benefit of the present generation, but for the economic, social, cultural and environmental health of future generations as well. It is a resource which needs and deserves more sensitive and far-sighted policy.

References

Adan de Yarza, 1913, La repoblacion forestal en el Pais Vasco, recopilado en *Euskadi Forestal*, 1984, Asociacion de Forestalistas del Pais Vasco, p. 24

Banco de Bilbao, 1986, 'Los deficits del sector maderero y papelero y el paro', *Actualidad Forestal del Pais Vasco*, **101–2**, 4–9

Clawson, M., 1975, *Forests for whom and for what?*, John Hopkins University Press, Baltimore, p. 175

Comision de las Comunidades Europeas, 1988, *El futuro del mundo rural*, Luxemburgo, p. 71

Echeverria Ballarin, I., 1933a, 'Fomento de la repoblacion forestal entre los particulares y empresas' en Asociacion de Ingenieros de Montes, *Aportaciones a la politica forestal de Espana*, 93–124, Rivadeneyra SA, Madrid, p. 318

Echeverria Ballarin, I., 1933b, 'El interes privado y la repoblacion de los montes', *Montes e Industria*, 28: 88–91

Elvira Martin, L.M. and Pellon Arregui, R., 1976, 'Analisis de metodos de trabajo en los aprovechamientos de *Pinus insignis* en el norte de Espana', *Montes*, 32 (185): 255–64

Eusko Jaurlaritza, 1988, *Baso Inbentarioa, EKMA, 1986*, Vitoria

FAO, 1964, *European timber trends and prospects. A new appraisal, 1950–1975*, New York, p. 233

Hutchinson, L.M. 1953, 'La calidad o la cantidad en la produccion forestal del futuro, *Montes*, 9 (50): 159–66

INIA-CTM, 1988, *Propiedades y tecnologia de la madera de Pinus radiata del Pais Vasco*, Victoria, p. 231

Kreysa, J. and Last, F.T., 1987, *Problems and opportunities for forestry in the EEC—Implications for research and development*, FAST Occasional Paper No. 165, Commission of the European Communities, p. 67

Leibundgut, H., 1960, ' "Orchard" versus "Naturalistic" silviculture', *Proceedings V World Forestry Congress (Seattle)*: 404–8

Llorca, A., 1984, 'Evolucion del bosque natural en el Pais Vasco', *Jornadas sobre la Defensa de la Naturaleza en la Cornisa Cantabrica*, Marzo

Mesanza Ruiz de Salas, B., 1987, 'Posibilidades de la Cornisa del Golfo de Vizcaya', *Montes* (nueva serie), 16: 5–7

Michel, M., 1984, *Anteproyecto de un programade mejora genetica del pino insignis en la Communidad Autonoma Vasca*, Gobierno Vasco

Ministerio de Agricultura, 1986, *Mapa de cultivos y approvechamientos de la Provincia de Navarra*, Madrid, Ministerio de Agricultura

Nair, P.K.R., 1983, 'Multiple land-use and agroforestry in *Better Crops for Food*, Ciba Foundation Symposium 97, Pitman Books, London, pp. 101–15

Pardo, R.D., 1985, 'Forestry for people: can it work?', *Journal of Forestry*, 83 (12): 732–41

Piera, A., 1985, Respuestas al cuestionario remitido por meimbros del Comite de Participacion Publica convenido por la CIMA, Mayo

Queen, E.W., 1949, 'La integracion de las industrias forestales', *Montes*, 5 (27): 239–41

Robins, J., 1981, 'Tropical timber: logging the losses', *South*, pp. 75–7

Ruiz Urrestarazu, M.M., 1986, 'Especies empleadas en las repoblaciones forestales del Pais Vasco', *Actualidad Forestal del Pais Vasco*, 102–102: 2–4

Secretariado VII Congreso Forestal Mundial, 1972a, *Declaracion del VII Congreso Forestal Mundial*, Buenos Aires, p. 3

Secretariado VII Congreso Forestal Mundial, 1972b, *Informes de las Comisiones del Congreso*. Buenos Aires, p. 51

Senft, J.F., Bendtsen, B.A. and Galligan, W.L., 1985, 'Weakwood. Fastgrown trees make problem lumber', *Journal of Forestry*, 83 (8): 476–84

Sholto Douglas, R. and Hart, R., 1985, *Forest farming*, Intermediate Technology Publications, London, p. 207

Susaeta, E., 1966, 'Alternativas entre bosques naturales y plantaciones', *Actas VI Congreso Forestal Mundial (Madrid)*, pp. 3877–85

Synott, T.J. and Kemp, R.H., 1976, 'Choosing the best silvicultural system', *Unasylva*, **18** (112–113): 74–9

Walford, G.B., 1985, 'In-grade testing of timber from young radiata pine trees', *New Zealand Forest Research Institute Report (1985)*, **61**

13 EC legislation on the environment and rural areas, March 1989- September 1990

David J. Briggs

1. Commission Regulation (EEC) No. 610/89 of 9 March 1989 amending Council Regulation (EEC) No. 3626/82 on the implementation in the Community of the Convention on international trade in endangered species of wild fauna and flora. *OJEC L66*, 24.

Updates CITES regulation.

2. Commission Decision of 10 May 1989 selecting rural areas eligible to receive Community assistance under objective 5(b) as defined by Council Regulation (EEC) No. 2052/88. (89/426/EEC). *OJEC L198*, 1–15.

Lists areas eligible to receive assistance from structural funds.

3. Council Regulation (EEC) No. 1609/89 of 29 May 1989 amending, with regard to the afforestation of agricultural land, Regulation (EEC) No. 797/85 on improving the efficiency of agricultural structures. *OJEC L165*, 1–2.

Extends aid for afforestation and increases levels of compensation.

4. Council Regulation (EEC) No. 1610/89 of 29 May 1989 laying down provisions for implementing Regulation (EEC) No. 4256/88 as regards the scheme to develop and optimally utilise woodlands in rural areas in the Community. *OJEC L165*, 3–4.

Defines types of woodland scheme to be supported from the Structural Fund, with the objective of diversifying agriculture and improving environmental protection.

5. Council Regulation (EEC) No. 1613/89 of 29 May 1989 amending Regulation (EEC) No. 3528/86 on the protection of the Community's

forests against atmospheric pollution. *OJEC L165*, 8-9.

Introduces technical and administrative amendments, and increases financial provision.

6. Council Regulation (EEC) No. 1614/89 of 29 May 1989 amending Regulation (EEC) No. 3529/86 on protection of the Community's forests against fire. *OJEC L165*, 10-11.

Supplements and strengthens protection measures and increases financial provision.

7. Council Regulation (EEC) No. 1615/89 of 29 May 1989 establishing a European Forestry Information and Communications System (Efics). *OJEC L165*, 12-13.

Establishes information system covering data on forest use, processing, marketing and afforestation.

8. Council Directive of 21 June 1989 amending Directive 80/779/EEC on air quality limit values and guide values for sulphur dioxide and suspended particles. (89/427/EEC). *OJEC L201*, 53-5.

Redefines limit values and measurement procedures for SO_2 and suspended particle concentrations in the atmosphere.

9. Council Directive of 18 July 1989 amending with regard to European emission standards for cars below 1.4 litres, Directive 70/220/EEC on the approximation of the laws of the Member States relating to measures to be taken against air pollution by emissions from motor vehicles. (89/458/EEC). *OJEC L211*.

Specifies stricter emission standards for carbon monoxide, unburnt hydrocarbon and nitrogen oxides.

10. Commission Directive of 17 July 1989 adapting to technical progress Council Directives 70/157/EEC, 70/220/EEC, 72/245/EEC, 72/306/EEC, 80/1268/EEC and 80/1269/EEC relating to motor vehicles. (89/491/EEC). *OJEC L238*, 43-9.

Redefines scope and test procedures set out in previous Directives on unleaded petrol.

11. Commission Regulation (EEC) No. 2295/89 of 4 October 1989 amending Regulation (EEC) No. 696/87 laying down certain detailed rules

for the implementation of Council Regulation (EEC) No. 3528/86 on the protection of the Community forests against atmospheric pollution (inventories, network, reports). *OJEC L287*, 11–12.

Redefines forests to be covered by the inventory; redefines procedures to be used when sample point is inaccessible: redefines procedure for classification of defoliation and discolouration.

12. Council Decision of 20 November 1989 on two specific research and development programmes in the field of the environment—STEP and EPOCH (1989–92). (89/625/EEC). *OJEC L359*, 9–22.

Establishes research programmes into science and technology for environmental protection (STEP) and European programme on climatology and natural hazards (EPOCH).

13. Commission Decision of 14 December 1989 amending Annexe 1 to Council Decision 77/795/EEC of 12 December 1977 establishing a common procedure for the exchange of information on the quality of surface freshwater in the Community. (90/2/EEC). *OJEC L1*, 20–2.

Revises sampling stations in France (7 sites), Italy (3 sites), Portugal (2 sites replaced, 1 deleted), Germany (1 site).

14. Council Regulation (EEC) No. 4003/89 of 21 December 1989 amending Regulation (EEC) No. 3955/87 on the conditions governing imports of agricultural products originating in third countries following the accident at the Chernobyl nuclear power station. *OJEC L382*, 4.

Extends regulation to 31 March 1990.

15. Commission Regulation (EEC) No. 197/90 of 17 January 1990 amending Council Regulation (EEC) No. 3626/82 on the implementation of the Convention on international trade in endangered species of wild fauna and flora. *OJEC L29*, 1–61.

Revises list of species covered by Regulation.

16. Council Decision of 26 February 1990 adopting a specific Community research and technological development programme in the field of competitiveness of agriculture and management of agricultural resources (1989–93) (90/84/EEC). *OJEC L58*, 9–14.

Establishes research programme on conversion, diversification and extensification of production; cost reduction; protection of the rural environment; product quality; socio-economic aspects of less developed regions; information dissemination.

17. Council Decision of 22 March 1990 amending Decision 85/338/EEC on the adoption of the Commission work programme concerning an experimental project for gathering, co-ordinating and ensuring the consistency of information on the state of the environment and natural resources in the Community. *OJEC L81*, 38.

Extends CORINE Programme for 2 years and increases funding to 10.5 m ECU.

18. Council Decision of 22 March 1990 concerning the conclusion of the Agreement between the Federal Republic of Germany and the European Economic Community, on the one hand, and the Republic of Austria, on the other, on co-operation over management of water resources in the Danube Basin. *OJEC L90,9*, 16–25.

Establishes procedures for co-operation, including exchange of data/expertise; joint scientific projects; co-ordination of monitoring procedures; establishment of Standing Committee on Management of Water Resources to recommend harmonisation of standards and control measures.

19. Council Regulation (EEC) No. 752/90 of 26 March 1990 amending Regulation (EEC) No. 797/85 as regards the rates of reimbursement for the set-aside of arable land. *OJEC L83*, 1–2.

Redefines levels of aid and commits member states to publicise scheme adequately.

20. Council Directive of 23 April 1990 on the contained use of genetically modified micro-organisms. (90/219/EEC). *OJEC L117*, 1–14.

Sets out measures for contained use of genetically modified micro-organisms with a view to protecting human health and the environment.

21. Council Regulation (EEC) No. 1210/90 of 7 May 1990 on the establishment of the European Environment Agency and the European environment information and observation network. *OJEC L120*, 1–6.

Agrees establishment of a European Environment Agency with responsibility to gather information on the state of the environment (especially in the areas of air quality and atmospheric emissions, water quality and

THE LIBRARY
BISHOP BURTON COLLEGE
BEVERLEY HU17 8QG
TEL: 0964 550481 Ex: 227

water resources, soil conditions, wildlife, biotopes, land use, natural resources, waste management, noise, hazardous chemicals and coastal protection).

14 Towards a European Environment Agency

David J. Briggs

Introduction

Since the adoption of its first Action Programme on the Environment, in 1973, the European Community's environmental policy has grown to become one of the dominant influences on rural areas in Europe. Quality objectives and standards agreed within the framework of this policy have often helped to shape national policies (e.g. on stream water quality, air quality). Specific legislation on environmental protection has led to direct action to conserve wildlife species and habitats: the so-called Bird Directive, adopted in 1979 (79/409/EEC), for example, has helped in the establishment of a network of over 600 protected bird sites in the European Community, many of which were previously unprotected at national level. Yet the policy has also had wider effects. The emphasis and publicity given to environmental issues (e.g. through the European Year of the Environment) has contributed to the evolution of public awareness, which itself has influenced national policy, not least in the United Kingdom. And attempts to integrate an environmental dimension into other EC policies, such as those on agriculture and the regions, have encouraged the development of more sensitive sectoral and structural policies relating to the rural environment (e.g. the Regulations on extensification and set-aside, adopted in 1988, and the proposal for control of nitrate pollution submitted in December 1988).

The political processes involved in formulating these various policy actions, and then implementing them in the member states are complex and often prolonged (e.g. Haigh, 1987; Johnson and Corcelle, 1989). At the start they were also frequently based on only a partial knowledge of environmental conditions and the distribution and magnitude of problems throughout the Community—a weakness which has undoubtedly contributed to the difficulties in policy formulation and, at times, the inefficiency of their effects. Improved environmental information has thus been a crucial need. In recent years a number of efforts have been made to provide an adequate information base for Community environmental policy, culminating in the recent agreement to establish a European Environment Agency. This paper examines the background to this development and assesses its ability to meet the Community's information needs.

The need for information

The need for information on the environment in the European Community arises for many reasons. As noted above, a major need is to direct Community policy towards issues and areas of greatest concern. The EC is a diverse and disparate region. It is a principle of Community policy that these regional imbalances should be reduced and eliminated. Yet, national policies are driven by relatively narrow, national perceptions. Lacking a consistent and reliable overview of the Community as a whole, EC policy then becomes a product of these competing national forces. The consequence, as Haigh (1987) clearly shows, is that individual policy actions are often the result of individual national pressures, modified and diluted during the process of collective ministerial bargaining. How rational or informed the resultant actions are is clearly open to doubt. Certainly their ability to address regional issues is limited.

Yet equally, this process has limitations at the broader scale. Many of the environmental problems facing the Community are not confined to national areas, but are international in origin or scope. Acid deposition, forest damage, climatic change and threats to migratory species are obvious examples. In these contexts, too, national perceptions are frequently either biased or blinkered, and knowledge available at a national level is often inconsistent or incomplete. Broader, more uniform information to direct policy is therefore required.

Environmental information, however, is needed for other reasons as well. One of the fundamental principles underlying the Community's environmental policy is that it should be preventative in approach. Problems should be controlled at source, and before they cause damage to the wider environment. To achieve this, however, clearly requires prior information—so that the sources can be defined and the effects predicted. As the continued debate over issues such as the health effects of nuclear installations on surrounding rural populations (e.g. Berel, 1990; Hill and Laplanche, 1990) show, this is impossible without precise data and adequate models of the transfer and response mechanisms involved. Moreover, because data collection typically takes a long time, these information requirements must be defined and planned far in advance of their need.

As already indicated, the Community's environmental policy is also intended to be integrative: as each of the Action Programmes has confirmed, environmental concerns must be allowed for, and built into, all other policies likely to impinge on the environment. Indeed, it is partly for that reason that environmental policy receives such a limited financial support. (The annual budget is still equivalent to no more than 2–3 weeks' expenditure on wine production under the Guarantee section of FEOGA.) Again, however, to achieve the objective of integration, environmental information must be available to set against the economic, social and other considerations which otherwise determine such policies.

A further need for information comes from the requirement to monitor the effects of environmental policy. This is no easy task, for policy effects may take many years to evolve, and are often masked by confounding factors, such as economic change or technological development. Moreover, policy initiatives are often pre-empted by the companies or authorities concerned. Aware of the probability of forthcoming controls, they may introduce the necessary innovations in advance of legislation either in an attempt to head off legal impositions, or in an effort to gain competitive advantage. Despite these difficulties, however, monitoring remains essential if policy development is to become a more formative process, and is to learn from previous experience. Information is therefore needed on environmental conditions both prior to policy implementation (as a baseline against which to judge its effects) and for the duration of the policy itself.

In addition, environmental information is required as a basis for informing the public. One of the commitments of Community policy, restated in each of its Action Programmes, is to raise public awareness of environmental issues. To this end, the EC has already published three reports on the state of the environment. As the most recent of these (Commission of the European Communities, 1987a) emphasises, however, consistent data on the environment remain scarce.

Information collection and exchange in the European Community

Faced with these various needs for information, the European Community has adopted a number of initiatives aimed at improving the availability and consistency of environmental data. Many of the earlier attempts were in the form of legislation requiring the collection and exchange of information on the quality of specified environmental media. Examples included the Decision on the Exchange of Information on the Quality of Surface Freshwater, adopted in December 1977 (77/795/EEC), a similar Directive on air quality (82/59/EEC) and a Decision to establish and update an inventory of sources of information on the environment (76/161/EEC). Additionally, various Directives—such as that on Bathing Water Quality (76/160/EEC)—have included provisions to collect and submit data in a consistent form.

In practice, however, these actions have met with only limited success. Generally, the regulations governing data collection have been insufficiently prescriptive. As a result, the data provided have varied substantially in their sampling design, measurement techniques, spatial location or reference and methods of processing. As a consequence, the data can rarely be compared with safety, and reveal little either about the distribution of environmental problems or the effects of Community policy. They have thus contributed little to policy development.

In an attempt to improve this situation, the EC adopted the so-called CORINE Programme in 1985 (Council Decision 85/338/EEC). This was a four year experimental programme, with the objective of 'gathering, co-ordinating and ensuring the consistency of information on the state of the environment and natural resources' in the European Community (Commission of the European Communities, 1985). Subsequently extended by a further year, this demonstrated again the formidable problems which face attempts to collect comprehensive and consistent environmental data in the European Community (e.g. Briggs and Mounsey, 1989; Briggs, 1990). Nevertheless, the Programme has succeeded in establishing a working prototype GIS on the environment containing a wide range of policy-related data (Whimbrel Consultants Ltd./Huddersfield Polytechnic, 1989; Wyatt et al., 1989). In this form it is already contributing to Community policy development in a number of areas. It was, for example, used to help identify monitoring sites for the Community network on forest damage (Regulation 1696/87; Commission of the European Communities, 1987b). Data from the system are also being used in the formulation of a Directive on habitat protection, and in routine applications to assess potential environmental implications of proposed regional policy development.

Proposals for an Environmental Agency

Against this background, the European Environmental Council met at Rhodes on 2–3 December 1988 and adopted a Declaration on the Environment, stressing the need 'to increase efforts to protect the environment directly and also to ensure that such protection becomes an integral component of other policies'. Following this summit, on 17 January 1989, the President of the European Commission, Mr Jacques Delors, called for the establishment of a 'European system of environmental measurement and verification which could be the precursor of a European environment agency'. This idea was subsequently restated by the Commissioner responsible for the environment, Mr Ripa di Meana, on 7 February, and included in the Commission Programme for 1989, presented to the European Parliament on 16 February 1989.

The nature of the proposed measurement and verification system—and the agency which would succeed it—were initially unclear. Mr Delors noted that the system should build on existing work undertaken in the CORINE Programme, and should be linked to existing national and regional measurement systems. He also suggested that it should have an 'alert' capability, which could give a rapid and effective response to environmental emergencies. How this was to be achieved, however, was not specified.

As with other policy proposals, therefore, the scheme provoked a variety of different interpretations by the member states. At one extreme was the notion of a broad 'club' of national agencies which would exchange information and expertise in reaction to specific events. At the other was the concept of a full environmental protection agency, rather like NEPA in the USA, with explicit legal powers and the responsibility to promote and police environmental action.

The Council Regulation

Objectives

The reality proved to be something between these extremes. On 7 May 1990—after what in EC terms was a relatively brief gestation period—a Council Regulation (No. 1210/90) was passed, agreeing 'the establishment of the European Environment Agency and the European environment information and observation network' (Commission of the European Communities, 1990). This defined the aim of providing both the Community and member states with:

objective, reliable and comparable information at European level enabling them to take the requisite measures to protect the environment, to assess the results of such measures and to ensure that the public is properly informed about the state of the environment. (p. 2)

To this end, the Regulation called for the creation of a 'European environment information network, which would be co-ordinated at Community level by a European Environment Agency'. These would have the tasks of:

i.   collection, processing and analysis of data on the environment;
ii. providing information to help define and meet policy needs, and to monitor the implementation of existing policy;
iii. improving the comparability of environmental data at a European level;
iv. encouraging the integration of European environmental information into international environmental monitoring programmes (e.g. UNEP);
v.   encouraging the widespread dissemination of reliable information on the environment;
vi. stimulating the development and application of environmental forecasting techniques;
vii. encouraging the development of procedures for assessing environmental damage and policy costs;
viii. stimulating the exchange of information on the best available technologies for environmental protection and amelioration.

Scope

As such, the Agency was clearly intended to build on and extend the work of the CORINE Programme, and, indeed, one of the specific tasks of the Agency was to be the continuation of this work. Echoing, likewise, the early philosophy behind CORINE (France and Briggs, 1980), the Regulation also stated that the Agency should describe the environment from three main points of view:

1. the quality of the environment;
2. pressures on the environment;
3. sensitivity of the environment.

Further, it specified the following priority areas of work:

1. air quality and atmospheric emissions;
2. water quality, pollutants and water resources;
3. the state of the soil, of the fauna and flora and of biotopes;
4. land use and natural resources;
5. waste management;
6. noise emissions;
7. chemical substances which are hazardous for the environment;
8. coastal protection.

Structure and working procedures

As noted, the European Environment Agency is intended to be an essentially co-ordinating body, overseeing—and serviced by—a network of national information centres. The structure of this network is outlined in Figure 14.1. At its base exists a series of so-called 'topic centres' (selected from nominations provided by member states), each of which would take responsibility for work in a specific thematic and/or geographical area. These would channel information via a national focal point, both to the Agency and to other institutions involved in the network.

The Agency itself is to be run by a management board, comprising sixteen members as follows:

1. 12 national representatives (one from each member state);
2. 2 representatives from the European Commission;
3. 2 scientists, designated by the European Parliament.

This management board will appoint a Director to be responsible for the day-to-day activities of the Agency, and who will, in turn, be assisted by a scientific committee.

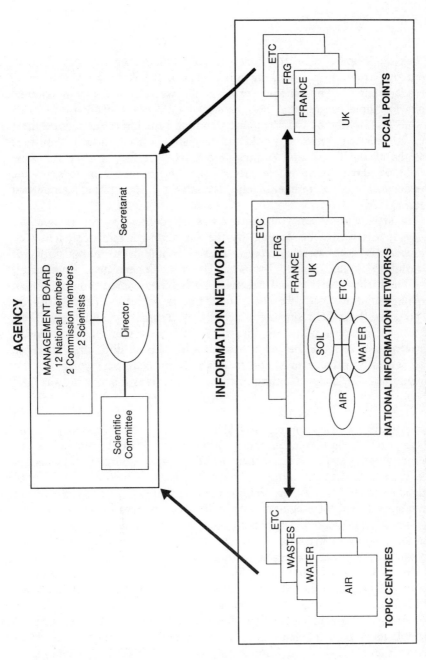

Figure 14.1 *Proposed structure of the European Environment Agency*

The work of the Agency will be defined by a 'multi-annual work programme', proposed by the Director and agreed by the management board.

The first work programme

When the Regulation on the European Environment Agency was adopted, both the structure and working procedures of the Agency were therefore broadly defined. The schedule of operation was also laid down: nominations for topic centres and designation of focal points were to be made within six months of the Regulation coming into force; six months later the information network would be formally defined; and within nine months of the Regulation coming into force, the first work programme would be agreed. The whole process (i.e. the coming into force of the Regulation) was to commence one day after the site of the Agency had been agreed.

The site of the Agency, however, was not defined by the Regulation. Instead, this was to be decided by the Environment ministers, following proposals by the member states. Eleven proposals were put forward: Strasburg, Berlin, Milan, Brussels, Utrecht, Copenhagen, Cambridge, Dublin, Lisbon, Madrid and Athens. The facilities offered ranged from an existing building, ready for occupation, free in perpetuity (in Madrid), to a proposed greenfield site for which the government would use its best efforts to secure a reduction in rent for the first year (in Cambridge). Nevertheless, selection between these sites has proved difficult. Preference has generally been expressed for locations in countries which do not already host a major Community office. A ready-made site was also favoured, since this would allow swift establishment of the Agency. Following some support for Berlin—largely in reaction to developments in Eastern Europe—Copenhagen and Madrid became the front-runners. The planned relocation of the European Parliament to Brussels, and the implications for the status of Strasburg, however, have confounded the issue, the French government refusing to agree a location for the Agency until this issue is resolved. At the time of writing, therefore, a site had still not been agreed, and the Regulation had still not come into force. Suggestions are now being mooted, as a result, that in interim site may need to be found, possibly in Brussels or Utrecht. If such a decision is taken, it may be doubted whether the Agency would in fact then ever move.

Meanwhile, in order to prepare for the Agency, a Task Force has been set up within the Directorate General for the Environment (DGXI) of the European Commission. This is developing proposals for a first work plan; is examining potential information, system and staffing requirements; is formulating a more detailed model for the structure and working procedures of the Agency; and is providing a link with the CORINE Programme.

Potentialities and problems

Given the need to improve the availability and quality of information on the environment, as a means of targeting and monitoring policy actions more effectively, it is clear that the European Environmental Agency has a major role to play. Without doubt, policy development in the Community would benefit from a better awareness of the distribution, magnitude and expected evolution of environmental conditions. Closer collaboration between national agencies is also required, not only in response to emergencies such as Chernobyl, but also to help identify and meet longer-term policy issues. The impacts of NEPA, in the USA, shows the influence which a powerful, central, co-ordinating agency can have—though whether entirely for the good is perhaps a matter of some debate.

The objectives of the European Environment Agency are admittedly less ambitious. The question nevertheless must be asked whether even this more limited role can be fulfilled, or whether the way in which the Regulation has been framed—and the manner in which it is being interpreted—will impair the work of the Agency and constrain its success.

The clash of national interests

The auguries to date do not bode well. The difficulties encountered in agreeing a location have already delayed the establishment of the Agency. These difficulties are, perhaps, not entirely surprising. Similar disagreements have dogged many other actions by the Community in the past, and often led to much more severe dilution or delay of the legislation involved. Indeed, many major pieces of Community environmental legislation (e.g. The Directive on EA) have taken far longer to come to fruition (see, for example, Haigh, 1987). The problems, however, derive from a common cause—the clash of national interests—and they may be expected to continue to affect the work of the Agency in the years ahead.

This interpretation is given force by the way in which the management structure of the Agency has been defined. As noted above, the management board—which is responsible for agreeing the Agency's work plan—is composed primarily of representatives of the member states (12 out of the 16 board members). This suggests that the Agency itself will continue to be dominated to a greater extent by relatively narrow, national interests. Negotiations about the work programme of the Agency may thus be protracted, and the work itself diverted away from more controversial issues which cannot gain the support of a significant number of member states. In this event, the ability of the Agency to act as an independent body, able to offer free-ranging advice on policy, is likely to be compromised. Equally, its capacity to respond rapidly to new environmental concerns will be impaired. The danger is therefore that the Agency may be used to support preconceived (national) political objectives, rather than to set new agenda for action based upon objective and independent research.

Problems are also likely to arise because of the manner in which the establishment of the Agency has been organised. As noted, member states are required to identify potential focal points and topic centres no more than six months after the Regulation comes into force. The first work programme, however, will not be agreed until a further three months later. Nomination of the organisations to be involved in the work thus precedes the specification of the work itself—the reverse of normal procedure. The risk is either that the topic centres initially proposed will not be appropriate to undertake the Agency's first work plan; or, more probably, that the definition of topic centres by national governments will tend to drive the delineation of the first work programme. In this latter case, national interests are again likely to prevail. It will certainly be surprising if, at this stage, a degree of 'horse-trading' does not take place, aimed at ensuring that each member state obtains responsibility for at least one major topic. Whether this will produce an appropriately balanced and incisive programme is open to doubt. It is also notable that criteria for the nomination and selection of topic centres have not been specified.

Foresight and authority

One of the objectives of the Agency, stressed in the Council Regulation, is that it should strengthen the preventive capability of the Community's environmental policy. This clearly requires that the Agency is able to act ahead of policy decisions, in an essentially proactive role. It must be able to identify problems before they become acute, and guide policy to appropriate responses. The need for this is undeniable. Given the long development times which most Community policies involve, it is essential that problems are identified early if any form of preventive—as opposed to remedial—action is to be taken. Whether the Agency can fulfil this role, however, is debatable.

A major difficulty is the time it takes to collect environmental data in a usable form. As the CORINE Programme has shown, this is a formidable, and frequently underestimated, task (e.g. Briggs and Mounsey, 1989; Briggs, 1990). The problem is not only that data are often incomplete—due to lack of measurement or survey, equipment failure, administrative inadequacies, confidentiality etc.—but that the data which do exist are typically highly inconsistent and of variable quality.

Differences in measurement methods, processing, spatial referencing, representation, scale, sampling design and basic definition abound (Briggs and Reeve, 1991). The conversion of such data to a standard form, and their integration into a consistent information system in which they may be analysed and used, are thus complex and time-consuming tasks. Especially in an area as large as the European Community, with its myriad of existing national and regional agencies, this process may take several years for any substantial data set.

If the Agency is to be truly preventive, therefore, it is essential that it begins to collect information well in advance of its policy need. Its first work programme, for example, should be attempting to lay the foundations for the policies of the mid and late 1990s. To achieve this, the Agency must have both the foresight and the authority to look ahead and predict potential policy needs. It must also have the technical capability to handle the data involved.

Whether it has any of these is uncertain. No facility has been established for predicting information requirements in an objective and rigorous way. The scope of work defined by the Regulation itself is both vague and somewhat unbalanced. There is, for example, no explicit mention of climate change, nor the marine environment—both topics of major and growing concern. Chemical hazards to the environment are specified, but radioactivity is not mentioned. Noise emissions are separately itemised, yet the much wider issues of soil, fauna, flora and biotopes are grouped as a composite set. There is no mention of impacts on human health. This list of topics thus shows little evidence of any broad of penetrating vision, or any clear evaluation of future needs. Rather, it reads as a set of traditional policy issues, hastily reassembled.

As the basis for tackling the environmental problems of the future, these terms of reference seem to leave much to be desired. What is needed instead are procedures for 'crystal-balling': for predicting potential policy issues and defining the information requirements they might imply. One such procedure would be to establish an advisory committee of environmental experts, with the duty to give longer-term guidance on the Agency's work. Another (and one already being conducted independently by the author) is to carry out Delphi-style surveys to identify a consensus on likely future environmental concerns, from which information needs can be deduced.

Even if such forward planning could be implemented, however, the ability of the Agency to exploit its results seems limited. As currently defined, the Agency is apparently forbidden from generating or proposing policy; instead it must merely provide the information to guide, support, monitor and implement it. Its ability to translate perceived problems into potential policy is thus severely circumscribed. Conversely, despite its obligation to be preventive in approach, it seems likely that the Agency will be an essentially reactive instrument, responding to policy proposals rather than defining policy needs in advance of political thinking.

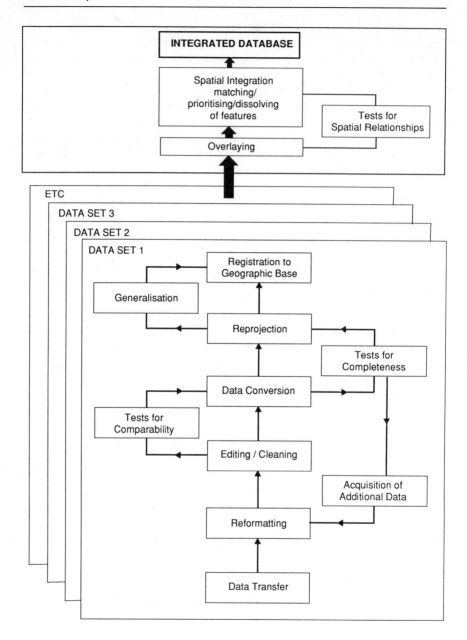

Figure 14.2 *Steps in the integration of multi-source data sets*

Capabilities for information handling

The final concern about the potential operation of the European Environment Agency relates to its ability actually to compile the information required. As has been mentioned, this is a complex and demanding task. It depends on the ability to bring together a wide variety of different data sets, and to convert them to a usable form. It means that clear and consistent data standards must be agreed and set; that data are checked for errors and discrepancies and corrected if necessary; that the data are then registered to a consistent geographic base; that the relationships between different data sets are properly established; and that any limitations or disparities in the data are clearly defined (Figure 14.2). It also requires that consistent methods are used for analysis or modelling, and that results are presented in a standard form.

The importance of these processes of integration and standardisation can hardly be overstated. Without them the information is at best of limited utility, and at worst misleading (see, for example, Briggs and Reeve, 1991). The ability to compare or combine different data sets—relating to different themes or geographic areas—is also impaired. Cross-sectoral or cross-boundary problems (often the most vital in terms of environmental policy) may thus be obscured. The types of models or analyses which can legitimately be used will be greatly constrained. Errors of interpretation are inevitable.

Nor will integration take place automatically. the experience of both the CORINE Programme and other, previous EC legislation demonstrates this clearly: irrespective of the standards or procedures defined, different national organisations tend to go their own way with regard to information collection. The data therefore end up discordant and incompatible. Consequently, it is unrealistic, within the context of the Agency, to assume that the various topic centres—each probably focusing on a specific area of work—will be able to create an integrated information base. Ultimately, consistency will need to be imposed, and this can only be done through a powerful, centralised body.

To some extent, the Regulation appears to have foreseen this need, for it commits the Agency to continue the work of the CORINE Programme. It may thus be assumed that the CORINE information system (a broad-scale GIS currently running on ARC/INFO) will be available to—or perhaps taken over by—the Agency. Nevertheless, to handle this work effectively will require much more than technical resources. It will need a substantial body of expertise, and a clearly defined organisation structure which ensures that topic centres collating information not only do so in close collaboration with this central team, but also transfer the data freely both vertically and horizontally through the network. As conceived, the structure of the Agency does not seem adequate for this function, and the links between the various topic centres, and the role of the Agency itself, remain unclear.

The commitment of the Agency to provide policy-related environmental information, and to use GIS techniques to that end, also raises a further question: namely the need for basic data. As the experience of the CORINE Programme has once more shown, policy-related information does not come ready made. It normally has to be computed from other, more basic sources, using appropriate models or assessment methods. Information on atmospheric emissions, for example, are rarely available; instead they must be derived from data on socio-economic activities (see, for example, Directorate General for the Environment, 1990). Similarly, information on the state of the soil (e.g. soil erosion, soil acidification (must generally be modelled on the basis of soil, climate, land use and other inputs. In addition, other basic data are inevitably needed to provide a geographic framework for data compilation; a backdrop for presenting of results; and an aid to information searching, retrieval and interpretation.

To meet the Agency's objectives, therefore, a wide range of basic data will be required. Who will be responsible for collecting these data is not clear. It is unlikely to be the topic centres, for the implication of the Regulation is that these will be specialist organisations, concerned with a relatively narrow set of policy issues. Nor, again, can it be left to the existing national agencies (e.g. the national geographic institutes), for these already work to different standards and time-scales. The data they produce thus tend to vary substantially in definition, classification, scale and representation. To make such data usable at a Community level will therefore involve co-ordination. As defined, it seems that the European Environment Agency will not meet this need: yet without such a facility it will not be able to achieve its own aims. If the Agency cannot itself fulfil this role, thought should perhaps be given to establishing a separate, independent European geographic institute, responsible for broad basic data collection.

Conclusions

It is, of course, easy to criticise any piece of Community legislation, and as yet the Agency is still too young to answer back. (Indeed, until a site is agreed and the Regulation comes into force, it remains *in utero*). The concerns expressed in this paper should thus not cloud the fact that the decision to set up the European Environment Agency represents a major step. Whatever its initial limitations, it is also clear that the Agency provides the opportunity to tackle many of the Community's environmental problems on a much sounder scientific footing than ever before.

If this opportunity is not to be missed, however, it is evident that the weaknesses in the Regulation need to be addressed. Chief amongst these is perhaps the problem, inherent in most Community legislation, of the paramouncy of national interests and influence. In environmental policy, especially—where problems tend to cut across national boundaries—these need to be subordinated. More appropriate would be to give the Agency itself greater freedom to define its own scope, and to seek out and pursue potential problems on the basis of scientific principles rather than political expedience.

In addition, however, this paper has argued that the provision of environmental information at a Community level is a complex process, requiring extensive facilities and support. In particular, it depends upon the availability of a whole range of basic data, and the ability to compile and integrate different data sets in a consistent form. The lessons of underestimating these needs have been shown by the CORINE Programme, from which the concept of the Agency in part derives. It is to be hoped that these lessons have been learned.

References

Berel, V., 1990, 'The incidence of childhood leukemia around nuclear installations in Britain: the Sellafield story', Paper presented to WHO consultation on data requirements for analysing spatial patterns of disease in small areas, Rome, 22–4 October

Briggs, D.J., 1990, 'Establishing an environmental information system for the European Community: the experience of the CORINE Programme', *Information Services and Use*, **10**: 63–75

Briggs, D.J. and Mounsey, H., 1989, 'Integrating land resource data into a European geographical information system: practicalities and problems', *Applied Geography*, **9**: 5–20

Briggs, D.J. and Reeve, D.E., 1991, 'Implications of incorporating environmental data into small area statistical analyses' in *Geographical database structures for small area statistical enquiries*, proceedings of a Technical Workshop, Small Area Health Statistics Unit, London School of Hygiene and Tropical Medicine, 22 June 1990 (in press)

Commission of the European Communities, 1985, 'Council Decision of 27 June 1985 on the adoption of the Commission work programme concerning an experimental project for gathering, co-ordinating and ensuring the consistency of information on the state of the environment and natural resources in the Community (85/338/EEC)', *Official Journal of the European Communities*, L176, pp. 14–17

Commission of the European Communities, 1987a, *The state of the environment in the European Community, 1986*, Luxembourg Office for Official Publications of the European Communities

Commission of the European Communities, 1987b, 'Commission Regulation (EEC) No. 1696/87 of 10 June 1987 laying down certain detailed rules for the implementation of Council Regulation (EEC) No. 3528/86 on the protection of the Community's forests against atmospheric pollution (inventories/network, reports)', *Official Journal of the European Communities*, L161, pp. 1–22

Commission of the European Communities, 1990, 'Council Regulation (EEC) No. 1210/90 of 7 May 1990 on the establishment of the European Environment Agency and the European environment information and observation network', *Official Journal of the European Communities*, L120, pp. 1–6

Directorate General for the Environment, 1990, *CORINE: examples of the use of the results of the Programme, 1985–1990*, Brussels, Commission of the European Communities

France, J. and Briggs, D.J., 1980, 'Environmental mapping of the European Community: a review of the proposed method', *Journal of Operational Research Society*, 31: 485–96

Haigh, N., 1987, *EEC environmental policy and Britain* (2nd edn), London, Longmans

Hill, C. and Laplanche, A., 1990, 'Overall mortality and cancer mortality around French nuclear sites', *Nature*, 347: 755–7

Johnson, S.P. and Corcelle, G., 1989, *The environmental policy of the European Communities*, London, Graham and Trotman

Whimbrel Consultants Ltd./Huddersfield Polytechnic, 1989, *CORINE data base manual. Version 2.1*, Huddersfield, Polytechnic of Huddersfield

Wyatt, B.K., Briggs, D.J. and Mounsey, H., 1989, 'CORINE: an information system on the state of the environment in the European Community', in H. Mounsey (ed.), *Building databases for global science*, London, Taylor and Francis, 378–96

Section IV:
Canada

edited by
Robert S. Dilley

Introduction
Robert S. Dilley

Canada is in a state of great turmoil. The growing alienation of Québec from the mainstream of Canadian life, coupled with regional restlessness in the western provinces, is threatening the fabric of the country. Closer economic ties with the United States—and now possibly with Mexico as well—have been promoted as an unprecedented opportunity for expansion, but are feared by many as the first step to total take-over by the southern giant. Concern about the environment has never been so high. The Federal Government's three-billion-dollar 'Green Plan', announced in December 1990 as 'the most comprehensive plan for environmental protection in the world' is already being dismissed as too little and too weak.

All of this is interlinked—often vitally—with rural planning and rural policy issues. In this section, Troughton takes a largely pessimistic look at the future of Canada's agriculture in a North American 'Common Market'. Elsewhere, Dykeman outlines the efforts of one institution to understand what is going on in rural Canada, and Hong looks at what Alberta is doing to encourage its rural communities to look to the future.

The summary of trends in rural Canada is compiled from many sources, including correspondents in most of the provinces. Anyone with something to say about planning and policy issues should contact the Canadian editor: in particular, contacts in British Columbia and Québec would be appreciated. Ideas for major articles or for short notes are always welcome. In the next issue it is hoped to provide an overview of the development of environmental assessment policy in Canada: another hot topic, given the dispute between Ottawa and Saskatchewan over dam construction. Suggestions are always welcome.

15 Canadian agriculture and the Canada-US Free Trade Agreement: a critical appraisal

Michael Troughton

Introduction

In January 1989 Canada and the United States signed a comprehensive Free Trade Agreement (FTA or CUSTA) which includes provisions for agriculture. Whereas agricultural provisions are only one section of the total FTA, they represent a significant alteration to the institutional and, potentially, the operating framework of Canadian agriculture. By adopting free trade, Canada reversed a policy whereby extensive areas of the economy, including agricultural production and processing, had operated under protective tariffs, and a political stance which had rejected several suggestions for free trade with the United States dating back to the nineteenth century and reiterated as recently as 1983. The effect was to place agricultural policy within a non-national context. Until 1989, and despite many strong trade linkages and technological transfers, North American agriculture operated as two distinct and separately controlled systems: this will no longer be the case.

Despite their significance, it is suggested that the agricultural provisions of the FTA were/are poorly understood and the implications not adequately evaluated. In part, this reflects the complexities of the modern agricultural (or agri-food) system, and direct involvement in it by only a small minority of the population; even within the agricultural community opinions were/are sharply divided. In part, it also reflects the fact that the FTA was debated more as an 'all or nothing' political decision than as an economic document. Unfortunately, the result was that no realistic appraisal of free trade in agriculture was undertaken in agricultural geographic terms, i.e., what the FTA means for Canadian farming with respect to actual characteristics of the national and continental agricultural systems.

The intent here is to attempt to provide an agricultural geographic appraisal. It is a critical appraisal, in so far as it is believed that failure to evaluate the provisions in this context allowed unrealistic and contradictory claims to be made for agriculture in the FTA, with potentially serious consequences for Canadian farming. The appraisal is presented in five parts: first, a brief review of agricultural provisions in the FTA; second and third, discussion of what are seen as inherent problems, namely, (1) premises that fail to recognize the reality of North American agriculture in which Canada is inherently the weak partner and (2) the inherent contradiction in the commitment made to facilitate free trade yet protect domestic production under 'trade-distorting' conditions; fourth, reference to studies and opinions voiced during the negotiating period; and fifth, reference to events since the signing of the FTA which underline the inherent problems and suggest difficult times ahead for Canadian farmers.

Agriculture provisions in the Free Trade Agreement

Agriculture is dealt with in Chapter 7 of the Canadian FTA document: it is a major chapter which contains a statement of Canadian objectives, the specific Articles and lengthy explanatory Schedules (External Affairs Canada, 1987, pp. 75–136). In so far as it relates to grape production, Chapter 8 'Wines and Distilled Spirits', is also part of the agricultural provisions. The Articles (as shown in Table 15.1) include a mixture of specific changes to terms of trade, together with some broad consultative arrangements that seem somewhat peripheral to the actual structure of Canadian agriculture. However, the prefatory statements, which outline Canada's objectives and expectations, are critical to that structure and provide the frame of reference for interpreting the Articles.

Canadian agriculture is fundamentally divided between its export and domestic-oriented production sectors. This division, which is based on particular regional and production characteristics, has become even more sharply defined in recent decades. It provides the rationale for an array of distinct agricultural policy and institutional arrangements, each designed to facilitate a particular sector. The critical importance of the division to the FTA is that while the export sectors seek new and/or freer trading opportunities (although not necessarily with the USA), the domestic sectors, which enjoy protection from competitive imports, seek to maintain that protection and, in fact, to curtail free trade, especially with the USA. This explains the dual nature of the stated Canadian objectives for trade in Agriculture in the FTA, namely to:

make access to the U.S. market more open and secure
and
to preserve Canada's (protective) agricultural policy instruments. (External Affairs, Canada, 1987, p. 75)

While these objectives satisfy the basic requirements of each set of

THE LIBRARY
BISHOP BURTON COLLEGE
BEVERLEY HU17 8QG
TEL: 0964 550481 Ex: 227

Table 15.1 *Provisions of the Canada-US Free Trade Agreement with respect to trade in agricultural commodities*

1. The two countries will not use direct export subsidies on agricultural products shipped to each other.

2. Canadian transportation subsidies under the Western Grain Transportation Act will be eliminated for products moving through western ports to US markets.

3. All tariffs will be eliminated within ten years, with a proviso that 'snapback' tariffs will be allowed for twenty years for fruits and vegetables.

4. Each country will exempt the other from its meat import laws.

5. Canadian import licences will be eliminated for US wheat, barley, oats, and their products, provided that US subsidies for these products are equal to or less than the respective Canadian subsidies.

6. Neither country will impose or reimpose quantitative restrictions on grain as long as there are no significant changes in grain support programs that lead to an increase in imports from the other country.

7. Canadian global import quotas for poultry, poultry products and eggs will be increased to equal the annual average of actual shipments in the past five years.

8. Canadian products with 10 per cent or less sweetener will be exempted from US quantitative restrictions.

9. The parties will work towards minimizing technical barriers (health, labelling, etc.) on agricultural, food and beverage products.

10. Each country agrees to consider the export interests of the other in any use of export subsidies to third countries.

11. The two countries agree to work together in the GATT to further improve and enhance trade in agriculture.

12. The parties agree to treat each other's wine and distilled spirits in the same manner. Differential charges on wine are to be reduced over a seven-year period and all other discriminating prices eliminated immediately.

13. Canada and the United States will consult semi-annually and at other times as mutually agreed on agricultural issues.

Source: External Affairs, Canada, 1987, Chapters 7 and 8

production sectors, they clearly operate in opposite directions, the latter in direct contradiction to the concept of trade liberalization, and includes arrangements the USA has explicitly identified as 'trade distorting' and which it is actively seeking to eliminate (USDA, 1987a).

Following the presentation of the Agriculture Articles (see Table 15.1), the Canadian government document contains a categoric statement as to how the North American agricultural system will change to benefit Canadian farmers:

By the end of the next decade, those agricultural and food products such as meat and livestock, grains and oilseeds, and potatoes, which we produce in abundance and which form the heart of our farm exports, will be able to compete on an equal footing in the huge American market without the burden of tariffs and other barriers at the border. At the same time, marketing systems, farm income stablization and price support programs remain unimpaired by the Agreement (External Affairs, Canada, 1987, p. 77)

In addition to underlining the distinction between export openness and domestic protectionism, this statement presents a highly selective interpretation. It makes no mention of the fact that US agricultural exports to Canada outweigh Canada's to the USA (see Figure 15.1) and that exports of Canadian grain compete with those of the USA in non-North American markets. It assumes that the removal of tariffs will create an agricultural version of a 'level playing-field', but with no explanation of how fundamental distinctions in terms of productivity and competitiveness, which favour the US, will be resolved.

Before reviewing the inherent characteristics and realities of North American agriculture, and examining Canada's protective policy instruments in more detail, one specific Article should be highlighted; Article 11 (Table 15.1) makes specific mention of the GATT (General Agreement on Tariffs and Trade) to which both Canada and the USA are signatories. During negotiations the FTA was hailed as a major breakthrough in international trade liberalization, with the FTA–GATT tie-in made explicit. However, incorporation of GATT into the FTA is two-edged. Canada is currently looking to GATT negotiations to pressure the USA and the European Community (EC) to end their trade subsidy 'war', which is having a major impact on Canadian grain (especially wheat) exports. At the same time, Canada uses Article XI of GATT to justify its protection of domestic production sectors (Gilson, 1989). Meanwhile, the USA pursues a policy of using GATT negotiations to pressure all its partners and competitors to liberalize trade, under its terms and with specific emphasis on items that it defines as 'trade distorting'.One commentator noted that understanding the FTA agricultural provisions required a detailed knowledge of GATT (Bowker, 1988). Unfortunately, very few people seemed to understand the connection, let alone the details. Nevertheless, by placing the bilateral agreement within this international context, Canada is open to wider pressures on its institutional arrangements, and especially to questions concerning the contradictory nature of its trading stance.

The FTA and the agricultural geography of North America

The FTA (including its agriculture provisions) was presented as a treaty between politically separate sovereign states, in order to create a 'level playing-field' across the continent, by not only removing barriers to trade but also establishing equal conditions on both sides of the border. While

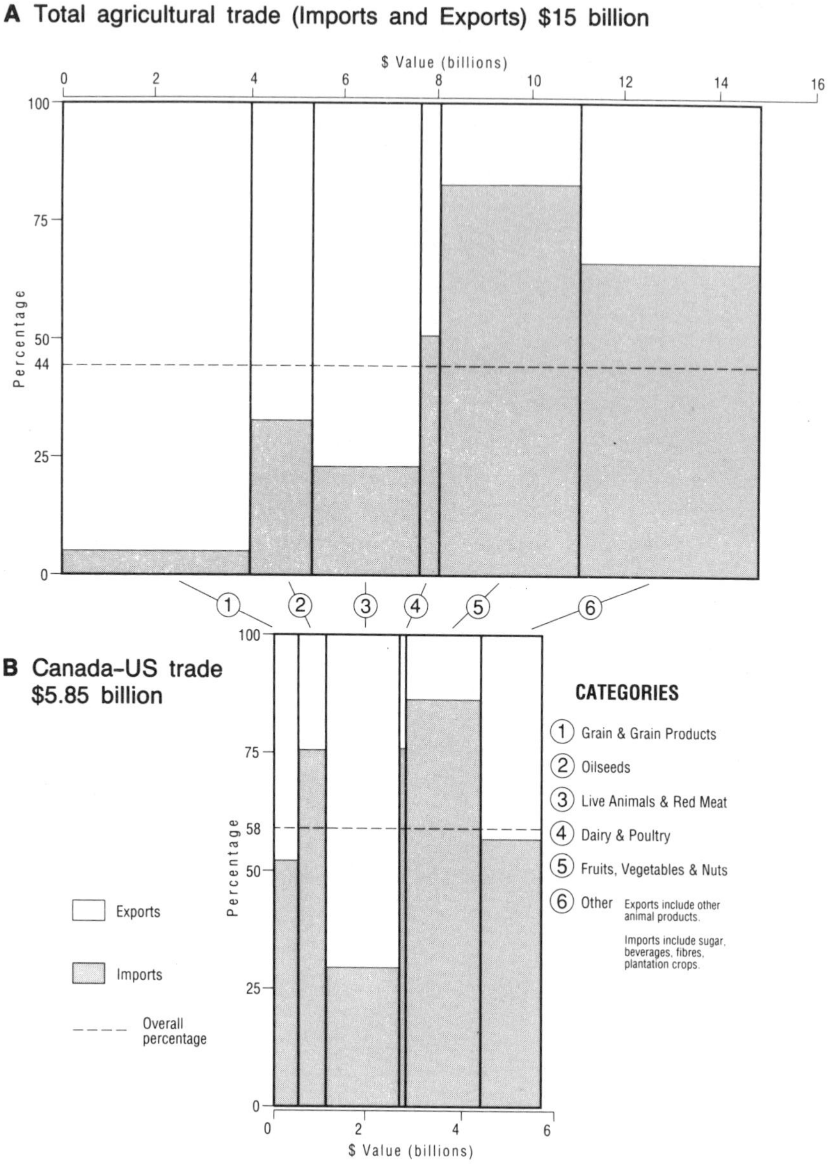
A Total agricultural trade (Imports and Exports) $15 billion
$ Value (billions)
Percentage
B Canada-US trade
$5.85 billion
Exports
Imports
Overall percentage
CATEGORIES
1 Grain & Grain Products
2 Oilseeds
3 Live Animals & Red Meat
4 Dairy & Poultry
5 Fruits, Vegetables & Nuts
6 Other
Exports include other animal products.
Imports include sugar, beverages, fibres, plantation crops.

Figure 15.1 *Canadian agricultural trade, 1986*

there was ample information with which the question this naïve assumption *vis-à-vis* agricultural conditions, most, and especially that pertaining to physical and economic geography was, it seems, ignored. In fact, North American agriculture comprises two very unequal systems, with inequality based mainly on inherent physical conditions which support significantly

Table 15.2   *Some gross dimensions of the Canadian and United States agricultural systems (1986)*

Characteristic	Canada	USA	Ratio
Total land area ('000 ha)	922,137	916,676	1:1
Total population ('000)	26,570	241,596	1:9
Total farmland area ('000 ha)	67,826	407,788	1:6
Farmland per capita (ha)	2.6	1.7	1:0.7
Total cropland area ('000 ha)	33,181	186,000	1:5.6
Cropland per capita (ha)	1.2	0.8	1:0.7
Total irrigated area ('000 ha)	748	18,102	1:24
Total number of farms ('000)	293	2,212	1:7.5
Total farm population ('000)	891	5,226	1:5.9
Total farm labour force ('000)	467	3,522	1:7.5
Gross farm receipts ($Can M)	20,785	194,560	1:9.4
Value agricultural exports ($Can M)	8,401	38,050	1:4.5

Sources: USDA, 1987c; Statistics Canada, 1987, 1989

different types and levels of production, with Canadian agriculture occupying the less productive and generally marginal situation.

Canada and the USA share the second largest block of arable land in the world, but the shares are unequal in both quantity and quality. In the mid-1980s, US farmland and cropland totals were 407 m ha and 186 m ha, respectively, compared to 68 m ha and 33 m ha in Canada (as shown in Table 15.2). Qualitative differences were even more marked and significant. The US cropland resource is rated at over 100 times the capacity of that of Canada based on agroclimatic factors, i.e. growing and frost-free seasons, moisture availability, area of high capability soils and the huge differential in terms of land suitable for intensive irrigated cultivation. As a result, the USA not only produces every crop and livestock item produced in Canada, but a range of crops that Canada is physically unable to produce. Furthermore, because of physical advantages, levels of productivity in US agriculture are consistently between 30 and 50 per cent higher than in Canada, despite similar levels of capital and technological investment at the farm level (Field, 1968; Auer, 1970; USDA, 1987c). As a result, US agriculture not only supplies a domestic market ten times that of Canada to a high level of self-sufficiency, but has become the world's largest agricultural exporter, eclipsing Canada in terms of both the range and value of its exports (USDA, 1987c). Even so, since the 1950s US agriculture has faced the problem of recurrent surpluses which has led to periodic curtailing of output. As of 1988 the USA had idled cropland equivalent to 60 per cent of the Canadian total (Brown, 1989). Finally, in so far as agricultural trading capability relies not only on production, but on elements beyond the farm gate, it is also noteworthy that the USA has developed the world's largest and most extensive agribusiness structure, which extends well beyond its borders, including into Canada, and which takes an aggressive 'free market' stance in both domestic and international markets (Vogeler, 1981).

By comparison, Canadian agricultural capability is quite limited. Over 80 per cent of the cropland base, including the Prairie granary, is physically marginal, plagued by extreme temperatures, a short growing period and inadequate and unreliable moisture (Williams, 1975). Nevertheless, because of the narrow range of crops able to be grown and the small domestic market, Canada had to develop and has remained reliant upon its Prairie grain exports. Whereas exports have increased, markets are primarily (erstwhile) socialist and Third World nations, with intense competition from other exporters, especially the USA. At present, because of global overproduction relative to effective demand and the export subsidy 'war' between the USA and the EC, Prairie grain farmers are experiencing real (i.e. unsubsidized) prices and incomes as low as those of the 1930s Depression (Fulton et al., 1989). In terms of numbers of farmers affected, these conditions are only partially offset by the situation of some cattle and pig (red meat) producers who, helped by cheap feed grain, efficient processing and a 'cheap' Canadian dollar, enjoy an advantage in the US market which, it was said, the FTA would exploit and enhance (External Affairs, Canada, 1987).

The remainder of Canadian agriculture, occupying less than 20 per cent of cropland, but contributing nearly 50 per cent value of production and concentrated mainly in Ontario and Québec, produces overwhelmingly for the domestic market. Output of a number of crops, notably corn (maize) and soya beans, is less than demand and the balance, imported from the USA, determines the price. Similarly, with respect to fruits and vegetables domestic production is markedly seasonal and the balance is imported for much of the year (see Figure 15.1). Tariffs which protected domestic horticulture will be eliminated (see Table 15.1, Article 3) with the likelihood that a proportion of production, including grapes, will be lost to cheaper, longer season, US imports. In other sectors, however, notably dairy and poultry, domestic production has come close to achieving self-sufficiency in both national and provincial markets. However, it has done so by operating within regulated marketing structures designed to maintain and protect the situation. These arrangements (discussed below) are currently upheld under Article XI of GATT, but are obvious targets for US pressure against 'trade-distorting' measures. Producers acknowledge that, without the domestic market protection, they would probably be overwhelmed by cheaper output from much larger, corporate dominated US sectors.

Thus contrasting the geographic realities of the two North American agricultural systems reveals two inherent problems that prevent the development of a 'level playing-field', as well as several other evolved advantages which the USA is unlikely to relinquish. First, while there may be some Canadian crop and/or livestock items currently in surplus and enjoying a relative competitive advantage, this situation is *not* an inherent one and cannot be predicted to continue. Based on surplus capacity and higher levels of productivity, US producers will tend to expand production not only to meet domestic demand on a competitive basis but with the potential to add the 10 per cent extra to meet Canadian demand. Second, nothing in the FTA can eliminate the situation whereby the US produces agricultural items that Canada cannot produce but which it consistently imports (e.g. citrus fruits, nuts), nor the longer growing season and higher output of items, particularly temperate fruits and vegetables, which compete directly with Canadian produce. For the former, Canada will continue to be a captive market; in the latter case Canadian producers will not only enjoy less tariff protection, but will have lost the rationale whereby horticultural processors have located in Canada to serve Canadian markets. Faced with lower prices of inputs in the USA these processors may, logically, relocate in cheaper supply areas, and still serve the Canadian consumer. With respect to the value of trade, the USA currently enjoys a 4:3 advantage in bilateral agricultural trade (Figure 15.1B); the factors just mentioned seem more likely to maintain that advantage than redress it, especially as imports of non-complementary items represent the fastest growing area of Canadian agricultural imports. In contrast, the reason why the total value of Canadian agricultural exports outweighs imports (Figure 15.1A) is because of sales of grain (mainly wheat) and oilseeds to countries other than the USA. Canada's major competitor is the USA and although the FTA calls for greater cooperation and elimination of export subsidies (Table 15.2, Articles 1 and 10), these, in fact, require success in wider (EC or GATT) negotiations. On the other hand, other provisions seek to eliminate transportation advantages for Canadian grain producers (Article 2) and provide a potential entry of US grain to Canadian domestic markets (Article 5); something US agribusiness has been seeking but which most Prairie farmers, farmer cooperatives (Pools) and some farm organizations have argued strenuously against.

Thus, rather than creating equal conditions, the FTA emphasizes the inherent advantages of US production. Obviously, while farmland cannot physically relocate, agricultural production and processing can. The geography of a tariff-free North American agricultural system suggests that significant parts of both intensive production and processing of output could, potentially move south to areas of surplus productive capacity in physically better areas, and to sources of cheaper raw materials, respectively. This shift, if realized, would leave the northern (Canadian) part of the continental system as the extensive margins of production (as shown in Figure 15.2).

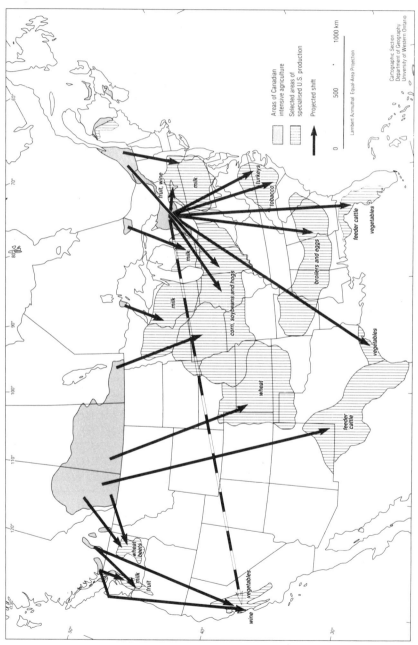

Figure 15.2 *Projected shifts in production of intensive agriculture from Canada to the USA based on combinations of physical base, scale economics and surplus capacity in the USA*

The FTA and Canadian agricultural institutional arrangements

In comparison with the failure to address geographic inequalities and the resultant inherent weaknesses of Canadian agriculture in a North American system, pre-FTA discussions did recognize the problems of particular institutional arrangements, especially those extant in Canada. However, the fact that many arrangements evolved because of the weaker or uncompetitive nature of Canadian agriculture was not made explicit. While the 'protective policy arrangements' are explicable and, to an extent, justified, by the distinct characteristics of Canadian agriculture, not only in physical, but also in socio-economic and political terms, to state categorically that they would 'remain unimpaired' within an agreement extolling free trade and seeking to eliminate trade-distorting measures is not only a contradiction, but a position which underlines the comparative weakness of the Canadian system.

Despite aspects of common heritage, US and Canadian agricultural systems evolved separately and in line with national political and institutional frameworks. The USA has always enjoyed the advantage of and looked first to its large domestic market. Its agri-food system developed in a domestic context, and agricultural exports were a secondary consideration until after World War II. Thereafter, however, exports have built upon a massive domestic production capability and an agribusiness structure which has expanded globally. The USA can pursue policies that combine aggressive expansion of exports with considerable domestic preference, and through its geo-political strength (including that of agribusiness) can define trade liberalization in its own terms. Because of the dominant role of agribusiness, successive US Farm Bills have stressed direct commodity-based payments to producers and processors. This decoupling of prices from income and/or socially oriented payments, allows the USA to separate agricultural and social policy instruments and to exclude the latter from consideration with respect to agriculture. Thus, despite its considerable restriction on imports (also using Article XI of GATT) and a high level of subsidy paid to producers, the USA takes a free-market, total trade liberalization stance at the GATT.

In contrast, the Canadian governments (federal and provincial) operating with respect to a much weaker and more fragmented physical economic and political base, have used agricultural policy and programmes in both a more socially comprehensive and a regionally differentiating manner. A consistent requirement has been the need to promote the export sector on one hand and protect domestic producers on the other. In both cases, the policies employed have combined social and economic objectives, not least in relation to the particular exigencies of national and regional conditions. Nevertheless, this allows a wide range of policies (including social programmes) to be identified as trade distorting, and for corporate interests to complain about the 'excessive' role of governments in Canadian agriculture.

Canada's major agricultural export region is that of the Prairies. While it contains the majority of Canadian farmers, was for long the world's largest wheat exporter and competes strongly in world markets, it is, nevertheless, a highly vulnerable and dependent region. From its late-nineteenth century beginnings, the federal government was heavily involved in its development and maintenance. The National Policy included immigration policies and massive subsidies for railway construction. Although attempting to leave production, marketing and transportation in private hands, federal and provincial governments were forced through combinations of adverse physical and economic circumstances to underwrite farmer cooperatives (Pools), to take over marketing through the Canadian Wheat Board (CWB) and to nationalize one major rail system (Canadian National), all by the 1930s and prior to more general government involvement in social and economic policies (Fowke, 1957). The CWB, granted a monopoly over wheat and barley exports, became a permanent institution seen as necessary to enable Canada to compete globally with both large private companies and other state trading organizations. Until recently, CWB payments represented profit from trading and sustained a reasonable farm income (albeit for decreasing numbers of farmers). However, since global surpluses and USA–EC trade 'war' depressed prices, government deficiency payments have represented an increasingly large proportion of farm income. State trading and income deficiency payments are both recognized as 'trade distorting' by both US and international bodies (USDA, 1987a; OECD, 1987). Western livestock producers have traditionally been more independent and less subsidized, but they too have recently (1989) become part of a Tripartite Red Meat Income Stabilization Plan which aims to stabilize fluctuating farm incomes. This latter programme typifies what has been identified as a basic Canada–US policy differentiation: Canada seeks to stabilize farm income and employment, whereas US programmes have moved to decouple income support and to emphasize markets and competition (Fulton, 1987) and the USA, as a result, labels stabilization programmes as 'trade distorting' (Miner and Hathaway, 1988). This difference is most obvious in the set of 'defensive' policies developed with respect to Canadian domestic production sectors.

While protective tariffs became a major part of Canadian policy following the lapse of the Reciprocity Treaty (1866), specific marketing arrangements with respect to domestic sector production date from the 1930s, with establishment of the first national and provincial product marketing boards. These boards sought to regulate prices through negotiation between producers and processors, and were a direct response to the growing oligopolistic power of agribusiness (Perkin, 1962). Until the 1950s the boards were relatively small and hardly affected demand and supply.

Thereafter, however, in the 1960s and 1970s they were transformed and became a major agent of government policy attempts to rationalize production and stabilize farmer income. Stimuli included the increasing power of agribusiness and the development of large-scale 'factory farming' of livestock, beginning with poultry in the USA, which threatened to eliminate all but a few individual farm producers. In response, marketing arrangements in the dairy sector (fluid, industrial milk and cream) and in poultry (eggs, broiler chicken and turkey production) were rationalized under supply management. Supply management is based on the identification of domestic demand and the allocation of production quotas to farmers which are tied to the price at which output is sold to processors. Supply management in Canada involves not only national agencies, but the division, allocation and regulation of each commodity at the provincial level (in effect, 10 regulated markets). Although the spread of supply management to other sectors stalled in the late 1970s, at the present time it contributes along with other forms of marketing boards, including the CWB, to the situation whereby about 60 per cent of all Canadian farm output (by value) is under some form of marketing board arrangement (Troughton, 1989). Although essentially a device to stabilize domestic sector production, it appeals to many farmers as a form of guaranteed income and a protection against the unequal competition of a corporate-dominated market-place. On the other hand, agribusiness processors and distributors have enjoyed secure supplies of raw material and preferred customer status.

Supply management is perhaps the most overt 'trade-distorting' protective policy instrument, but during the post-war period Canadian governments initiated several other forms of policy with the same broad aims of income protection and output stabilization. Stablization programmes have been applied to a range of products, along with access to cheaper credit, various forms of insurance and subsidization of specific inputs and costs, including transportation. In many cases these have been applied differentially, at the provincial level and/or in respect of areas which are physically and/or economically less advantaged. These programmes run parallel to the wider set of welfare economic programmes, including health and unemployment insurance, and by the range of broadly based equalization payments, each of which differentiate Canada from the USA.

While not universally popular within Canada, these protective agricultural policy measures had evolved over 50 years prior to the FTA negotiations and represented the corner-stone of federal government policy. Although the extension of supply management had stalled under the Conservative administration, that government had, nevertheless, explored its extension with respect to national tobacco and beef plans, whilst continued commitment to policies of stabilization were demonstrated with respect to the red meat sector. Furthermore, although directions changed somewhat, there was a major programme in effect of subsidization to aid in upgrading the rail transportation system and on-going commitments to provide aid to farmers in all regions affected by both economic and physical hardship.

Assessments of free trade in agriculture prior to January 1989

As late as 1983 Prime Minister Mulroney repudiated the whole idea of Canada–US free trade. However, by 1985, following pressures from the Reagan administration, and reaction to fears of increased US protectionist policies, the MacDonald Royal Commission on the Economy in 1985 concluded that free trade was the 'superior alternative', and the policy decision to go ahead was taken. After the about-face, events moved quickly. Negotiations were placed on a 'fast track' by the US Congress and free trade became the issue on which the Canadian federal election of November 1988 was fought. The free trade document became generally available late in 1987, so that when the FTA was signed in January 1989, it had been seriously examined for less than 18 months, and as an election issue had been reduced to a simple 'Yes' or 'No' proposition.

Agriculture represents only one part of the FTA and it received less general attention than other sections, notably the automobile industry, energy and such sensitive impact areas as social services and culture. On the one hand this reflected the small number of people affected directly, i.e. a farm population which is less than 3 per cent of total population. On the other hand, in terms of employment in agriculture and food-related industries, not to mention consumers, the attention was light. While much was made of the leadership agricultural trade liberalization would represent internationally, the obvious parallel to difficulties experienced with the Common Agricultural Policy (CAP) in the EC were largely ignored. Many comprehensive FTA reviews, both *pro* and *con*, chose not to assess agriculture, seeing it either too complex and variable (Bowker, 1988), or automatically desirable if it led to dismantling of marketing boards (Crispo, 1988). A major review by the Economic Council of Canada (ECC) took government assurances on safeguards at face value, albeit noting that an array of non-tariff barriers would remain after implementation (ECC, 1988).

The agricultural community was divided, with the majority uncertain and generally opposed. Key issues were whether the pact would benefit trade, and what would be its effects on marketing boards and supply management. Attitudes to these issues polarized two minorities, whose opposing views emphasized what was/is the primary contradiction, namely how to match the ideal of broad, liberalized free trade, with Canadian 'trade-distorting' institutional arrangements, in both the bilateral (Canada–USA) and international (GATT) contexts. Pro-free trade were those who perceived direct advantages, notably cattle and hog producers and processors, oilseed processors and private grain handlers. Their main concentration was in western Canada but included eastern hog producers. However, the Pools, some organizations representing western grain and oilseed producers and the CWB saw few bilateral advantages and were wary of US agribusiness competition. Strongly opposed to free trade were those groups whose livelihood was tied to supply management or who already felt the pressures of US competition in such areas as vegetable and fruit production and processing. The absolute contrasts could be compared in two full-page national newspaper advertisements in September and October 1988 (as shown in Figure 15.3). The statement of the FTA opponents was one of the few places where specific mention was made of inherently higher production capacities in US agriculture.

Provincial governments tended to sit out what was, technically, an area of federal jurisdiction (i.e. foreign trade), despite potential impacts to a key sector of provincial activity, and the underlying issue of inter-provincial trade barriers. However, in the two provinces most affected by supply management, the response was negative. In Québec, with a heavy reliance on dairying, the 30,000 member Coopérative Fédérée voiced fears that weaker safeguards in the FTA or GATT negotiations could impact drastically on agriculture in eastern Canada (Bergeron, 1988). The Ontario government made a more substantive argument. The Ministry of Agriculture and Food (OMAF) issued three reports that indicated significant potential negative effects to horticulture (OMAF, 1987a), the food and beverage sector (OMAF, 1987b) and the provincial food processing industry (OMAF, 1988). Ontario was especially upset at removal of protection for the wine industry and pointed out that, with the possible exception of some beef and pork exports, provincial agriculture, which accounted for over 28 per cent of Canadian farm receipts, was threatened by any relaxation of control over imports and any weakening of supply management.

The largest body of material examining the FTA and agricultural trade came from agricultural economists. While almost completely ignoring the varied physical and operational characteristics of the two systems, they did explore institutional arrangements and the linkage with GATT. The Canadian situation in a potential free trade context had been laid out by Warley (1985), who clearly identified the wide range of trade-affecting elements in the Canadian system. Attention was drawn to USDA (1987a) and OECD (1987) studies which comprehensively categorized agricultural policy instruments as to the degree of trade distortion (Miner and Hathaway, 1988) and the US-developed measure of Producer Subsidy Equivalent (PSE) (USDA, 1987b). US negotiators made no secret of intent to use this 'ammunition' in both bilateral and GATT negotiations and it was identified as part of the US position (see Bonnen, Robinson et al. and Blandford and Johnson, in Allen and MacMillan, 1988).

FREE TRADE SHOULD BE FAIR TRADE

The U.S.A. wouldn't have signed the present agreement if their farm and factory workers were treated like our Canadian farmers and factory workers.

There's nothing wrong with the concept of free trade but this contract is a disaster for the agrifood industry in Canada.

It's not fair... that the current free trade contract will negatively affect three quarters of a million Canadians who earn their living in farm production and food processing industry. We anticipate that over 150,000 jobs will disappear.

It's not fair... that our Government should appoint a blue-ribbon panel of agriculture experts (called SAGIT) and then ignore their expert advice and this warning: The experts unanimously agreed that Canadian Food Processing and ultimately the Canadian Farmer "will be in a perilous position if the tariff and regulatory structure for food processing is altered while existing agricultural policies are maintained for the primary sector." The Government turned its back on this warning and this is going to undermine the poultry and dairy industry.

It's not fair... that the Government should be telling Canadian farmers that under the Free Trade Agreement "We will protect farm incomes and jobs in agriculture. Our Marketing Boards are safe." At the same time, the Government is telling food processors that they "will have access to competitively priced goods". These two Government claims cannot both be true at the same time.

It's not fair... that the Government should be telling Canadian farmers "The deal gives you tariff-free trade and secure access to the U.S. markets". When at the same time President Reagan says "there is nothing in the agreement" stopping the United States from limiting imports of beef and pork" (or any other farm products?....)

It's not fair... but it is a fact of life, that California gets more than its share of good weather. An acre in South Western Ontario can grow 19 tons of tomatoes in a year, in Quebec it grows only 10 tons. In California, the same amount of land will produce 31 tons. New Brunswick and P.E.I. yield 11 to 13 tons of potatoes per year per acre. Quebec, 9 tons, Manitoba, 6 to 7 tons. In the state of Washington, the average yield is 26 tons per acre. It takes only simple arithmetic to figure out that American tomatoes and potatoes come to market a lot cheaper than ours; that ketchup and french fry manufacturers would have little choice in where to purchase and process their products. We farm in the top half of the continent, the cold half. Now the Free Trade Agreement, as currently written, will make the Canadian farmer pay an unacceptable penalty.

It's not fair... that the U.S. can limit the imports of further processed products containing sugar (like cookies and candies) from Canada but Canada cannot limit the import of most further processed products containing grain, poultry, egg, horticulture and dairy products from the United States. This is particularly difficult to understand when you consider that the export of U.S. sugar and sugar-bearing products to Canada has increased 500% since 1982.

Don't wait until you or your neighbour lose your job

Add your signature below and send the coupon to your Member of Parliament as soon as possible.

Under the present Free Trade Agreement signed by the Government, food processors can move their factories closer to the lower-cost materials in the United States. But our farmers and factory workers don't have the same alternative.

We have a responsibility to make the facts clear regarding their future.

The current trade contract requires major surgery and needs to be re-negotiated.

If this is not possible, we need to reject the total contract.

Signature _____

This ad sponsored by the following: Nova Scotia Chicken Marketing Board • McCain Foods Limited • David Lord Limitée • Union des Producteurs Agricoles du Québec • Rolopage Inc. • Ontario Federation of Agriculture • Hunt-Wesson Canada • Golden Valley Processors Inc. • Fraser Valley Frozen Ltd. • Glen   ne Farms

Open Up the U.S. Border... Watch Canadian Farm Exports Soar

When you produce some of the *best* quality farm commodities in the world, don't you want the freedom to sell to the *wealthiest* consumer market in the world — the United States of America?
    Of course, you do.

That's why most Canadian farmers and processors want free trade with the United States. We want it because Americans will pay for that unique quality.

Canada's premium commodities include:

✓ Red spring wheat for bread
✓ Durum wheat for pasta
✓ Canola for the healthiest oils and margarines
✓ Heavy oats for race horse feed and milling
✓ Malting barley
✓ Flax for linseed oil

✓ Natural Christmas trees
✓ High-quality lean beef
✓ Canadian bacon and lean pork
✓ Maple syrup
✓ Honey
✓ Breeding cattle, hogs and horses

Those opposing free trade talk about lost jobs, social programs, identity.
    Rubbish!
    Free trade is about business. The business of business is to provide a product or service that best meets the customer's needs.
    We're proud to produce the best farm commodities in the world. And we want to sell them to the U.S. as well.

SPONSORED BY:

Alberta Pork Producers Marketing Board
Saskatchewan Hog Marketing Board
Manitoba Hog Marketing Board
Western Stock Growers Association
Alberta Cattle Feeders Association
Alberta Cattle Commission
Saskatchewan Stock Growers Association
Manitoba Cattlemen's Association
Alberta Sheep and Wool Commission
Lamb Feeders of Canada
Western Barley Growers Association
Western Wheat Growers Association
Lakeside Farm Industries
Gainers Ltd.
Alberta Women in Support of Agriculture
Canadian Cattlemen's Association
Nova Scotia Cattlemen's Association
Manitoba Farm Business Association

Ontario Pork Producers Marketing Board
United Grain Growers Limited
Nova Scotia Christmas Tree Council
Western Hog Growers Association
Fletchers Fine Foods
Britco Export Packers Ltd.
Deli Flavor Foods Ltd.
XL Foods
Springhill Farms Limited
East-West Packers (1969) Limited
Manitoba Canola Growers
Saskatchewan Canola Growers
Alberta Canola Growers
Prairie Canola Growers Council
Flax Growers Western Canada
Pioneer Grain Company Limited
James Richardson & Sons Limited
Canadian Agricultural Policy Alliance

Help Canada prosper. Support free trade.

FARMERS FOR FREE TRADE

Figure 15.3 *Newspaper advertisements for and against the Canada-US Free Trade Agreement*

Canadian agricultural economists were fully aware of the institutional framework and spent time explaining the different orientation of Canadian agricultural policy (Fulton, 1987; Coffin in Allen and MacMillan, 1988). Both a major review of Canadian competitiveness (Brinkman, 1987) and a comprehensive review of the FTA sector by sector (Warley and Barichello, 1987) indicated major problems if protection measures were to be withdrawn. Warley and Barichello saw this as both an explanation for farmer opposition to the FTA and as a possible reason for withdrawing all or part of agriculture from the pact. The agricultural economists also spent time examining the situation *vis-à-vis* GATT, especially the problems faced by Canada in advancing international trade liberalization while seeking to retain, and even enhance, protection underr Article XI (Warley, 1987; Menzie and Prentice, 1987). It was also pointed out that Canada's broadest interests lay outside the continental framework, and that these might be compromised by a US-dominated continental agreement (Oleson, 1987; Coffin, 1987). However, while there was clearly an awareness of problems for agriculture within the FTA by the economists, many of whom worked for or were advisors to the federal government, and despite evidence which supported farmers' fears and indicated real threats to Canadian institutions, there is no evidence of any attempt to modify the FTA Agriculture section. A broad, theoretical consensus favouring free trade seemed to outweight empirical findings of major problems for Canadian agriculture both nationally and internationally. When the election of November 1988 confirmed the Agreement *in toto*, the only voice raised was that of a political scientist. Why, he asked, had it not been possible to take a 'middle ground' which, he suggested, would have accepted tariff reductions *except* on agricultural products and processed foods (Young, 1988).

Agriculture and Free trade following the Agreement

Since November 1988 several events have tended to confirm fears and dampen optimism in Canada with respect to agriculture and the FTA. Problems have arisen both within the direct, bilateral provisions and indirectly through ongoing GATT negotiations which pose direct threats to both agriculture trade and to safeguards for domestic production and processing. Furthermore, there are signs that the Canadian government, faced with the inherent contradiction in the FTA between commitment to free trade on one hand, and support for domestic farm programmes on the other, is searching for ways to modify the latter.

Indicative of the inherent contradictions was the fact that, even between the November election and formal signature of the FTA in January 1989, dispute arose. In December 1988, Canada hosted meetings of the 'Uruguay Round' of GATT, in Montreal. The primary Canadian concern, together with other members of the 'Cairns Group', was to persuade the USA and EC to end their 'trade war' based on export subsidies. Under the FTA, the USA should have agreed with Canada, in so far as 'the two governments agree to take account of each other's export interests when using export subsidies on sales to third markets' and 'to work together in the GATT' (see Table 15.1, Articles 10 and 11). In Montreal, however, the USA took an intransigent position on trade subsidies, and launched a counter-attack on Canada, calling for alterations to its marketing arrangements, specifically the monopolistic operation of the CWB. Since January 1989, the USA has continued a hard-line approach, both in the international trade context and bilaterally. It has challenged Canada both in GATT and directly *vis-à-vis* institutional arrangements. In GATT negotiations in Geneva (May 1989) the USA, although entering into a tentative agreement with the EC, emphasized its intention to use Export Enhancement Subsidies on wheat sales to the USSR, where it competes directly with Canada, and ignored 'Cairns Group' requests to the contrary. In addition, the USA exploited Canada's weak position over GATT Article XI, fighting Canada's request to have ice cream and yogurt included as restricted imports, despite maintaining similar restrictions itself (Gilson, 1989). The GATT sided with the USA, forcing Canada to refuse to comply; a position which undermined its credibility with other 'Cairns Group' members. The US position was seen as a direct challenge to supply management in the Canadian dairy industry.

Another dispute which has broad bilateral implications concerns Canadian exports of pork to the USA. Pork production was identified as an area in which Canada was competitive (Brinkman, 1987) and the perceived trade was a major factor in garnering some industry support for the FTA. However, US pig producers, facing cheap Canadian imports, appealed to their Trade and Commerce Department. This agency determined that Canadian pork was subsidized to an equivalent of 8c per kg and applied a countervailing duty. The concern here, besides the impact on pork exports *per se* and the issue of retaliatory duties, was the range of subsidies identified as 'trade distorting'. Although pork is not under supply management, the USA cited no fewer than 16 federal and provincial programmes, including the recently signed Tripartite Livestock Stabilization Plan, as well as other stabilization, feed freight and regional development programmes. This unilateral action completely ignored counter-claims that US hog producers are heavily subsidized by their own domestic programmes, and seems to suggest that the USA is prepared to put its own domestic interests over free trade, while being aggressive towards Canada's domestic policies and programmes.

There are growing indications that that type of pressure, plus inconsistencies in the GATT context, are weakening Canadian government resolve. Despite avowals to the contrary, the government has become sensitive to food processors who claim loss of markets and employment due to higher priced Canadian inputs, and to consumer groups who emphasize lower cross-border costs of certain food items, notably those produced in Canada under supply management. Several government statements have called for more flexibility, and three documents issued in 1989 seem to indicate an attempt to change the domestic situation. In March a report which addressed only processor concerns was released (de Grandpré, 1989), followed in June by one suggesting that, in response to global pressures, Canadian farmers might have to renounce subsidies (Gilson, 1989). This was followed, in November, by the government's first post-FTA policy statement (Agriculture Canada, 1989). This document, despite its title (*Growing Together*) and statements indicating continuing attention to the 'opportunities' and 'safeguards' of the FTA, lays repeated stress on the need to re-assess marketing arrangements, to make sure that they do not hinder trade. While attention is paid to better integration within Canada, what has made farmers suspicious of the government's intentions are references to the need to be competitive, even though supply-managed sectors operate in a purely domestic context. Other references attack the levels of transportation subsidy and question the validity of deficiency payments (Agriculture Canada, 1989). The inferences are of pressure from processors, from the USA, and the ongoing problems in the GATT. In March–April 1990, Canada engaged in further GATT negotiations in Geneva, and it is noteworthy that, in a statement on the eve of talks, Canada's International Trade Minister finally acknowledged an inconsistency of current Canadian agricultural policy, specifically seeking to protect supply managed producers, while calling for other countries to drop barriers to Canada's exports; 'some will argue it's inconsistent, but we have to represent our industry as a whole. And *there are two real separate groups*' (Crosbie, 1990). This fact is not new, but it is arguable that by failing to recognize it, and the inherent and evolved structures of the system in the context of FTA negotiations, Canada placed itself in an impossible box. Having done so, given the commitment to GATT, and the pressures that are already coming from the USA, one can only predict modification to supply management and related policies, which, in effect, suggests that the whole agricultural geography of Canada will be subject to change.

References

Agriculture Canada, 1989, *Growing Together. A vision for Canada's agri-food industry*, Pub. 5269.E, Ottawa

Allen, K. and MacMillan, K. (eds), 1988, *US–Canadian agricultural trade challenges: developing common approaches*, Resources for Future/CD, Howe Institute, R.f.F. Washington DC

Auer, L., 1970, *Canadian agricultural productivity*, Staff Study No. 24, Economic Council of Canada, Ottawa

Bergeron, J-M., 1988,'Implications of trade liberalization for the Canadian food industry', *Market Commentary, December 1988*, (Proceedings of the Canadian Agricultural Outlook Conference), pp. 165–70

Bowker, M.M., 1988, *On guard for thee: an independent review of the Free Trade Agreement*, Vogageur Pub., Hull

Brinkman, G.L., 1987, 'The competitive position of Canadian agriculture', *Canadian Journal of Agricultural Economics*, 35(2): 263–88

Brown, L.E., 1989, 'Reexamining the world food prospect', in L. Brown, *et al.* (eds) *The state of the world 1989*, Norton, New York, pp. 41–58

Coffin, H.G., 1987, 'The internationalization of Canadian agriculture', *Canadian Journal of Agricultural Economics*, 35(4), Part II: 691–707

Crispo, J., (ed.) 1988, *The free trade story*, Macmillan, Toronto

Crosbie, Hon. J., 1990, quoted in the *Globe and Mail*, Toronto, 16 March 1990

de Grandpré, A.J., 1989, *Adjusting to win*, Report of the Advisory Council on Adjustment, Ottawa

Economic Council of Canada (ECC), 1988, *Venturing forth: an assessment of the Canada–US Trade Agreement*, ECC, Ottawa

External Affairs, Canada, 1987, *Trade: securing Canada's future* (the Canada–US Free Trade Agreement), Government of Canada, Ottawa

Field, N.C., 1968, 'Environmental quality and land productivity: a comparison of the agricultural land base of the USSR and North America', *The Canadian Geographer*, XII(1): 1–14

Fowke, V.C., 1957, *The national policy and the wheat economy*, University of Toronto Press, Toronto

Fulton, M., 1987, 'Canadian agricultural policy', *Canadian Journal of Agricultural Economics*, 34: 107–25

Fulton, M., Rosaasen, K. and Schmitz, A., 1989, *Canadian agricultural policy and prairie agriculture, a study for the ECC*, Supply and Services, Ottawa

Gilson, J., 1989, *World agricultural changes: implications for Canada*, C.D. Howe Institute, Toronto

Menzie, E.L. and Prentice, B.E., 1987, 'Formal and informal barriers to trade in agricultural products, Canada-United States', *Canadian Journal of Agricultural Economics*, 35(4): 946–53

Miner, W.M. and Hathaway, D.E., 1988, 'World agriculture in crisis: reforming government policies', in W.M. Miner and D.E. Hathaway (eds), *World agricultural trade: building a consensus*, IRPP and IIE, Halifax, pp. 35–110

OECD, 1987, *National policies and agricultural trade*, Paris

Oleson, B.T., 1987, 'World grain trade: an economic perspective of the current price war', *Canadian Journal of Agricultural Economics*, 35(3): 501–14

OMAF, 1987a, *Competitiveness of Ontario's horticultural industries*, K.F. Harling and Associates, Toronto

OMAF, 1987b, *Canada–US trade negotiations: implications for Ontario's agriculture, food and beverage sector*, Discussion Paper, Toronto

OMAF, 1988, *Competitiveness of selected industries in Ontario's food processing sector under the Canada–US Free Trade Agreement*, Woods Gordon, Toronto

Perkin, G.F., 1962, *Marketing milestones in Ontario 1935–1960*, Ontario Department of Agriculture, Toronto

Statistics Canada, 1987, *Census Canada 1986: agriculture, Canada*, Supply and Services, Ottawa

Statistics Canada, 1989, *A profile of Canadian agriculture census Canada 1986*, Supply and Services, Ottawa

Troughton, M.J., 1989, 'The role of marketing boards in the industrialization of the Canadian agricultural system', *Journal of Rural Studies*, 5(4): 367–83

USDA, 1987a, *Government intervention in agriculture*, ERS Staff Report, Nov. 229, April 1987

USDA, 1987b, *Preliminary estimates of producers and consumer subsidy equivalents, 1982–86*, mimeo

USDA, 1987c, *Agricultural statistics 1987*, US Government Printing Office, Washington

Vogeler, I., 1981, *The myth of the family farm: agribusiness dominance of US agriculture*, Westview, Boulder

Warley, T.K., 1985, 'Canada's agricultural and food policies', in D.G. Johnson (ed.), *Agricultural policy and trade: adjusting domestic programs in an international framework*, Trilateral Commission, NY University Press, New York

Warley, T.K., 1987, 'Issues facing agriculture in the GATT negotiations', *Canadian Journal of Agricultural Economics*, 35(3): 515–34

Warley, T.K. and Barrichello, R.R., 1987, 'Agricultural issues in a comprehensive Canada–US trade agreement: a Canadian perspective', *Canadian Journal of Agricultural Economics*, 34(1): 213–27

Williams, G.D.V., 1975, *An agroclimatic resource index for Canada and its use in describing agricultural land losses*, Agriculture Canada/Science Council, Ottawa

Young, R.A., 1988, 'Why did we ignore the middle ground?', *Globe and Mail*, Toronto, 24 November

THE LIBRARY
BISHOP BURTON COLLEGE
BEVERLEY HU17 8QG
TEL: 0964 550481 Ex: 227

16 Canada: the rural scene
Robert S. Dilley

Introduction

These are uneasy times for rural Canada. Agriculture, the mainstay of the rural economy, is struggling in an age of low farm prices and fierce international competition in Canada's staple: wheat. Elsewhere in this volume (chapter 15) Troughton deals with the fears Canadian farmers have of the long-term effects of free trade with the United States. Certainly there is little confidence in the true levelness of the cross-border playing-field: Canada has seen too many protective tariffs raised against it, immediately its farm products begin to make an impact in the US market. There is also some scepticism about US demands for other countries to end unfair subsidisation of agriculture: demands coming from a country that spends billions of dollars in agricultural price support.

The Canadian government itself has not been especially sympathetic to the needs of rural areas. Cuts in social services have often impacted more seriously in small towns and the countryside than in metropolitan areas. Rural post offices, long the centre of social life, are being subject to wholesale closure, and rural mail deliveries are being curtailed. Passenger rail transport has been slashed, leaving large parts of the country with no service at all. The federal government is not alone in arguing that these cuts were economically justified; but there is no doubting that the smaller and remoter rural communities have suffered disproportionately in both cases.

There is concern, too, about the introduction in January 1991 of the Goods and Services Tax (GST), Canada's version of VAT. No-one knows what the effect of this new tax—proposed at an initial 9 per cent and then dropped to 7 per cent in the face of immense opposition—will be. Agriculture may get off lightly: agricultural products are to be zero-rated, and farmers who buy farm supplies and services will be able to claim the GST back. Since the GST is replacing the current 13.5 per cent Manufacturers' Sales Tax, this could result in an overall gain for farmers. It may be significant that the Ontario Federation of Agriculture, representing some 21,000 Ontario farmers, refuses to condemn the tax, despite polls showing some 85 per cent of the national population opposed even to the scaled-down amount. There is, however, concern that administrative costs may well rise as farmers have to handle additional paperwork, complicated by the refusal of the provinces to roll GST into their own sales tax.

Underlying all these political moves is a growing uneasiness about the possibilities of global climate change: the 'greenhouse effect'. Much of Canada's agricultural land is already at the margin, and a change of only a few degrees could have a devastating effect. Such long-term changes—from increases in drought on the Prairies to changes in fish migration patterns in the Gulf of St Lawrence—are discussed in an Environment Canada Publication, *Toward a common future: a report on sustainable development and its implications for Canada* (Supply and Services Canada, Ottawa, 1989). Also of concern is the loss of prime farmland to urban and industrial expansion. Canada, the second largest country in the world in area, has only limited amounts of prime agricultural land—less than 5 per cent of the country's land area. Between 1966 and 1986 well over a thousand square miles of that land was lost to urbanisation. Nearly sixty per cent of this was land of the highest class for agriculture—over four per cent of the best land in Canada (*Urbanization of Rural Land in Canada, 1981–86*, State of Environment Fact Sheet 89–1, Supply and Services Canada, Ottawa, 1989).

Problems in farming

Nowhere is the problem of farming more acute than in Saskatchewan. Taxpayers have spent at least $6 billion to prop up Saskatchewan farm incomes over the past decade, and the provincial government is looking for more aid. Drought and low wheat prices have knocked the bottom out of farmers incomes—total net farm income in the province in 1990 is expected to be little more than half the 1989 figure. On the other hand, continuing to pay subsidies encourages farmers to stay in wheat mono-culture, whereas a market-induced switch—probably to forage and live-stock—might be better in the long run (Thunder Bay *Chronicle–Journal/Times News*, 15 April 1990). Without waiting to see if Ottawa will bail out Saskatchewan farmers again, the provincial government has taken a number of steps to try to ameliorate the situation. Efforts are continuing to establish new rural development programs. A soil conservation program is to be instituted, with a focus on education. The major emphasis of farm management policy is to be on business management, marketing and maximising economic yield. The Lands Branch of the Department of Agriculture has been transferred to the Department of Rural Development, and several policy changes have resulted. The Provincial Land Lease Allocation Policy and Assignment Policy have changed so that the applicant does not have to have an income principally derived from farming operations—this recognises that many farmers have been forced to supplement their incomes off the farm. The Lease Utilization and Payment Policy now requires lessees of government land who had a lease cancelled for non-payment to clear the debt before they can participate in any provincial farm operation programs. The Provincial Land Sales Tender Policy provides that land previously tendered twice is open to all producers.

A series of rural service centres has been established to improve communication to rural residents about rural development initiatives and programs. A new magazine has been developed—*Rural Developments*—which is distributed to the rural service centres. The Pollution Control Act was established to promote environmentally sound sites for new livestock facilities. The Fieldworker Program Act was introduced to control weeds, rats and other pests. Finally, Agricultural Diversification Bonds have been developed to help fund rural development projects.

Alberta is also concerned about farming, and its Soil Conservation Act strengthens and clarifies legislation aimed at reducing soil degradation losses—which affect 10–15 per cent of the province's agricultural land. The Act provides a framework for encouraging sound soil conservation practices, helps preserve Alberta's agricultural land base, and ensures that the farming sector can sustain current levels of productivity. Penalties for contravention have been increased from $200 to $5,000. In Ontario work continues on completion of a provincial policy statement under section 3 of the Planning Act to guide municipalities in protecting prime food lands. When adopted by Cabinet all municipalities and provincial agencies will be required to have regard to this policy.

Rural reorganisation

Several provinces are reacting to the problems of rural areas by reorganising their government organisations. In April 1989 the government of Manitoba created a new Department of Rural Development, incorporating the former Department of Municipal Affairs with the added responsibilities of water and sewer services, the conservation districts program and regional development. The 'Mission Statement' of the new Department is to strive to enhance the future of rural Manitobans and to foster regional income stability, in partnership with local government and the community, by promoting environmentally sound development and diversification.

A number of major changes were incorporated into the Alberta Planning Act in 1988 (Bill 50). The amendments had several objectives. One was to increase municipal autonomy in land-use decisions. This involved giving greater discretionary powers to municipal and planning authorities in determining procedures to change land-use by-laws, in processing development applications, and in approving power lines and pipelines on public reserve lands. Bill 50 was also concerned to deregulate the planning process by simplifying administrative requirements and clarifying existing provisions. The procedure for preparing regional plan amendments by regional planning commissions, and approval by the Alberta Planning Board, was simplified to save at least 30 days in the process. Greater flexibility and efficiency were provided for the Department of Municipal Affairs in setting subdivision fees, and in administering the Alberta Planning Fund. Finally, there was concern to introduce new provisions to address planning issues. Problems relating to the recovery of front-end costs of oversize municipal facilities were ratified. Technical concerns regarding the granting of land titles for parcels severed by roads or streams were addressed.

The Subdivision Regulation was substantially revised in 1989, primarily to further the Alberta government's objective of deregulation. Amendments included technical revisions to clarify the policy intent of the farmstead and first-parcel subdivision approval; reduction of parcel size for country residential subdivision to protect the agricultural land base; simplification of procedural and administrative provisions; and the elimination of obsolete provisions. Most importantly, a new 'fast-track' approval process was introduced for the subdivision of parcels severed by roads and streams. Most of these subdivisions occur in rural areas. Elsewhere in this volume (Chapter 18) Hong reports on Alberta's 'Vision 2020' program, designed to encourage communities to look to the future.

The government of Saskatchewan has adopted and implemented a number of new municipal planning and zoning by-laws; including basic planning statements under the Planning and Development Act. The principal aim is to give more power to municipalities with regards to development control.

In January 1989 the Consultative Committee to the Ontario Minister of Municipal Affairs produced its report, *County Government in Ontario*. The report makes 41 recommendations on the representation and functions of the 26 counties in southern Ontario, excluding the restructured county of Oxford (rather less than a quarter of the area of southern Ontario is organised into regional, district or metropolitan municipalities: all of the north of the province is in territorial districts). Recommendations include the strengthening of the role of the counties by, among other things, adding sole responsibility for waste management and social services, and with general responsibility for economic development and sewer and water services. Counties would adopt official plans and administer the consent granting process, though local municipalities would be responsible for local planning implementation. Provincial grant programs will encourage larger units of local government, and counties would be enabled to receive levies from local municipalities without having to get all of them to agree on the instalment payments. If approved, these proposals could have a profound effect on how rural southern Ontario is organised. More specifically, a provincial policy statement on wetlands is anticipated soon, to assist municipalities in drawing up their official plans (which must be approved by the province). Existing policy statements cover mineral aggregates and floodplains.

Recognising the massive changes that are occurring within rural communities on the island, the government of Prince Edward Island established a Rural Development Board of Cabinet. The Board is charged with the responsibility of identifying policies and programs that will help to sustain rural communities within the Province. The first task of the Board is the preparation of a rural community development strategy. Consultation meetings have been held throughout the island. Key questions focused on during the meetings included: how should housing needs be addressed within rural communities? how can tourism be developed to optimise benefits for rural communities? what is needed to retain people in rural communities? what are local development priorities? how can the government and the community decide what is appropriate for rural development, and how can it be achieved? Preparation of the rural community development strategy is ongoing, and will be an important document in terms of providing the provincial government with guidance for rural development.

The most comprehensive attempt to reorganise government approaches to rural—indeed, to provincial—planning is taking place in New Brunswick. The Province has adopted a development strategy entitled *Toward 2000: An Economic Development Strategy for New Brunswick*. This document provides a framework for the development of provincial policy and programs and is being used as a guide for major government decisions. The underlying reason for the Strategy is to assist the Province to make adjustments to maintain competitiveness within a global economy, and to preserve unique aspects of the New Brunswick quality of life. The achievement of 'real and self-sustaining economic growth' is an important goal of the Strategy, as is the need to support 'a new spirit of self-reliance among people and a sense that [the Province has] . . . a social and physical environment that can offer the best of all worlds'.

The strategy has six main themes:

i.   to invest in people through education programs focused on youth, on literacy, on upgrading and training and on curriculum development within the school system;

ii.   to promote entrepreneurship and small business development through the establishment of a small business directorate, the development of a small business strategy, strengthening of the regional economic development commissions (of which there are twelve covering the entire Province), establishing centres of excellence for industry, encouraging self-employment, and reducing the paper burden for small businesses;

iii.   to strengthen infrastructure as the basis for attracting investment; involving reliable and reasonably priced electricity, upgrading of the provincial highway system, provision of a municipal economic development funding program for Mainstreet projects and the utilisation of local firms for government contract work;

iv.　to preserve and enhance the environment and natural resources, including more effective management and protection of natural resources, re-evaluation of the penalty structure for environmental offences, consideration of recycling programs and the establishment of a process to bring rural land under a planning framework;

v., vi.　the last two parts of the Strategy deal with equity in regional development within the Province and the development of a clear identity and image for the Province as a corporate unit.

The document provides an important framework for government initiatives and sectoral plans that are currently being prepared. With the resulting sectoral plans it will provide an important framework for local rural plans within the Province.

This provincial initiative has already resulted in the development of one major sectoral strategy—*Tourism Strategy: Towards the Year 2000*. This document was prepared in consultation with the tourism industry within the Province. It outlines a vision for the sector, identifies weaknesses and strengths, and outlines an action plan that is built around the topics of research, marketing, product development, organisational support and standards and training. One of the key initiatives within the tourism strategy is the development of theme regions within the province that would serve as the basis for development planning, promotion and marketing. During the summer of 1990, a series of consultation meetings were held with industry to help to identify theme region boundaries, names, organisation structures and appropriate supporting programs and services. Given the very rural nature of the Province as a whole, the leadership being provided by the Province will have a profound influence on rural community leadership in these management areas.

Consistent with New Brunswick's commitment to grass-roots or community-based development, regional economic conferences are being supported by the Province. Leadership—and two-thirds of the funding—for the conferences must come from the regional level. The purpose is to build regional plans through consensus among diverse regional interests and to this end the conferences will be based on locally developed sectoral work groups. The results will be used to develop a plan that will then be presented to Cabinet for final endorsement. This plan will then serve as a guide for provincial government investment decisions.

Mining

Mining is a concern in some jurisdictions. In Manitoba the government is planning a complete replacement for its 60-year-old Mines Act. The new Act, as well as detailing the powers of the relevant government authorities, would establish two separate and independent bodies: a Minerals Research Advisory Council, to advise the Minister on research opportunities to improve the performance of the mineral industry, and the Mining Board, which will act as a board of arbitration in disputes. Further sections of the Act deal with mine development from exploration to payment of royalties to rehabilitation of the landscape. Quarry minerals have a section of their own.

The federal government has made changes to the Canadian Mining Regulations in the Northwest Territories. Among the changes are the removal of the requirement for specific types of exploration work prior to leasing; the simplification of staking procedures and the maintenance of company records and the removal of the 50 per cent Canadian content requirement for companies applying for 21-year mining leases. Mining is the largest private sector employer in the Northwest Territories, and these changes should encourage foreign investment, especially in the uranium industry, which is suffering from low world demand.

The environment

Another area of concern is environmental pollution. On 30 June 1988 the 149-clause Canadian Environmental Protection Act (CEPA) was proclaimed; it is described as the most comprehensive piece of environmental legislation the country has even seen. The product of extensive public consultation, CEPA addresses pollution problems on land, in water and throughout the atmosphere. It deals with organic and inorganic substances, giving the federal government the power to protect Canada's environment and its population from toxic substances. The Act establishes a list of substances to be assessed for health and environmental impacts; requires industry to provide information on all substances new to Canada; gives the public access to reports and data and the right to intervene at all levels—from asking for a substance to be added to the list to suing for compensation. The corner-stone of CEPA is prevention, and to ensure this, Environment Canada has established regional investigation officers.

A new fund has been established by Environment Canada to encourage all Canadians to play their part in protecting and preserving the environment. Funds are available for clean-ups that restore and conserve, and for waste-recycling and waste-reduction initiatives. Community projects will be eligible for up to half the money required (up to a maximum). One of the federal government's priorities for 1990 is the completion of the *Green*

Plan: A National Challenge. This will identify the policies, programs, laws and other methods the government will use in its aim 'to make Canada, by the year 2000, the industrial world's most environmentally friendly country'.

On a smaller scale, in August 1989 the Yukon government announced funding for conservation demonstration projects: small-scale projects involving such schemes as recycling waste, demonstrating soil conservation, fish stocking and fish conservation awareness programs. Approval depends on the viability and educational value of the project, which may be initiated by individuals, non-profit organisations, business firms, Crown corporations, municipalities, Indian bands and government agencies. On a much broader scale, the Yukon Council on the Economy and the Environment was established in 1989 November to 'take a lead role in encouraging environmentally sound economic development' in the territory. In January 1990, the Alberta Environment Minister released a public consultation document designed to lead to comprehensive new environment legislation in the province.

Social services

Through the Minister responsible for the New Brunswick Housing Corporation a Housing Task Force was sponsored, charged with the responsibility of examining housing needs within the Province. The Task Force, in a report entitled *Home Sweet Home*, called for the government to adopt innovative solutions to housing problems, increased community involvement and responsibility, and an overall approach that perceives adequate housing as a positive environment for personal growth and development. As a result of this report, the government has introduced a number of new programs. These include: Home Completion Loan Program, Downpayment Assistance Program, Rent Supplement Program, Emergency Repair Program, Home Orientation and Management Program and Community Involvement Program. The Housing Corporation is working on developing a partnership with communities and business to share responsibility for social housing solutions.

The Ontario government has announced the creation of 53 new provincial parks. This will bring the total to 270 and the area covered to 6.3 million ha (24,000 square miles). A new parks policy will provide added protection for the wilderness areas and nature reserves which make up 80 per cent of the system. No logging, hunting, trapping, mining or hydroelectric development will be allowed (except traditional activities by status Indians). Any new tourist operations will require extensive consultation. Trapping, mining and HEP development will also be prohibited in all other provincial parks, as will logging in all but Algonquin and Lake Superior parks.

One of the major developments in transport planning has been the establishment in rural Saskatchewan of a computerised transport data base. This provides up-to-date and accurate information on over 50,000 km of designated road in 299 rural municipalities. If roads are added or improved the data base will be updated. This makes it a very important decision-making tool. There has already been a revision of several maps as a result of the data base.

Conclusions

Rural Canada is not flourishing, except in those areas close enough to metropolitan centres to accommodate urban workers looking for a rural lifestyle. Governments at all levels, rarely looking beyond the next election, are tinkering with policies and planning in the hope that things will improve. It may need more radical solutions. There is understandable concern about the economic future of farming and mining, and there is overdue concern about the state of the environment. Unfortunately, policies proposed to improve the former are often at the expense of the latter. The federal government comments that 'A century ago Canada had a national dream to unite the country physically with a railroad. Now we need a new national dream of a secure future for Canadians in a healthy environment' (*Toward a Common Future*, p. 46). However, passenger rail travel is now but a dream, or a memory, for most rural Canadians, and the country's environmental efforts were rated (July 1989) second worst of the seven major industrial countries (a conclusion hotly disputed by Ottawa). Rural communities in southern Ontario may be flourishing, with their injection of yuppie commuters, but there are now few places in the country where it is still an appealing prospect to become a farmer's boy.

Acknowledgements

I am grateful to the following individuals for providing information used in preparing this report: W.A. Bardswich, Director of Mines, Manitoba; Floyd W. Dykeman, Mount Allison University, New Brunswick; Gerald W. Fitzpatrick, Municipal Affairs, Ontario; Tom Hong, Municipal Affairs, Alberta; Jack Penner, Minister of Rural Development, Manitoba; Adrian Seaborne, University of Regina, Saskatchewan. Further information came from *Sustainable Development* (formerly *Land*), the newsletter of Environment Canada, Ottawa.

17 Promoting community development Atlantic Canada group focuses on rural areas and small towns

David Bruce

At the centre of the Mount Allison University Campus lies one of its oldest buildings, the historic President's cottage. The 'cottage' provides a unique setting for the work undertaken by the six-member staff of the Rural and Small Towns Research and Studies Programme (RSTRSP); it houses the workspace for a team of researchers dedicated to the expansion of knowledge of rural and small town communities.

RSTRSP is an independent, university-based research and resource centre established in 1984 at Mount Allison University, Sackville, New Brunswick. The principal funding source for the Programme is the Canada Mortgage and Housing Corporation: in 1989 the two signed a renewal contract committing long-term funding.

The work at RSTRSP is primarily focused on, but not restricted to, the Atlantic Canada region. The nature of the research (both applied and theoretical) allows for the results to be used in other geographical settings throughout the world. The high quality of research has drawn attention from national and international researchers and interest groups alike.

Rural and small town communities play an important role in the social and economic fabric of our society. However, the problems facing rural areas and small towns are different from those of larger urban centres. The economic and social bases of these communities are often placed at risk by national and international forces beyond their control. As such, innovative solutions are required not only to address the changing economic and demographic characteristics of rural areas and small towns, but also to ensure the continued viability of these communities. The management of these changes is crucial to the continued survival and success of these settlements: RSTRSP has dedicated its efforts to meeting this management challenge.

Three approaches

RSTRSP uses three approaches: research, outreach, and academic studies. In each of these capacities RSTRSP contributes not only to the immediate university community, but also to local, regional, national and international development issues.

The Programme's primary focus is on community development in general, with special attention paid to two areas—housing, and community and rural development. These two are closely intertwined and have resulted in a wide range of issues being addressed by the group. From a development perspective these issues include land use, the environment, demographic change, tourism, small business and industry development, local government roles and entrepreneurship. RSTRSP has effectively addressed many pressing concerns of rural and small-town communities, stressing key themes such as self-help, local community leadership and initiatives, partnership building and networking, the use of strategic, integrated and coordinated planning as problem-solving approaches and local capacity-building.

Tackling the issues

RSTRSP has developed and maintained a commitment to ensuring that its work has practical application as well as academic relevance. As such, the staff has made every effort to address the real problems unique to rural and small-town communities.

Sustaining growth and development in rural areas and small towns is a difficult and challenging task. In view of the Programme's limited human and financial resources a survey was conducted of residents in Atlantic Canada, to determine what were seen as the key issues and problems faced by rural residents. Workshops have addressed the issue of local capacity building and sustainable development. Another related problem is the high cost of service delivery due to the low-density scattered settlement pattern. Demographic changes within rural and small-town communities are placing additional demands on the communities and their services. To assess this problem a review of rural planning and development in New Brunswick was conducted to determine possible planning directions.

In many cases, rural and small-town communities have little control over the local economy and are often dependent on a few large, externally-controlled industries. In addition, an entrepreneur base exists that is most often small and unsophisticated, but with untapped potential. In an effort to remedy this situation, a preliminary examination of home-based businesses has been completed in Atlantic Canada, with a follow-up study proposed. It is here, through the little-known world of independent micro enterprise, that there lies a great source of untapped expertise and local control.

Unfortunately, there are only limited resources available to assist the private and public sectors to identify development options and opportunities, or to manage and plan for their community. Few state-of-the-art techniques in community development/planning/management have been developed for rural areas and small towns. RSTRSP has tackled this problem by conducting workshops and seminars on the topic. A survey of community leadership training needs is currently being completed to identify the areas and skills local leaders themselves feel need to be improved.

There are only limited housing options in rural and small-town communities, especially for those outside the standard nuclear family. Very little is understood about the housing market in rural areas and small towns in general. In response to these problems, RSTRSP has recently completed a study of single-parent families and their housing needs, a profile of the elderly and a study of the residential renovation industry: all for Atlantic Canada. Initiatives under way or scheduled for the near future include: a study of the alternative financing options for social housing projects; an examination of self-help housing in Atlantic Canada; an assessment of the contribution of volunteers in community-based housing organisations; determining the impact of the elderly on rural and small-town housing markets; a look at the rural and small-town rental market; a study of how to meet local housing needs while addressing the 'Not In My Backyard' syndrome; and assessing local housing regulations (policy versus implementation) in New Brunswick.

Keeping in touch

The Programme is much more than a research body. Staff are committed, through a number of initiatives, to establishing and maintaining links with all levels of government, the private sector and the public at large. Staff serve as directors on boards for several organisations which have a rural and small-town interest, and act as members of editorial boards for relevant journals. Closely associated with this function, staff also design and deliver performance workshops commissioned by professional and community groups. Past topics have included tourism planning, preparation of municipal housing strategies and the utilisation of performance zoning. In addition, staff regularly participate in national and international conferences.

RSTRSP annually sponsors a regional housing workshop: the theme for 1990 was *Using Housing as a Community Development Tool*. These and periodic national and international conferences have attracted leading speakers from all over the world. The two most recent international conferences were entitled *Integrated Development Beyond the City* (1986) and *Resolving Rural Development Conflicts* (1988). Both conferences have been extremely useful in providing a forum for the exchange of ideas and for networking with other individuals and groups. Building on these experiences, the next conference (set for 23–26 June 1991 in Charlotte-town, Prince Edward Island) is to be on *Innovative Rural Communities*.

One of the most important facets of the Programme is its publication series. This series covers not only reports of research results, but also the contents of workshops and conferences, and material from solicited and unsolicited external studies. Through this series and a broad association with other organisations, RSTRSP has developed extensive and thorough library holdings on housing and community development.

Through its many activities RSTRSP has rapidly become one of the leading forces in the practice of rural and small-town economic development, and one of the most respected sources of information and instruction. For more information about the Programme or its publications, contact:

Floyd Dykeman
Director, RSTRSP
Department of Geography
Mount Allison University
Sackville, New Brunswick
EOA 3CO
Canada
Phone: (506) 364–2394
Fax: (506) 354–2601
Bitnet: KCOSSEY@MTA or BRUCED@MTA

List of recent rural and small town research and studies programme publications

Papers

Ashton, B., with F.W. Dykeman and L. Benson, 'Integrative planning praxis: the Swan Hills Colloquium case', 1990

Carter, J.H. and Griffin, H., 'Levels of rurality in the Southwest: identifying the field of study', 1990

Corbett, R. (ed.), 'Protecting our future: conflict resolution within the farming community', 1989

Corbett, R. (ed.), 'Resolving rural housing policy conflicts: case studies from Canada, United States and Britain', 1989

Cossey, K.M. (ed.), 'Rural environments and the elderly: impact, contributions and needs fulfilment', 1989

Cossey, K.M. (ed.), 'Cooperative strategies for sustainable development in distressed communities: building and strengthening community-based development organizations', forthcoming

Cossey, K.M., with R. Corbett and F.W. Dykeman, 'The residential renovation industry in Atlantic Canada: policy and market implications of self-help, new technology and local regulation', 1989

Cossey, K.M., with R. Corbett and F.W. Dykeman, 'The residential renovation industry in Atlantic Canada: summary report of frequency runs and selected crosstabulations', 1989

Dykeman, F.W., 'Home-based business: an incubator for small business and employment development', 1989

Dykeman, F.W. (ed.), 'Rural tourism opportunity recognition: insightful marketing and development concepts', 1989

Higgs, E.S., 'Planning as technological change: impacts on the autonomy of rural communities', 1989

Kingsland, S. and Eddy, M.H., 'Laying aside the magnifying glass: city, country, and regional design', 1989

Leung, Hok Lin, 'Reflections on planning beliefs and practices', 1989

Books

Corbett, R., (ed.), *Addressing housing issues: the role of local government*, 1989
Corbett, R., *Coming of age: a profile of the elderly in Atlantic Canada*, 1989
Corbett, R. (ed.), *Building partners within the housing community*, 1990
Dykeman, F.W. (ed.), *Entrepreneurial and sustainable rural communities*, 1989/90

THE LIBRARY
BISHOP BURTON COLLEGE
BEVERLEY HU17 8QG
TEL: 0964 550481 Ex: 227

18 Alberta's Vision 2020: communities choosing futures today

Tom Hong

In 1988, the Government of Alberta introduced a new program for all local government entities, including rural municipalities, to help them better prepare for the uncertainties of the future and for the rapidly-changing operational environment within which municipal governments would likely be operating. The program—called *Vision 2020: Communities Choosing Futures Today*—was designed as a self-help program which would have a grass-roots focus and be locally driven. The program was conceived by the Minister of Municipal Affairs as a tool which would enable locally elected officials to become aware of future research, provide a simple yet effective means of fostering a strategic thinking approach and improve short and long-term decision-making by undertaking a community 'visioning' process and developing a Vision Statement for the community.

This visioning process comprises four steps:

1. Assessing the current status of the community;
2. Agreeing upon a 'Preferred Future' state;
3. Identifying future trends which might affect the community, positively or negatively;
4. Choosing an achievable future state for the community, written as a Vision Statement.

Vision 2020 was designed to be a strategic thinking and planning process, initiated, managed, facilitated and implemented by local people and not by the provincial government or professional planners (though the program was designed by planners). The program is not mandatory, and no provincial government funds or grants are provided to participating communities.

Of the 365 municipal governments in Alberta, 285 sent one elected and one administrative official each to comprise the 'facilitation team'. Each team of facilitators attended a two-day workshop to learn how to lead their own councils through the four steps of the visioning process. To ensure that all municipalities were informed of this important new planning program, a complete set of Vision 2020 material was sent to each locally elected municipal councillor and to the Chief Administrative Officer of all 365 municipalities.

The Vision 2020 program material, intended to provide every elected council with all the resources needed to undertake the visioning process, comprised two short videocassette tapes and five technical resource booklets:

i.   Discussion Guide (which is a self-explanatory guide to the four-step visioning process, showing that it can be completed in as little as one or two days of council meetings). The Guide includes a Summary of Future Trends;
ii. Trends Guide to Vision 2020 (a compilation of national and international future trends research);
iii. Compendium of Trends Selected by Agencies of the Alberta Government;
iv. Guide to Public Involvement;
v.   Putting Your Vision to Work—Implementation Guide.

By the end of the 1989/90 fiscal year, approximately 135 municipalities had indicated that they were using or intending to use the Vision 2020 program, and approximately 60 municipalities had completed the program, producing a Vision Statement for their community.

Feedback from elected councillors and municipal administrators who have completed the program has been extremely favourable. It is estimated that more than one half of Alberta's population resides in communities which have completed or are intending to participate in the Vision 2020 program.

Section V:
Australasia

edited by
Geoff McDonald

Introduction
G.T. McDonald

This section covers that region of the world in the south-west Pacific, west of the date-line and south of Indonesia, the largest in area but by far the smallest in population of all regions covered in this volume of PIRPAP. Unfortunately, the sub-editor was unable to find a correspondent from the Pacific Island countries in the region (Polynesia and Melanesia), and the review is limited to the very westernized countries of Australia and New Zealand. This is regrettable, and hopefully will be rectified in future volumes.

Contributions in this section are in two parts: reviews of recent events and a major article on Australia's premier rural region, the Murray/Darling Basin. As always, planning in Australia is disjointed and confusing, resulting from the mixture of politics and State parochialism that has always been present. The panel of contributors to the review is drawn from each State, and provides a brief discussion of trends and events in their States. No synthesis is attempted, although the role of the Commonwealth (Australian) Government in rural policy matters is expanding and this influence has been noted in all States.

The New Zealand situation is fascinating to all rural planners. The experiment there with restructuring and co-ordination of government resources and environment administration is of global significance. A major article on New Zealand will appear in one of the next volumes of PIRPAP.

Planners and researchers from the south-west Pacific are urged to write to the regional editor with comments, suggestions and offers of contributions. People from Pacific Island countries are especially urged to do so.

In time, hopefully, PIRPAP will assist in drawing together rural planning practitioners and researchers, giving some focus to an eclectic area of interest that we know to have a core and which definitely has a diverse following in all countries.

19 The Murray-Darling Basin: a case study in cooperative policy development
Neil S. McDonald*

Introduction

In our society it is only through the political process that individual and corporate resource use decisions can be reconciled with the larger judgment of public interest. The current initiatives in the Murray–Darling Basin in Australia provide an example of the political economy of natural resources management, that is to say, the integration of technical, environmental and social policies into an effective management strategy. At the farm level rational economic choices for an individual may not always be consistent with the public interest in the long-term sustainability of resource use. Similarly, differing community values for economic, environmental and quality-of-life objectives cannot be reconciled purely on objective, technical grounds.

In terms of Australia's federal three-tiered system of government, the multiplicity of jurisdictions and institutions impinging on the management of the Basin's resources has not been conducive to consistent integrated management. Under the Australian Constitution, State governments have prime carriage for the planning and management of the nation's natural resources. It is, however, at the local government or community level that the critical resource use decisions are taken.

After a review of the current state of the Basin's natural resources, this paper examines the history of its resource management, in particular its intergovernmental dimensions. Major facets of the current cooperative initiative between the respective responsible governments are reviewed. Lastly comments are provided on what may be termed 'the unfinished agenda'.

* The views expressed in the paper are those of the author and do not necessarily reflect the official Government position.

The Murray–Darling Basin

The Murray–Darling Basin lies at the heart of Australia's rural economy and accounts for about one-third of the national output from rural industries. Within its confines fall 25 per cent of the national cattle population, 50 per cent of the sheep and lambs and over 90 per cent of the irrigation cereal and 67 per cent of irrigated fruit. The Basin spans over four States, New South Wales, Queensland, Victoria and South Australia as well as the Australian Capital Territory. The Basin covers one-seventh of the Australian continent (1 million square kilometres), and supports directly or indirectly over two million people. The Basin, in particular its rivers and their floodplains, are important habitats for unique flora and fauna. On this basis, associated tourism has become an important part of the regional economies.

History of management

Disputes over the sharing of the waters and navigation rights of the River Murray and its tributaries were prominent in Australia's early colonial history. Fundamental to these disputes has been the designation of the River Murray as part of the boundary between the then separate colonies of New South Wales and Victoria. In 1855 the boundaries were amended to:

the whole watercourse of the said River Murray, from its Source . . . to the Eastern Boundary of the Colony of South Australia is and shall be within the Territory of New South Wales. (cited by Clarke, 1971a, p. 14)

Even with this definition, disputes over water rights between the three colonies were prevalent. In the following fifty years leading to Federation, use of the River Murray provided continual aggravation between the three independent colonies of New South Wales, South Australia and Victoria.

South Australia, reliant on adequate flow across its border to maintain its blossoming river-trade, protested against any proposal to direct water from the Murray. The ceding of water rights to the Chaffey brothers for the first commercial irrigation scheme near Mildura in northern Victoria, brought bitter protests from South Australia. Despite New South Wales' early claim to exclusive use of the waters in the Murray above the South Australian border, they agreed with Victoria that the waters of the Murray 'shall deemed to be common property of the Colonies of New South Wales and Victoria and each of them was entitled to divert one half of the available water' (Clarke, 1971a, p. 27). From time to time this apparently simple agreement was the centre of disputes between New South Wales and Victoria. As will be shown later it took until 1990 to reach agreement on a method of allocation of the respective water rights to implement this agreement.

The River Murray question remained prominent in debates leading to the Federation of the Australian colonies in 1901. Subsequently, an interstate Commission, to which the new Commonwealth became a fourth party, was promoted, though the matter was not finally resolved until 9 September 1914 with the signing of the River Murray Waters Agreement and the establishment of the River Murray Commission (RMC).

The Agreement provided for water rights for the three States and gave responsibility to the River Murray Commission for the management of the main stream of the River Murray in accordance with formulae laid in the Agreement (Clarke, 1971b). The RMC was, however, a servant of the signatory governments, and was almost devoid of independent planning, executive, regulatory and financial powers. The management of tributary flows remained in the hands of State government as did responsibilities for the management of other natural resources.

The Agreement was amended eight times in the subsequent 75 years with only the latest two amendments substantially changing its role. In 1982, the amendments to the Agreement empowered the RMC to have consideration of all relevant water quality management objectives, including water salinity. This had the effect of broadening its hitherto sole concern of water supply to water quality, with its clear interaction with irrigation and water-related land management concerns. At that time, salinity increases were beginning to threaten not only the quality of water for downstream urban and industrial users but also the productivity of large tracts of land, especially in the extensive irrigation areas.

As a consequence of the 1982 amendment, together with the emerging land and water degradation problems, the River Murray Commission, along with the State Premiers of South Australia and Victoria, called for cooperation to address their concerns. Although the need to integrate land, water and environment issues was beginning to be acknowledged, it was however, beyond the capacity of the 1982 Agreement to influence this in any meaningful way.

This was the setting then for the four signatory governments, who at that time were of the same political persuasion, to undertake what is now termed the Murray–Darling Basin Initiative.

The Murray–Darling Basin Initiative

In November 1985, with the support of the Prime Minister and the respective Premiers, Ministers from each of the four governments of Commonwealth, New South Wales, Victoria and South Australia with responsibility for land, water and environmental matters met in Adelaide and agreed to establish a new Commonwealth/State forum to develop collaborative action to tackle serious resource management problems in a basin-wide approach. In the official Joint Communiqué issued after the meeting, the outcome was described as a 'historical breakthrough to ensure the long term viability of Australia's most productive natural resource, the Murray–Darling Basin'. Given the previous one hundred and seventy years of mistrust and squabbling between the parties, the outcome of the meeting can be rightly termed a milestone decision, for it agreed to a program of further action based upon three important planks: the establishment of sound administrative arrangements to provide a focus for political direction and technical cooperation; the definition of mutually supportive management strategies; and for an involvement by the diverse Basin community. A factual account of the progress to date on the development of the agreed action plan is outlined below.

Administrative framework

Legislative changes One of the first steps under the Initiative was to amend the River Murray Waters Agreement to reflect the new cooperative natural resource management directions. The resulting amendment which was passed by the parliaments of the four governments in late 1987 established three new bodies in legislation, a Murray–Darling Basin Ministerial Council, a Murray–Darling Basin Commission, incorporating the River Murray Commission, and a Murray–Darling Basin Community Advisory Committee.

The legislative change maintained the long established agreement between the four parties for the operation and management of the waters of the main stream of the River Murray but added an advisory capacity in relation to land, environment and other water resources in the Basin. The overriding responsibilities for the management of the Basin's natural resources were nevertheless retained by the State governments. With these amendments in place, the opportunity now exists to enhance the management of the Basin's resources and this has provided a focus for the cooperation in developing mutually supportive activities and goodwill between the four governments.

Concern has been expressed on the effectiveness and robustness of the Agreement should parties be of different political persuasion. Experience to date, where New South Wales is governed by the Coalition parties and the other three governments by Labor, has nevertheless been promising for a long-term cooperation and gives credence to the robustness of the arrangements despite the historical interaction between the four parties. Further amendments to the Agreement are being developed in light of the first four years' experience, though these are likely to be minor and procedural.

The 1987 amendments expanded the area covered by the River Murray Waters Agreement from the main stem of the River Murray to the whole of the Murray–Darling Basin. Despite provision being made in the amendments for Queensland to be included in the Initiative, initially that State saw no advantage in joining with the other four governments. Queensland has, however, recently indicated its willingness to join and negotiations are currently under way on its potential role in the Initiative.

The Murray–Darling Basin Ministerial Council From the outset it was agreed that the emphasis in any revised institutional arrangements would have to be greatly enhanced, with high level consultative arrangements across the full range of key water, land and environmental issues. Against this background, Ministers agreed that a political focus for cooperative decision-making was essential. This would reflect the principle of cooperative action, the complexity of management issues and the likely frequent requirement for trade-off decisions on an intersectoral and intergovernmental basis.

The Murray–Darling basin Ministerial Council comprises up to three Ministers from each of the governments of New South Wales, Victoria, South Australia and the Commonwealth with prime responsibilities for matters relating to land, water and environment. The Council, chaired by a Commonwealth Minister, meets at least once annually and has under its charter to have

general oversight and control over the major policy issues of common interest to the contracting Governments in relation to the Murray–Darling Basin. (River Murray Waters Agreement, clause 7B)

To date Council has provided leadership in setting the directions of the Initiative and has taken a prominent role in the establishment of resource management strategies, which will be discussed later. As well, Council oversees the financial budget pertaining to the Initiative. For example, Council recently approved the 1990–1 budget for activities under the Initiative of $43.1 million.

Despite some cynicism of political motives it will nevertheless be in the political arena where the basic directions for the management of the Basin's resources are ultimately determined. This positive political direction provides an ongoing level of commitment and support not common in other similar resource management administrative arrangements.

Murray–Darling Basin Commission In addition to the traditional sources of advice provided to Ministers from their bureaucracies, Council receives technical advice and secretariat support from the newly formed Murray–Darling Basin Commission. The Commission coordinates advice from the various government agencies in the respective Ministerial portfolios. Unlike its predecessor, the River Murray Commission, a four-member body not subject to direct political control, the Murray–Darling Basin Commission is under the direction of Council. While this Commission provides the formal mechanism for cooperation between government agencies, a significant windfall flowing from the initiative has been the vast improvement in communication at officer level both within and between governments. This cooperation has been instrumental in resolving a number of long-standing issues such as groundwater, water allocation, riverine vegetation and other matters, as will be shown later.

Murray–Darling Basin Community Advisory Committee The 1987 Amendments to the River Murray Waters Agreement make provision under Clause 7F for the establishment of a Community Advisory Committee (CAC).

Public involvement in resource management has not been a common fixture of past management practices. Consistent with trends overseas, however, there has been mounting pressure for communities to have a say in broad management policies likely to influence their collective futures.

Established in 1986, the CAC sought to bring advice to Council representatives as far as is possible for such a far flung and diverse community as exists across the Basin. With no overseas role model to follow, the CAC was a bold venture. Its role was to sensitise Council to community concerns and aspirations and to act as a two-way channel of communication between Council and the Basin Community. The initial Committee of 18 members consisted of a chairperson, eight members from regional areas and nine members drawn from bodies representing a range of national community interests such as the Australian Council of Trade Unions, the Confederation of Australian Industry, as well as those bodies representing resource sector interests, namely the National Farmers Federation and the Australian Conservation Foundation. The Committee's role was not to duplicate technical advice despite the considerable background of its members, nor was the Committee to duplicate existing mechanisms where sectoral interests are promoted in a political arena. Rather, the CAC's role was to provide advice on the more social aspects of resource management and the implications of changes to that management. The need to formulate advice on the balance of advantage and 'fair play' across the Basin was novel to most of the new Committee.

Not surprisingly the CAC has been perceived by many as a body not living up to its expectations. After two years its composition has been altered to provide a greater environmental voice in the Committee's deliberations.

Concurrent with the development of the CAC there has been an upsurge in the role of the community in State and regional resource matters, particularly in integrated or total catchment management. Though the future role of the CAC could well be shaped by these State-based initiatives, a Basin community perspective is still required.

THE LIBRARY
BISHOP BURTON COLLEGE
BEVERLEY HU17 8QG
TEL: 0964 550481 Ex: 227

Management strategies

At the outset, Ministers identified the following key issues as requiring the coordinated attention of governments: inappropriate land management which has adversely affected the land, water and ecological resources of the Basin; concern for poor water quality especially salinity; and degradation of the natural environment.

In response to these identified concerns the Council has undertaken three significant tasks: the identification of the major environmental resources of the Basin (MDBMC, 1987); the agreement to a Natural Resources Management Strategy for the Basin (MDBMC, 1990); and the acceptance of a salinity and drainage strategy for the Basin (MDBMC, 1989).

With these three important strategic documents agreed by all parties, the umbrella for the strategic management of the Basin has largely been determined. In contrast to the lengthy negotiations in the early history of cooperation between the respective parties, these agreements have been reached relatively quickly. Though conditioned by the urgency to address the resource degradation, they represent significant progress.

Each of the three strategic documents is briefly reviewed below.

Environmental Resources Study The publication of the *Environmental Resources Study* represented a valuable synthesis of information on the environmental resources of the Basin. Although its scope covered the entire Murray–Darling Basin, albeit with a limited attention to resources in Queensland, the primary focus was on the implication of resource management for the river systems. While appreciating that the thread that links the four governments is the river system and the problem it faces, the study acknowledged that many of the problems derived from the way the catchments were managed.

The study, based on existing information, identified: sensitive environmental resources; the actions which should be taken to safeguard those resources; further investigations needed to overcome deficiencies in knowledge for making planning and management decisions; and the requirement for a Basin-wide monitoring program. As such, the study provided a base document for the development of a broadly based Resource Management Strategy for the Basin.

Natural Resources Management Study The *Natural Resources Management Study* was agreed to by the Ministerial Council in August 1990 after earlier consideration of community views on the detail and direction of the Strategy brought forward by the Community Advisory Committee. A draft strategy was widely publicised throughout the Basin and was promoted by a comprehensive campaign of public, well attended workshops at regional centres.

The objective of the strategy is to accelerate and complement existing State and national resource management programs. The strategy document does not contain a solution to every resource issue within the Basin but rather provides a framework under which such issues may be addressed. The strategy thus provides a framework for coordinated government and community action but relies on the community to implement a significant component of on-the-ground works and measures, and seeks to accelerate action through a program of community works and measures and community education. For problems that cross-state boundaries or have interstate implications the strategy provides for coordinated government action. An initial program of works and measures was begun in the 1989–90 fiscal year at a cost of $7.7 million with each government contributing in accordance with an agreed cost sharing formula. $13.5 million has been allocated for the 1990–1 program. The current program is wide ranging, with 185 separate projects receiving financial support. Some of the more significant programs are briefly discussed below.

Under the strategy, a program of vegetation management has been developed to complement existing State programs. The clearing of indigenous vegetation over the Basin to provide for agricultural expansion was a prominent part of early Australian settlement. The extensive clearing has left less than 50 per cent of the original vegetation with markedly less in the productive wheat/sheep areas. As a consequence, a number of land and water management concerns have gradually emerged. The Strategy is also supporting community revegetation programs in the more humid rim of the Basin where dryland salinisation is emerging as a significant problem.

Further restrictions on clearing residual native vegetation have been brought forward in each of the three States. The benefits of vegetation retention or revegetation relate to reduced groundwater recharge and lower soil erosion risks together with the enhancement of the overall environment for flora and fauna.

The strategy has identified a number of aquatic and riverine issues requiring attention as a matter of urgency, including related wetland and fish management. The natural watering of the large stands of river red gum (*E. camaldulensis*) have been disrupted by river regulation and, in places, their viability as a natural ecosystem is threatened. Combined government forest management plans are thus being developed under the Strategy.

As a result of widespread clearing and extensive irrigation across the Basin, there are increasing waterlogging and salinity problems, especially in the shallow Murray Groundwater Basin. This consists of a series of sedimentary deposits, where the aquifers are relatively thin with very flat gradients and so can fill quite quickly (for details, see Evans and Kellett, 1989). Hydrogeological mapping has revealed that with increasing groundwater recharge, high water tables are becoming common in the east of the Basin, together with an enhanced discharge of highly saline ground-waters in the South Australian reaches of the River Murray.

Under the strategy, a detailed hydrogeological mapping program at a scale of 1:250,000 has been accelerated and a program of hydrogeological modelling is under way. Not so long ago, the relevant State authorities were reluctant to cooperate in what is a Basin-wide problem. Regional aquifers do not now stop at State borders.

Salinity and Drainage Strategy   One of the priority tasks recognised early in the life of the new Ministerial Council was the need to coordinate action on the interrelated problems of salinity and drainage across the Basin. The development of a *Salinity and Drainage Strategy* was the first test of the cooperation between the governments under the Initiative. Significant progress has been made, given the early history of lack of cooperation on water matters.

The *Salinity and Drainage Strategy* aims to strike an equitable balance between the competing needs to discharge saline drainage from upstream irrigation areas and the maintenance of acceptable salinity levels in the downstream, or South Australian reaches, of the River Murray.

Current production losses from land salinisation and water logging in the major irrigation areas of the Basin are estimated to be $65 million per year. Without intervention through improved drainage, the area affected by high water tables could increase by 500,000 hectares. Though the River Murray has naturally occurring high background levels of salinity, widespread clearing and intensive irrigation have exacerbated the problem. It is estimated that current river salinity levels cost water users $37 million per year. As Adelaide and the industrial centres of Whyalla and Port Pirie rely heavily on River Murray Water, South Australia's concerns on salinity levels is an extension of their historical concerns to maintain access to waters of adequate quality and quantity. An emerging problem is that of high levels of nutrients in the river leading to occasional algal blooms. These have occurred in recent years when the flow in the river system is fully regulated and has the potential for high levels of toxicity harmful to animals and humans.

The initial program concentrated on the construction of a jointly funded program of salt interception schemes. These schemes are located adjacent to the river between Morgan, South Australia and just upstream from Mildura, Victoria. Their purpose is to intercept the naturally occurring groundwater discharges referred to earlier and to pipe the highly saline water to large evaporation basins some kilometres away from the River. Overall, it is anticipated that river salinity in the lower reaches will be reduced by 15–20 per cent of current median values. The proposed major scheme at Woolpunda in South Australia costing some $25 million is nearing completion. Other schemes to complete the initial package are at the investigation stage.

As a consequence of their contributions towards the initial package, the upper States, NSW and Victoria, will receive a limited salinity credit to allow them some saline drainage into the river. How these salinity credits are to be dispersed will be a matter for the individual States to determine.

The *Salinity and Drainage Strategy* also outlines some new and significant principles. Most important amongst these has been the agreement that in future each State will be responsible for actions that affect river salinity. The impacts of future actions will be quantified against a set of baseline conditions which has been agreed by all parties. These principles are to be incorporated in legislation by adding a Schedule to the River Murray Waters Agreement.

One of the obstacles faced before the *Salinity and Drainage Strategy* was accepted was the issue of how their respective shares of the available waters of the River Murray should be accounted for. Within the Agreement provision is made for the sharing of the waters on an annual basis. Allowing for an entitlement for South Australia as set out in the Agreement together with an agreed volume of water retained for future storage, New South Wales and Victoria share the remaining water much as they had done a century ago. While this may be equitable on an annual basis, the procedures allow for no flexibility and opportunity for the two upper States to follow differing aspirations. In order to meet both parties' needs, and to enhance the overall productivity of the area, both parties have agreed to a continuous accounting process for the allocation of their share of the River Murray waters.

Victoria, with a high proportion of horticulture and permanent pasture, has in recent years underused its quota, preferring to reserve water as a shield against possible future dry years. New South Wales, on the other hand, with extensive areas of rice production, has adopted a more opportunistic approach of using available water.

Conclusion

Bedevilled by over a century of interstate rivalries interlaced with regional and local politics, the history of the management of the natural resources of the Murray–Darling Basin could hardly have been termed effective. In the relatively short time of five years, however, action promoted through the Murray–Darling Basin Initiative is a demonstration of how to integrate policies and practices to resolve conflicts between competing demands and interests. Progress has been underpinned by, and will continue to require, strong political leadership and commitment, together with an increasing acceptance of a land stewardship ethic based on sustainable resource management concepts at all levels of the community. This political commitment and ongoing involvement is essential but was missing previously.

With the essential framework firmly in place, there are several immediate strategic concerns that should guide the consolidation phase of the Initiative.

First, close linkage of community actions with an overall Basin strategy is necessary to promote the economic and social changes that are ultimately the aim of the Initiative. The 'people factor' will need to remain high on ongoing agendas. Community groups will require continuing support in terms of resources and guidance on strategic directions; and their activities will need to be linked so as to maintain a mutually supportive approach at a Basin level.

Next, although containing river salinity was the first step in managing salinity in the Basin, land protection from salinisation is probably the most important issue in the long term. History is replete with failed irrigation schemes. While overall costs are high, drainage policies and practices need to be resolved and are probably the single most important strategic issue in the rehabilitation of the Basin. The irrigation infrastructure in the Basin, together with drainage needs, have been estimated to be in the order of $800 million. These apparent needs will need to be integrated into the more difficult context of long-term regional viability and sustainable resource use.

Finally, there remain considerable potential gains to the nation from further rationalisation and introduction of greater flexibility in relation to water allocation. If water delivery charges do not reflect true costs or policies are not responsive to market realities and opportunities, then water usage could run counter to overall basic management objectives. Implementing market-oriented policies will not be easy.

This paper has shown an approach set within the Australian constitutional framework that promises to place the management of the Murray–Darling Basin, an agricultural region whose produce is significant in world market terms, on a sound basis for future generations. In a comment on the management initiative the Chairman of the Ministerial Council, Mr John Kerin, in a press release issued after the ninth meeting of the Council, noted that the Initiative's achievements had been to 'catalyse community support for a genuinely cooperative and strategic attack on Basin issues, undistracted by parochial self-interest'. With respect to the future Mr Kerin said, 'In the consolidation phase we need to draw on the lessons of our success and apply them well in the future . . . Our resources are too threatened, our funds are too scarce and time is too pressing for us to do otherwise.'

References

Clarke, S.D., 1971a, 'The River Murray question: Part I—colonial days', *Melbourne University Law Review*, **8**: 11–40

Clarke, S.D., 1971b, 'The River Murray question: Part II—federation, agreement and future alternatives', *Melbourne University Law Review*, 8: 215–53

Evans, W.R. and Kellett, J.R., 1989, 'The hydrogeology of the Murray-Basin, southeastern Australia', *BMR Journal of Australian Geology and Geophysics*, 11(2/3): 147–66

Murray-Darling Basin Ministerial Council (MDBMC), 1987, *Murray-Darling Environmental Resources Study*, NSW State Pollution Control Commission, Sydney

Murray-Darling Basin Ministerial Council (MDBMC), 1989, *Salinity and Drainage Strategy*, Murray–Darling Basin Commission

Murray-Darling Basin Ministerial Council (MDBMC), 1990, *Murray–Darling Basin Natural Resources Management Strategy*, Murray–Darling Commission

20 Recent developments in rural planning in Australia

G.T. McDonald

The national perspective

Australia is a federation (Commonwealth) of six States and a number of territories. The States, at the time of federation, ceded to the new Commonwealth powers over a number of specific areas, including external trade, defence and foreign affairs, communications and the financial system; retaining for themselves all other powers including urban development, land, water, minerals and forestry resources—the bulk of the subject matter of land-use planning. As in all federal systems, the distribution of power between levels of government is under constant tension and conflict, and one of the most important developments in Australia over recent years has been the evolution of this power balance, and in particular the trend towards increasing power at the national level in relation to resource use and environmental issues. This is happening irrespective of the political party in government and the Commonwealth has increased its involvement in rural planning dramatically in recent years by using its powers in traditionally accepted areas such as trade and finance to have far-reaching consequences on land use and production in Australian agriculture, mining, forestry and even urban development.

Several principles have been common themes in Commonwealth control over rural planning, most importantly:

i. Australia has been very active in international fora in promoting the cause of free trade in agricultural products and has translated this belief in the 'free market' to deregulation of many industries and marketing arrangements such as those for sugar and wheat.

ii. The Commonwealth government, under Hawke, has demonstrated a very strong commitment to environmental issues, especially nature conservation, and has become involved in controls over logging (World Heritage areas in New South Wales, Queensland and Tasmania), National Heritage listing of forests in Victoria and environmental controls over pulp mill projects in several States. In fact, the Commonwealth government is now the dominant player in Australian forest policy.

iii. There is continued commitment to positive discrimination towards

Australia's aboriginal people, and high levels of funding for social and economic development programs for them including land acquisition.

No issue better illustrates the tension between the three levels of government in Australia than environment decision-making, where public policy intervention is needed to achieve the social goals of conservation of resources and ecosystems at the expense of narrow parochial interests or development biases. The consequence is an increasing centralisation of control over the environment, despite the apparent lack of Commonwealth jurisdiction and increasing confusion and conflict over the extent of the States' rights over land matters. The Commonwealth has made use of the Australian Heritage Commission and the listing of sites on the Register of the National Estate to reduce or halt the logging of forests in most States over the past year. The listing of the tropical rainforests of Queensland on the World Heritage List effectively prevented further logging there. Logging of 'old growth' forests in the heritage-listed forests of Tasmania, Victoria and southern New South Wales has also been halted.

On the positive side, the Commonwealth has, since the introduction of income taxation during World War II, always been more affluent than the States and recently has used financial inducements to farmers and State governments to promote the Land Care program—a program of joint funding for community land conservation and farm planning. This program has proved to be most successful, based on the right balance between self-help and government inducement without mandatory controls. Controls are indeed viewed with caution as they have never been successful in controlling soil erosion in Australia.

Whether controls or inducements are used, there is, however, evidence of increasing tensions between environment interests and economic interests, even within the various governments. The response of the Commonwealth government has been to establish the Resources Assessment Commission (RAC), which is charged with the responsibility of incorporating both environmental and economic perspectives in providing advice to the government on matters referred to it. So far, the RAC has been given commissions to inquire into Australian forestry, coastal zone management and mining at Kakadu stage III. It is too early to speculate on whether the RAC will be successful, although many people, especially on the development side of the conflict, believe that more effective means are required to resolve the trade-offs between conservation and development.

Despite the rapidly changing distribution of powers in Australia, the States still have the dominant influence over rural planning matters, and the remainder of this review discusses each State in turn.

THE LIBRARY
BISHOP BURTON COLLEGE
BEVERLEY HU17 8QG
TEL: 0964 550481 Ex: 227

New South Wales

Since the election in 1988 of the Greiner State Government, rural planning has been relegated to a position of less urgency, in face of the problems of the Sydney metropolis, and many of the initiatives of earlier in the 1980s have lost impetus.

Comprehensive planning in particular, with its requirements for comprehensive visions, co-ordination and monitoring, has suffered from the reductions in real funding which have been experienced by the Department of Planning since 1985. In consequence, there has been little progress on broad matters such as planning for State-wide distributions of populations and settlement, and for forecast overspills from the Sydney and Canberra metropolises. Much of the so-called comprehensive planing by the Department for its regions, such as embodied in the latest Hunter REP (1989), is little more than provisions for the regulation of physical development and conservation.

The most concerted initiatives in rural planing recently have involved the Departments of State Development and of Business and Consumer Affairs in economic development planning. The Department of State Development is preparing regional strategies for the Hunter and Illawarra regions and for the rest of country New-South Wales and, while their content is still uncertain, it is possible that these might embody strategic visions. The Department of Business and Consumer Affairs, through its Minister, has recently put forward a proposal for programs of infrastructure development, labour market development, regional business development, enterprise development and support by regional development boards, aimed at promoting regional development and decentralisation. The Minister's paper (*Regional Development and Decentralisation*, Department of Business and Consumer Affairs, February 1989) is short on targets or other visions of the future (so, strictly, is not a plan) and is rather vague on specifics such as the provision of resources to the regional development boards, so it is too early to judge how effective the programs might be. The commitment of the Minister to regional development and decentralisation is certainly in question when the growth centre development corporations of Albury-Wodonga and Bathurst-Orange under his control are being disestablished.

Overall, the new State government appears to have no co-ordinated view of economic development in the regions. As initiatives quite separate from those mentioned above, the State government is planning to move the head offices of its Department of Agriculture and Rural Affairs (to Orange), and Department of Lands (to Bathurst and Dubbo) by the end of 1992. These moves will give considerable fillips to growth in the larger country towns involved, as well as saving considerable sums for the State government. Since the election of the Greiner government, appreciable numbers of small schools, hospitals and other community-service facilities have been closed or transferred to larger country towns. Apart from protesting, rural communities have generally done little about this, but there have been interesting initiatives: Yeoval (with a population of 300) has reopened its community hospital as a registered co-operative; and the State government, in anticipation of deregulation of local government under a proposed new Local Government Bill, is considering either, using local government as agents for community services, or their offices to provide space for more specialised services such as the police; while the transfer of postal services from post offices to general stores in some smaller towns and villages has actually been the salvation of some stores.

The philosophies of economic rationalisation which have been behind the closures and downgrading of community services have been reflected in government initiatives in relation to physical infrastructure. Government agencies have transferred responsibility for some village water supply systems to local communities; funding to local councils for roads and bridges has been cut, with a consequence that sealed roads are being allowed to revert to gravel; and deregulation of bus and air services has led to increased competition on higher volume routes, but withdrawals on low volume routes. The most significant initiative relates to the State Rail Authority, which is closing stations grossing under $300,000, transferring freight and passenger services to roads, withdrawing formerly subsidised services such as night sleeper services, closing some rail lines and privatising its bus services.

In the Department of Planning during the 1980s, there has been some emphasis on the development of policies for rural planning. The Department has commissioned important studies of non-urban planning policy (1981), rural subdivision and residential planning (1983), rural services and servicing costs (1983) and demand for land and rural subdivision (1985), as well as producing a model rural local environmental plan (1987), but since the election of the new government, the Department has been preoccupied with metropolitan planning issues and it is unlikely, despite the continuing encouragement of the Department of Agriculture and Rural Affairs, that other developments, such as that of the State Environmental Planning Policies (SEPPs) on subdivision in non-urban areas, will continue. The Department has revised SEPPs on multiple occupancies of rural lands (1988) and coastal wetlands (1989), but the only new SEPPs which affect non-urban lands are those restricting development near littoral rainforests (1988) and making cattle feedlot developments subject to consent (1989). The Department has gazetted a number of REPs in addition to the 'comprehensive' ones mentioned earlier, but most of these have been concerned with minor matters such as controlling land use in riverine lands (Murray REP, 1988), improving water quality (Hawkesbury-Nepean REP, 1989), setting guidelines for the establishment of extractive industries (Western Division, 1989) and controlling light emissions in areas adjacent to a major telescope complex (Orana REP, 1990). There appears to be no comprehensive scoping of issues as a basis for identifying issues for most of these REPs.

In local councils, by contrast, there has been some activity in the production of scheme plans in LEPs, reflecting pressures on these authorities from the Department of Planning to prepare rural planning schemes. However, despite lip-service paid to innovations such as flexible zoning, most of these LEPs exhibit neither vision nor innovation. Most are simply policy statements about the control of physical development. Some more interesting developments either adopted or proposed include:

1. bringing agriculture and forestry within developments requiring consent (Blue Mountains);
2. extending a Tree Preservation Order to a whole shire (Wellington);
3. requiring developers to meet performance criteria rather than minimum area requirements in subdivision of rural areas (Jerilderie);
4. requiring consultation and concurrence by, *inter alia*, the department of Agriculture and Rural Affairs for subdivisions.

Possible amendments to the Environmental Planning and Assessment Act 1979, which is under review, may allow local physical planning to be more innovative.

In other government agencies, the climate of fiscal pragmatism has led to reduced real funding for many activities relating to planning of physical development and conservation. Management planning by agencies responsible for reserved Crown lands has extended only to major reserves, especially in the National Parks and Wildlife Services which lost more than ten per cent of its staff in a recent twelve-month period. Resources mapping, such as the floodplain mapping programs of the Department of Water Resources, has been curtailed, although the Soil Conservation Service has completed much of its program of mapping capability across the State. However, the Minister for Natural Resources (covering the Forestry Commission and Lands Department) has recently promulgated a policy to encourage but control recreational uses in these lands, especially recreational vehicles in sensitive environments.

Catchment management, through total (or integrated) catchment management, has become a major thrust of the activities of the Soil Conservation Service and Department of Water Resources.

Victoria

Since 1988, the State government has introduced a number of policy documents and new pieces of legislation, all of which have significant implications for planning in rural Victoria. The main policy documents as shown in Table 20.1 are: the State Conservation Strategy, the State Economic Policy, the State Agricultural Strategy, the State Salinity

Table 20.1 *Contemporary policy documents in Victoria*

The main State policy documents relevant to rural planning are:

State Conservation Strategy

1. Maintain essential ecological processes and life-support systems.
2. Preserve genetic diversity.
3. Ensure the sustainable use of renewable resources.
4. Ensure the wise use of non-renewable resources.
5. Protect natural areas and ecosystems for the non-material needs of society.

State Economic Strategy

1. Ensure that the substantial importance of agricultural production to the State's economy is recognised and a prosperous and viable rural sector is maintained.
2. Build on the major competitive strengths associated with Victoria's rich and diverse agricultural bases.
3. Ensure that Government policies and programmes are more effective in meeting the economic and social needs of rural people.

State Agricultural Strategy

1. Maintain a diverse agricultural base with a wide range of soils and climates close to transport and water resources.
2. Increase the contribution of agriculture to the development of the Victorian economy.
3. Promote income and employment growth in agriculture from which all Victorians will benefit.
4. Ensure agricultural systems are sustainable in the long run in that basic resources of soil and water are maintained in a suitable state for production purposes.
5. Ensure that agriculture is sustainable in the sense that economic development proceeds in accord with the Government's Conservation and Salinity Strategies.
6. Ensure that agricultural development takes place in a way that is consistent with the broader objectives of society, such as improvement of the welfare of animals and the objectives in the Social Justice Strategy.

Social Justice Strategy

1. Reduce disadvantage caused by unequal access to economic resources and power.
2. Increase access to essential goods and services according to need.
3. Expand opportunity for genuine participation by all Victorians in decisions which affect their lives.
4. Protect, extend and ensure the effective exercise of equal legal, industrial and political rights.

Strategy, the State Social Justice Strategy and a draft Greenhouse Strategy. The main legislative initiatives have been the introduction of a Planning and Environment Act, a Water Act and a Flora and Fauna Guarantee Act, and the preparation of a new Mineral Resources Bill.

The Planning and Environment Act, which was proclaimed in February 1988 (replacing the Town and Country Planning Act), makes it obligatory for planning authorities to consider environmental matters when processing permit and rezoning applications and provides a framework for the municipalities to introduce their own planning schemes and associated controls. A new Water Act was passed by Parliament in 1989 and became effective during 1990. The Act is designed to simplify the management of the water industry and make it more efficient. Like the Planning and Environment Act, the Water Act also requires that environmental considerations are taken into account during the processing of approval applications (for example, water licences), and that responsible authorities carry out their functions in an environmentally sensitive manner. The third piece of legislation, the Flora and Fauna Guarantee Act which was proclaimed in 1988, provides mechanisms for listing species or communities in danger of destruction, and for identifying potentially threatening processes. It is intended that regulations relating to protection and preservation will soon be introduced. The fourth piece of legislation, the draft Mineral Resources Development Bill, is intended to replace the Mines Act. When introduced, the new Act will streamline administrative and planning procedures, with benefits for the mining industry (e.g. speedier decision-making), for the community (e.g. greater consultation) and for the environment (e.g. National, State and wilderness parks will be exempt from exploration and mining).

In addition to introducing new legislation, the State government has introduced a number of policy initiatives and programs during the past two years that will affect planning in rural Victoria. The government's 'Greenhouse Challenge', with its focus on sustainable development, refers to the need for long-term planning to cope with future climatic change and to reduce dependence on fossil fuels through a variety of measures, including land-use planning. New land-use planning initiatives include a State-wide review of rural land use and an investigation of urban growth potential for selected rural centres.

Much attention has been focused on forestry, vegetation retention and land degradation. A Code of Forest practice that will guide and control timber production throughout the State has been endorsed and a review of plantation forestry undertaken. Initiatives to revegetate critical areas and to halt vegetation loss include a 'Tree Victoria' plan that aims to have more than 100 million trees planted by the year 2010 and a proposed amendment to all planning schemes in Victoria requiring a permit to be obtained before native vegetation can be cleared. The serious problem of soil degradation is being addressed through a Land Care Program which has more than 2,500 participating landholders, and the problem of salinity is being tackled through a State Salinity Strategy—'Salt Action: Joint Action'—which will see the preparation of community-based salinity management plans.

In April 1990, immediately following the federal election, the State government made a number of administrative changes that will impact on rural planning. The federal Labor government fared poorly in the election in Victoria and the State Labor government responded by creating a new Department of Planning and Urban Growth and a new 'mega'-Department of Conservation and Environment. The Department of Conservation and Environment embraces forestry; water resources—including drainage and floodplain management; national parks and the management of other public land; flora, fauna and fisheries; and environmental policy. Perhaps somewhat anomalously, the Environment Protection Authority and responsibility for administering the Environment Effects Act remain with the Department of Planning and Urban Growth (formerly the Ministry for Planning and Environment).

Western Australia

The most significant development over the past twelve months has been the announcement by Mr Barry Carbon, Director of the Environmental Protection Authority, that no further land would be released for agricultural purposes (*The West Australian*, 12/4/90). It was reported that, with about 2 m. ha of the 15.5 m. ha of land released to agriculture in Western Australia being badly degraded, the State 'had reached the arable land limit both ecologically and agriculturally'. Mr Carbon was also reported as saying that he did not believe there would be any further pastoral land releases either. Despite some question as to whether he has the authority to make such a statement on behalf of the State, or the power to see that it is implemented, outraged reactions by the President of the Western Australian Pastoralists' and Graziers' Association (*The West Australian*, 14/4/90) and by a Western Australian Liberal Party Senator (*The Countryman*, 26/4/90), suggest that his statement is to be taken seriously. Indeed, it appears that all land release proposals over the past four years have been referred to the Environmental Protection Authority for its assessment and recommendation, which have been negative in each case.

In order to appreciate the significance of this announcement, it is necessary to recognise that since European settlement of Western Australia in 1829, there has been a widespread perception in the community—urban as well as rural—that there is ample land available for further 'development'. This perception has been reinforced by the fact that only some 6 per cent (40 m. ha) of Australia's land mass is used for agriculture, and CSIRO's (1977) estimate that a further 25–30 m. ha are available for agricultural purposes (that is, land which can be periodically cropped and sown to improved pasture), but those areas are in the subtropic eastern region of the continent away from the coast, not in Western Australia.

Acceptance of the Environmental Protection Authority's decree by farmers and rural planners and administrators will represent a major (and overdue) switch in attitude. From now on, increases in total production will have to be obtained by increasing productivity per unit area, and not by simply clearing additional land as has been done in the past.

This may not be too easy if the degradation of agricultural land highlighted by the release of the most recent saltland survey data for 1989 continues. According to this survey secondary soil salinity in the dryland, wheatbelt region of Western Australia has increased from 264,000 ha in 1979 (the date of the previous survey: see Henschke, 1980) to 443,000 ha (George, 1990). The degraded area has increased by more than 500 per cent since the first saltland survey was undertaken in 1955, and it constitutes a huge loss of agriculturally productive land from farmers who, on average, are making a lower return on their capital investment than the current inflation rate in every wheatbelt shire of the State.

The major response by the State to land degradation has been the formation of Soil Conservation Districts, recently merged with the (also Australia-wide) Land Care concept, closely related to total (or integrated) catchment management (TCM), and funded by the Federal Government's National Soil Conservation Program (NSCP). There are now over 100 Soil Conservation districts in Western Australia, including more than 70 per cent of all farmers and pastoralists, and covering approximately 75 per cent of the agricultural lands and about 80 per cent of the pastoral areas (Robertson, 1989). However, there has been some questioning as to the effectiveness of this program, welcome and appropriate as it undoubtedly is (Conacher and Conacher, 1988, p. 133).

Alarm continues to be expressed in certain quarters over pesticide residues—particularly in meat destined for the North American market, but also in free-range eggs and mothers' milk. With a few exceptions, official or agency support for farmers who wish to reduce their dependency on synthetic pesticides is negligible. Indeed, there is active encouragement at all levels for their continued use.

The terms of trade continue to operate against farmers in Western Australia, as is true for Australia as a whole, with costs paid by farmers exceeding prices received in every year since 1980/81 (Cribb, 1989, Table 1). Saudi Arabia's continuing refusal to allow live sheep to be landed there is currently exacerbating matters (although this trade, which is more important for Western Australia than for any other State, continues to be strongly opposed by environmentalists and animal liberationists), as will the Soviet Union's reneging on wool payments and the currently mooted drop in wool prices, if continued for any length of time.

There is a continuing decline of most country towns and localities. The primary cause is probably continued losses of farm populations as a result of farm amalgamations in response to the cost/price squeeze, although this major issue urgently requires a significant research input. The most recent inter-censal period, 1981–6, shows nearly all wheatbelt centres continuing to lose population, sometimes at remarkably high rates. The Williams locality, for example (located only 160 km south-east of Perth), lost over 24 per cent of its admittedly small population (343 in 1986). Narrogin, Katanning and Merredin, all with populations over 3,000, each lost more than 14 per cent of their inhabitants over the same five-year period. One of the State's responses to this problem, the formation of Regional Development Authorities, cannot deal with the underlying, macro-economic situation.

Although there are still many efficient and profitable farmers in Western Australia, heretical questions are starting to be asked as to whether we can afford to continue with an agricultural industry in its present form.

South Australia

The past five or six years have seen a variety of interesting developments related to the management and planning of the rural environment in South Australia. These initiatives have involved reviews of resource management legislation and policy affecting soils, water and vegetation, as well as re-evaluation of land-use planning arrangements. While all this activity might convey the impression of a great leap forward for the state of the rural environment in South Australia, the net results are very recent and remain largely untested, if not unfinished. Consequently, it remains to be seen how effective all these initiatives will be.

One area of policy where the results are well known, however, is in the control over the clearance of native vegetation, by way of the Native Vegetation Management Act 1985. This is an acknowledged highlight of rural environment policy in South Australia, albeit a very controversial one amongst the farming community. The Act makes clearance of any native vegetation without consent illegal. Where farmers are refused permission to clear land, they become eligible for 'financial assistance' (compensation) if they undertake to enter into a Heritage Agreement for the management of that land and its vegetation. To date, in excess of 140,000 hectares are covered by about 350 agreements which have cost $18.6 million.

Introduced at a time when satellite imagery showed that more than 80 per cent of the State's rain-fed agricultural area had been cleared of original vegetative cover, these controls were met at first with loud protest from the farming sector. More recently, though, a growing acknowledge-ment of the need for rural land conservation, together with the payment of financial assistance in what are otherwise difficult economic times for the rural sector, has led to greater acceptance.

Adding weight to the rural land management push started by the Native Vegetation Management Act are the very recent amendments made to legislation covering soil conservation, pastoral (public) lands and water resources management. The Soil Conservation and Land Care Act 1989 marks an important shift in philosophical emphasis away from the threat of punitive action for mismanagement after the event, to the establishment of mechanisms intended to raise proactively the level of land management on farms. It does this in large part by enshrining the notion that agricultural land use should be based on land capability criteria. This fundamental change is facilitated by provisions in the legislation for the preparation of District Soil Conservation Plans, intended to reflect land capability parameters; three-year programs for rehabilitation, conservation or extension projects to be undertaken by the Soil Conservation Board of each district; and voluntary Property Plans intended to formalize management regimes for individual farms.

The Pastoral Land Management and Conservation Act 1989 controls the leasing of the semi-arid and arid rangelands in the north of the State for extensive grazing of cattle and sheep. Similar to the soil conservation legislation, this Act also espouses a more direct conservation philosophy than previously, though by emphasizing the notion of sustained yield as opposed to land capability. Likewise, there is also an emphasis on raising the standard of management at the level of individual holdings. To implement this, a program of systematic lease assessments by government rangelands personnel is under way. This will establish a baseline statement about the land condition of all leases in the State and provide a uniform basis for monitoring management recommendations, all of which the Pastoral Board may require to be formalised in a Property Plan.

Finally, water resource management in the State is undergoing a metamorphosis due to legislative and policy changes contained in the Water Resources Act 1990. This will have a variety of implications for those rural industries which have the potential to impact upon water quantity and quality. Farmers involved in taking water from proclaimed watercourses or lakes (surface water) or well areas (groundwater) or, disposing of wastewaters in proclaimed water protection areas, will in future be required to pay more substantial licence fees and charges. The rationale for this 'user pays' approach lies in a desire to encourage more conservative use and better management practices, while at the same time boosting funding for monitoring in these key resource areas.

As pointed out already these last three initiatives are still relatively new and untried. It remains to be seen how they will work in practice. Critical to their effectiveness will be the State government's commitment to adequate resourcing of the administration and programs involved and its response to any adverse reaction by the farming community.

Regarding land-use planning initiatives, the three regional policy reviews of the last five years or so (Flinders Ranges, Mount Lofty Ranges and Murray Valley) represent the high points, albeit qualified, of rural planning activity in recent times. All three have been comprehensive in nature, attempting to resolve a multiplicity of conflicting interests involving a large number of government departments, as well as industry and community groups across very large areas (e.g. the Flinders Ranges

Review area is the largest at 62,000 km²; the Mount Lofty Ranges Review area the smallest at 6,500 km²). Common to all three reviews has been the emphasis on the need to resolve resource management problems arising where agriculture, mining, tourism and, to a lesser extent, residential development, have led to deteriorating soil, water and vegetation resources, as well as overall landscape and conservation values.

Part of the impetus for these reviews has come from the emerging realisation that, while many of these impacts have militated directly against the achievement of environmental goals, either implicit or explicitly stated in the statutory land-use plans for these regions, those same plans (and the planning system infrastructure, based around the Planning Act 1982 have been ineffectual in addressing these problems. During the process of these reviews, this has prompted some rethinking of the philosophies, mechanisms and administrative arrangements that have shaped rural planning in South Australia to date. Unfortunately, the scale and complexity of these exercises has meant that agreement on policy has been difficult to reach and, as a consequence, there is little to show for all this planning effort to date.

Queensland

In December 1989, a State election occurred in Queensland, resulting in the replacement of a National Party government (rural Conservative) which had been in power for 32 years and its replacement with a new (Labor) government. Naturally, after such a long period of one government, the new government began a period of review and reform across most areas of government, not the least being rural planning.

At the most fundamental level, the new government is reviewing the basic electoral system itself, which was previously weighted in favour of rural electorates at the expense of the cities, a cause of undemocratic parliamentary processes, lack of accountability and even corruption in the development of the State's rural lands. A new electoral system, sure to be introduced within the first term of the new government, will have far-reaching consequences on the nature of the government process, making planning more open and responsive to community opinion.

At the time of writing, the process of change had only just begun, but included a significant restructuring of the government by reducing the number of ministries from 27 to 18. A new Department of Land Management was created by merging the land administration (Lands, Titles, Valuation) and mapping departments into one, thus allowing a more efficient land administration system. The new Department immediately instituted an Inquiry into the land tenure system, at least as it relates to the leasing of land from the State.

A new Department of Resource Industries was created by the merger of mines and water resources, resulting in efficiencies of mostly a bureaucratic rather than operational nature. The first task of the new Minister was to try to resolve the conflict created just before the election with a Mineral Resources Act which had given rights of access to mining prospectors to land in private ownership, regarded as unacceptable by farmers and graziers. A sister Department, Primary Industries, was created by the merger of the old Department of Primary Industries (fisheries, agriculture and livestock) with the Department of Forestry, which became the Queensland Forestry Service within the new Department.

Significant changes occurred with the environment portfolio with the reinstatement of the National Parks and Wildlife Service within the new Department of Environment and Heritage. The new government was elected on a platform of more environmentally sensitive policies and the first action by the Minister was to drop the legal action taken in the High Court by the previous government challenging the right of the Commonwealth to place the Wet Tropics (rainforests) on the World Heritage List. A management scheme for the region has now been established which prevents logging and requires the area, which has outstanding conservation values, to be managed for conservation and recreation purposes. The Minister has also expressed a commitment to establish an Environmental Protection Authority and thus make Queensland the last State in Australia to acquire an effective environmental management agency. For national parks, the government is committed to the goal of increasing the conservation estate to 5 per cent of the State over the next six years.

Apart from these administrative changes and the promise of a redirection of policies in many areas, the recent events in the State have been dominated by the review process itself, with an emphasis on formal and informal inquiries. For urban and regional planning, the whole development control process is under review, a 'systems review', with the aim of streamlining the process and making it more responsive to community needs. A revised planning bill will be enacted in 1990 which essentially improves and polishes the procedures in the existing act. A whole new bill will be likely to follow in future years. Formal inquiries are dealing with coastal management, the land tenure system, the electoral system, the allocation of water rights and the future of Cape York and of logging on Fraser Island. There are many less formal reviews and interdepartmental committees considering other revisions to the rural planning in the State. The outcomes of all these reviews cannot be predicted, although many in the community are becoming impatient for the new government to begin making decisions.

Perhaps the only general conclusions that can be drawn from these events is that Queensland will emerge with a much more open if not efficient planning system, with greater consideration of social and environmental values reflected in policy. A total change from the previous Bjelke-Peterson era. The government is entitled to a period of grace, since it spent so long in opposition and it has so much catching up to do.

Acknowledgements

Prepared by G.T. McDonald with assistance from A.J. Conacher (WA), P. Houston (SA), C.H. Leigh (Victoria) and I.J. Bowie (NSW). Unfortunately, no contribution was available from Tasmania.

References

Commonwealth Scientific and Industrial Research Organisation (CSIRO), 1977, 'On food and the future', *Ecos*, **12**: 3–13

Conacher, A. and Conacher, J., 1988, 'The exploitation of the soils', in R.L. Heathcote (ed.), *The Australian experience*, Longman Cheshire, Melbourne, pp. 127–38

Cribb, J., 1989, 'Agriculture in the Australian economy', in J. Cribb (ed.), *Australian agriculture, Volume 2, 1989/90*, Morescope Pty Ltd., Camberwell, pp. 11–48

George, R.J., 1990, 'The 1989 saltland census', Western Australian Department of Agriculture (draft)

Henschke, C.J., 1980, 'Saltland in statistics—the 1979 saltland survey', *J. Agric. WA*, **17**(2): 42–9

Robertson, G., 1989, 'Community involvement in land conservation—the Western Australian Experience', *Australian Journal of Soil and Water Conservation*, **2**: 19–23

THE LIBRARY
BISHOP BURTON COLLEGE
BEVERLEY HU17 8QG
TEL: 0964 550481 Ex: 227

21 Review of recent developments in rural planning in New Zealand

Richard Willis

Since the election of the Labor government in 1984, and particularly since their re-election for a further term in 1987, New Zealand rural areas have received probably their biggest policy and planning shake-up since the abolition of provincial government in the 1870s as shown in Table 21.1. This has come about through two sets of policies: firstly, the speedy removal of all subsidies and government assistance to agriculture under the market-oriented economic policies of the government, commonly known as 'Rogernomics' after the then Minister of Finance, Roger Douglas; secondly, the wholesale restructuring of local government which took place from 1987 onwards, with accompanying legislative changes in related areas of resource management (not yet passed), the devolution of power and resources to communities of indigenous people, the Maori (not yet passed), the rationalisation of regional health and education services (not yet finalised) and the deregulation of the transport industry. The far-reaching nature of these legislative changes, of course, means it is difficult to disaggregate their separate effects on 'rural' policy and planning. This review does not propose to discuss the subject of the removal of agricultural support because this process is by now studied in the literature (see Sandrey and Reynolds, 1990). Suffice it to say, there can be few examples where such regulatory change has been so extreme or so fast.

The issue of local government reform and accompanying changes deserves more mention. As at November 1988, before the implementation of the new legislation, New Zealand had 213 territorial authorities, 22 regional authorities and over 400 special-purpose boards and authorities administering such issues as harbours, health, education, water catchments, drainage and pest destruction. It was often felt that this level of local democracy provided a balance to the power of central government in a small country with only three million people, and only one House of Parliament with no Constitution (see Bush, 1989: 88). Under the new scheme, all the previous local government functions plus some new ones will be carried out by 14 regional councils made up of 72 constituent territorial authorities. The most obvious change for rural areas is the

Table 21.1 *Contemporary rural policy and planning issues in New Zealand*

Issue	Level of government
Removal of agricultural subsidies	Central government decision
Provision of drought and flood relief	Central government decision
Policies for assisting debt-ridden farmers to leave the land	Central government
Local government reform	Central government
Macro-economic policies affecting rural areas including: 1. floating of exchange rate 2. removal of industrial protection 3. transport deregulation 4. changes in the tax system	Central government
Resource Management Law Reform including: Soil and water planning	Change from special local authority to new regional authority based on river catchment boundaries
Pest destruction and noxious weeds	Change from special local authority to new regional authority
Overall land-use planning	Abolition of many smaller territorial local authorities. New and enlarged district schemes and new regional schemes. Town and Country Planning Act to be abolished but new legislation not passed

boundaries map where the nineteenth century county boundaries have been abolished and new regional boundaries based on river catchments have been instituted. In one sense, the desire to bring in water and soil resource management under the regional government umbrella can be said to have driven the implementation of the legislation. Spatial change alone has meant less 'rural' influence on decision-making because the smaller amount of regional councils are now centred in either metropolitan or provincial cities of considerable size and urban character. There is provision for 'rural service' committees within the region, but they have only an advisory role, and rural people worry that they may be powerless to affect major decisions (Kelly, 1990, p.7). Another concern of rural dwellers is that initial regional rate (tax) demands have been high in a scheme which boasted efficiency due to economies of scale as its major advantage, and many farmers are concerned that the basis of regional taxation will now be changed in ways that disadvantage them.

Of even more concern to some are the other pieces of the legislative jigsaw, without which the restructuring picture will be incomplete but which it now appears are unlikely to have passed before the general election in 1990. The Resource Management Law Reform Bill, for example, is a huge piece of legislation with actual and potential far-reaching consequences for rural planning policy making. A key feature of the new system is that it is the impact of activities rather than the activities themselves which are to be controlled. The legislation consolidates 54 statutes governing New Zealand's land, air and water resources, including major resource management laws such as town and country planning, water and soil, clear air and noise legislation, drawing all these into a single resource management act based on the principle of sustainable management. The problem at present, of course, is that the new Regional Councils have been set up to administer this act, but must operate under the disparate provisions of the old legislation until the act is passed. The impact of these changes will be assessed in a major paper to be published in this publication in 1992. However, the general drift is away from central government involvement in planning, although much of the legislation empowering this devolution had yet to be passed by the end of 1990.

References

Bush, G., 1989, 'The revolution of local government restructuring in New Zealand', *Planning and Administration*, 2: 88–102

Kelly, M., 1990, 'Rates just one area of rural concern', *New Zealand Farmer*, 20 June, pp. 7–8

Sandrey, R. and Reynolds, R., 1990, *Farming without subsidies*, M.A.F. G.P. Books

THE LIBRARY
BISHOP BURTON COLLEGE
BEVERLEY HU17 8QG
TEL: 0964 550481 Ex: 227

THE LIBRARY
BISHOP BURTON COLLEGE
BEVERLEY HU17 8QG
TEL: 0964 550481 Ex: 227